T0315001

SCHOOL CHOICE AND THE BETRAYAL OF DEMOCRACY

RHETORIC AND DEMOCRATIC DELIBERATION
VOLUME 26

EDITED BY CHERYL GLENN AND STEPHEN BROWNE
THE PENNSYLVANIA STATE UNIVERSITY

Co-founding Editor: J. Michael Hogan

Rhetoric and Democratic Deliberation focuses on the
interplay of public discourse, politics, and democratic action.
Engaging with diverse theoretical, cultural, and critical
perspectives, books published in this series offer fresh
perspectives on rhetoric as it relates to education, social
movements, and governments throughout the world.
A complete list of books in this series is located at the back
of this volume.

SCHOOL CHOICE AND THE BETRAYAL OF DEMOCRACY

HOW MARKET-BASED EDUCATION REFORM
FAILS OUR COMMUNITIES

ROBERT ASEN

The Pennsylvania State University Press | University Park, Pennsylvania

This volume is published with the generous support
of the Center for Democratic Deliberation at The
Pennsylvania State University.

Library of Congress Cataloging-in-Publication Data

Names: Asen, Robert, 1968– author.
Title: School choice and the betrayal of democracy
  : how market-based education reform fails our
  communities / Robert Asen.
Other titles: Rhetoric and democratic deliberation ;
  v. 26.
Description: University Park, Pennsylvania : The
  Pennsylvania State University Press, [2021] | Series:
  Rhetoric and democratic deliberation; volume 26 |
  Includes bibliographical references and index.
Summary: "Examines political calls for market-based
  education reform and explores the efforts of public-
  school advocates to build democratically spirited
  connections between schools and communities"—
  Provided by publisher.
Identifiers: LCCN 2021021739 | ISBN
  9780271091396 (cloth)
Subjects: LCSH: School choice—Political aspects—
  United States. | Education and state—United
  States. | Privatization in education—United States. |
  Democracy and education—United States.
Classification: LCC LB1027.9 .A77 2021 | DDC
  379.1/11—dc23
LC record available at https://lccn.loc.gov/2021021739

The Pennsylvania State University Press is a member
of the Association of University Presses.

It is the policy of The Pennsylvania State University
Press to use acid-free paper. Publications on uncoated
stock satisfy the minimum requirements of American
National Standard for Information Sciences—
Permanence of Paper for Printed Library Material,
ANSI Z39.48–1992.

To my mother, Fela, who has taught me compassion, courage, critical thinking, and so much more

CONTENTS

ACKNOWLEDGMENTS

In this book, I argue for the value of community as a democratically oriented way of living our lives together. Communities may promote individual growth while fostering group solidarity. For public education, communities may support learning, and students, teachers, and others may build empowering communities inside and outside of classrooms. In vibrant, diverse, inclusive, and just societies, individuals may participate in many communities, exploring diverse interests, developing different aspects of their selves, and promoting various affiliations. In writing this book, I have been fortunate to draw from the strength of many communities that have made me a better scholar and a better person.

At Penn State Press, Ryan Peterson has been a supportive and thoughtful editor. At an early stage in this project, Ryan shared his view of the value of this project and indicated his interest. Throughout the revision process, Ryan offered important advice and feedback, answering my questions quickly and clearly and providing me with regular updates and information. Nicholas Taylor has been an excellent copyeditor. Series editors Steve Browne and Cheryl Glenn expressed strong support for this book to join the titles in Rhetoric and Democratic Deliberation. I cannot think of a better home for this project. Catherine Chaput and Patricia Roberts-Miller read the entire manuscript for the Press, offering specific and insightful feedback that enabled me to clarify my arguments and bolster my contributions. More generally, I have learned a great deal from Cathy's and Trish's scholarship, and these lessons also have informed this work.

In Madison, I have benefited enormously from a vibrant intellectual community of colleagues who have supported my scholarship on this project and others. Rob Howard, Jenell Johnson, Steve Lucas, Sara McKinnon, Allison Prasch, Sue Zaeske, Louise Mares, Jonathan Gray, Eric Hoyt, Lori Lopez, Jeremy Morris, Christa Olson, Zhongdang Pan, Catalina Toma, and Mike Xenos all have supported this project in numerous ways. Both as audience members for presentations and in interpersonal conversation, some of these colleagues have patiently listened to me discuss the limits of market-based reforms of public education and the possibilities for more democratic alternatives. They all have sustained a collegial environment that encourages scholarly exploration of important issues. I also have appreciated conversations with Maryam Ahmadi, Vipulya Chari, Shereen Yousuf, and Megan Zahay in which we have addressed the implications of market governance for the conduct of public life and possibilities for meaningful public engagement. A special thanks goes to Kelly Jensen, who not only has discussed these issues but worked with me to interview public education advocates across Wisconsin in the summer of 2019. In this work and through other activities, Kelly has exemplified the qualities of a dedicated researcher and teacher.

I am fortunate to work at a university that values and promotes faculty research. Support for this research was provided by the University of Wisconsin–Madison Office of the Vice Chancellor for Research and Graduate Education with funding from the Wisconsin Alumni Research Foundation.

I discussed ideas for this project and presented earlier drafts of portions of this book at various colleges and universities, including Pennsylvania State University, the University of Bergen, the University of Colorado Boulder, the University of Nevada, Reno, the University of North Carolina at Chapel Hill, the University of South Florida, the Virginia Military Institute, and Wayne State University. At the University of Wisconsin–Madison, I gave talks to the Communication Arts Department and participated on a panel discussion organized by the Department of Educational Policy Studies and the Center for Ethics and Education. I also delivered presentations to the Southeast Wisconsin Schools Alliance, the Wisconsin Rural Schools Alliance (with Kelly Jensen), and the Wisconsin Public Education Network (again with Kelly Jensen). I am grateful to all the people who attended these talks for their excellent observations, feedback, questions, and suggestions. The process of discussing this work in different venues has sharpened my conceptual framework and analysis.

Although they did not serve as early versions of chapters, I did write a few scholarly journal articles that contributed importantly to the development of my thinking about some of the topics I explore in this book. I am grateful to Mary Stuckey for providing me with great feedback on an article about neoliberalism and the public sphere that was published during her editorship of the *Quarterly Journal of Speech*. I am also grateful for the editorial support and feedback that Susan Jarrett and Michelle Ballif offered on an article addressing relationships and the public sphere that appeared in a special issue of *Rhetoric Society Quarterly*.

Countless conversations with and other forms of support from many colleagues and friends have helped me during the various stages of writing this book. In particular, I thank the following people for their various contributions:

Alec Baker, Bill Balthrop, Jeff Bennett, Carole Blair, Heather DuBois Boure-nane, Maegan Parker Brooks, Dan Brouwer, Karma Chávez, David Cheshier, Crystal Colombini, Pam Conners, Jim Dillard, Rebecca Dingo, Jeff Drury, Jer-emy Engels, Lisa Flores, Whitney Gent, Charles Goehring, Phillip Goodwin, Ron Greene, Debbie Hawhee, Florence Hsia, Michelle Iten, Kelly Jakes, Mer-edith Johnson, Nathan Johnson, Paul Johnson, Kim Kaukl, Michele Kennerly, Zornitsa Keremidchieva, Abe Khan, Jens Kjeldsen, Brian Lavendel, Michael Lee, Chris Lundberg, Steve May, Christina McDonald, Chuck Morris, Kevin Musgrave, Cate Palczewski, Trevor Parry-Giles, Phaedra Pezzullo, Damien Smith Pfister, Kendall Phillips, Terri Phillips, Angela Ray, Peter Simonson, Denise Solomon, Brad Vivian, Michael Waltman, Eric Watts, Isaac West, Scott Wible, Kirt Wilson, Jen Wingard, Carol Winkler, Luke Winslow, Misti Yang, David Zarefsky, and Laurie Zimmerman. Across a network of relationships, these people manifest what John Dewey envisioned as a Great Community.

My family has provided me with incredible support during the writing of this book. My mom, Fela Asen, to whom this book is dedicated, has exempli-fied the virtues of education and community by building innumerable gen-erative relationships. My sister, Karen Hirsch, has shown steady interest in and support for this project. My children, Simone and Zac, have engaged the transformative power of education in their own lives, and have demon-strated concerns for the importance of education for others. They also have reminded me of the diverse relationships of life. Our dog, Bini, has been a great exercise partner and a welcome distraction. My wife, Sue Robinson, has supported this project in many ways, as a source of encouragement, a sounding board for ideas, a sharer of resources, a valued interlocutor, and an enthusiastic and dedicated advocate for a more just world.

INTRODUCTION: COMPETING DISCOURSES
AND CONTRASTING VISIONS OF EDUCATION

Two recent news stories, one inviting sympathy for public school teachers and the other describing cynicism toward public education, offer important lessons about some of the current challenges facing K–12 public education in the United States. The first item, a 2018 cover story in *Time* magazine, detailed the insufficient pay, uncertain support, and difficult circumstances for many of the nation's public school teachers. The story noted that the pay gap between teachers and comparable professionals had reached record levels, with teachers experiencing "some of the worst wage stagnation of any profession." Beyond salaries, twenty-nine states spent less per student in inflation-adjusted dollars than before the late-2000s Great Recession. Dramatizing these trends, the circulation of this *Time* issue included three different magazine covers, each featuring an image of a female public school teacher (Latina, white, and African American) in a classroom or school building, and each superimposed with a troubling statement cast in the voice of the person pictured: "My child and I share a bed in a small apartment, I spend $1,000 on supplies and I've been laid off three times due to budget cuts. I'm a teacher in America"; "I have a master's degree, 16 years of experience, work two extra jobs and donate blood plasma to pay the bills. I'm a teacher in America"; "I have 20 years of experience, but I can't afford to fix my car, see a doctor for headaches or save for my child's future. I'm a teacher in America."[1]

The second item appeared in a local newspaper in Madison, Wisconsin. The 2019 article recounted the advice offered by an administrator at a religious school outside of Madison for families at the school to take advantage of a loophole in state law to qualify for private school vouchers. Under the law, families with children currently attending private schools could apply for vouchers only when their children enter specified grade levels. To work around this constraint, Community Christian School administrator Dale Lempa advised families that they could become eligible by enrolling their children in a public school for as little as one day, since public school students could apply for vouchers across all K–12 grade levels.[2] Lempa remarked, "Our mission is to support parents in their responsibility to raise godly children. We therefore carry an obligation to provide parents with all the information they need to make the best decision for their own families. We will not make those decisions for them."[3] Presumably, staff at the Community Christian School have sought to fulfill their mission by identifying a legal loophole without rendering a judgment on the ethics of employing this loophole.

Considered together, these two news stories paint a picture of public school systems struggling to obtain sufficient resources for meeting basic needs and achieving critical goals while confronting the growth of an education marketplace funded, in important respects, by public tax dollars. Images of teachers living austerely and sacrificing personal needs for their students' learning comport with wider trends of cutting public education funding by reducing teacher pay and benefits. In 2011, Wisconsin governor Scott Walker argued that facilitating these outcomes by eliminating collective bargaining rights for public employees would give local school districts the flexibility they needed to adjust to funding cuts in the state's biennial budget.[4] Reduced state support in Wisconsin has shifted more of the burden of funding public schools to local districts, exacerbating the influence of local wealth disparities on children's education. Meanwhile, Walker and others, including former US secretary of education Betsy DeVos, have employed the language of freedom and choice to advocate for expanding education markets. The remark from the Community Christian School administrator aptly encapsulates this argument: because families know their children best, families should decide how to direct educational resources, through vouchers and other tools, to private and public options. Advocates also claim that this exercise of choice would reward successful schools, goad other schools to improve, and shutter failing schools. Further, they maintain that markets would appropriately position families as consumers choosing among education providers. In this light, the potential contradiction of engaging in disingenuous behavior to finance religious instruction resolves as consistent action attuned to the market principle of the pursuit of self-interest.

These news stories and their wider implications raise important questions about the state of US public education in an era of market hegemony that asserts its superiority as a model for public policy and public life. Intimating wider discourses, these stories express divergent values and commitments to public education. Engaging in public argument and campaigns that advance different visions, advocates from different backgrounds representing diverse interests have broached questions about the very structure and purpose of public education. What is public education for? How should we imagine the proper relationship of schools and society? Who is responsible for public education? How should we value public education? What values should guide public education? These questions do not necessitate mutually exclusive answers that foreswear context-specific applications of particular tools, such as the use of residential and curricular enrollment strategies in some local districts.[5] However, as John Dewey wrote, we need to align our means and ends in light of the educational goals we wish to achieve. Without purposeful engagement, education reduces to rote training, offering little benefit to students, teachers, and communities.[6] We cannot avoid the question of what we want to accomplish, and this requires articulating a vision for education and human relationships.

Advocates from academia, government, business, and elsewhere have confidently asserted a vision of a bustling education marketplace that includes traditional public schools, private (religious and nonreligious) schools, charter schools, and more. As early proponents of a market vision, economists Milton Friedman and Rose Friedman co-authored a series of books challenging what they regarded as a restrictive government education monopoly.[7] In their early writings on this topic, the Friedmans supported government financing but not government provision of education. They drew a harder line in later writings, rejecting the very existence of compulsory education laws. In contemporary politics, figures like Scott Walker and Betsy DeVos have represented themselves as allied with parents against bureaucrats, urging education reforms that draw on the competitive spirit of the market and its embrace of individual freedom and choice. Corporations like the office-sharing company WeWork have financed and organized market-based schooling. In 2017, the company announced the creation of a private New York City elementary school for "conscious entrepreneurship." WeWork cofounder Rebekah Neumann asserted that "there's no reason why children in elementary schools can't be launching their own businesses." Along these lines, Neumann described herself as "rethinking the whole idea of what an education means."[8] As these examples suggest, a variety of people and organizations have articulated market visions for education in their advocacy at national, state, and local levels. As this discourse reveals, education markets value communication and public activity, but, as I argue in this book, these modes of communication and publicity diverge from practices of democratic deliberation and decision-making.[9]

Affirming different goals, alternative visions imagine public-spirited and democratically engaged schooling. Invoking historical perspectives and contemporary advocacy, these visions acknowledge problems with educational institutions and practices but retort that only public action for public schools can foster vibrant relationships inside and outside of school buildings that position public schools as keystones of local communities. These advocates insist that a nondemocratic education will not advance democratic values of equality, freedom, and justice. From John Dewey to contemporary local people and organizations, these visions assert an essential, multilayered relationship of education and democracy. For his part, Dewey defined education and democracy as resonant, mutually informative and beneficial processes. Local advocates in Wisconsin and elsewhere have expressed a capacious vision of education as the coproduction of schools and communities, associating successful education with inclusive processes and participatory decision-making, community deliberation and accountability, and responsive and dynamic relationship networks. Indeed, a 2018 *Washington Post* story identified "a new public education movement" in Wisconsin involving "parents and teachers and local grassroots activists coming together to fight for the public schools in their communities."[10] For Dewey and contemporary local advocates, communication serves critical roles inside and outside the classroom. Dewey regarded communication itself as educative and thus central to the school experience.[11] Through a variety of communication modes— letters to the editor, marches, postcards, legislative testimony, public forums, group deliberation, campaigns, and more—local advocates have created and strengthened relationships among students, teachers, parents, and other community members. They have connected communities across Wisconsin in support of public education.

School Choice and the Betrayal of Democracy addresses the prospects for vibrant public discourses for a democratic education in an era of expanding markets and local modes of resistance. I bring together academic texts, federal and state legislative speeches and hearings, and ethnographic interviews with local advocates. As highly influential public intellectuals who wrote about education in the broader context of society, John Dewey and Milton Friedman and Rose Friedman serve as conceptual case studies, respectively, of democratically oriented and market-oriented visions of education. Although their visions differ, Dewey and the Friedmans recognized the power of education to facilitate, sustain, and promote particular forms and networks of human relationships. At a national level, Betsy DeVos has emerged as a high-profile critic of public education and an enthusiastic supporter of technological innovation directed toward expanding education markets. Although DeVos was not the first secretary of education to push for market-based reforms, she was represented in media and policy circles as the least "public"—first among education secretaries never to have attended a public school nor to have sent a child to a public school.[12] At the state level, Wisconsin has pursued legislative innovations in implementing vouchers to support education markets, initially through bipartisan legislation in the early 1990s directed at Milwaukee, and more recently through partisan efforts to expand vouchers statewide. Serving in a representative democracy, state legislators nevertheless have employed nondemocratic means to achieve market expansion. At the local level, I worked with Kelly Jensen in summer 2019 to conduct interviews with thirty-seven local public school advocates across Wisconsin.[13] In these interviews, advocates explained the importance of relating and critically engaging education, democracy, and community. Together, these cases reveal textured, multivocal discourses of democracy, markets, and education.

Democratic Relationships, Publics, and Education

In my recent work, I have characterized publics as networks of relationships that include local, direct interactions as well as indirect connections that sustain wide-ranging, large-scale discourses and discussions.[14] A polysemous term connoting a range of related but distinct ideas, "public" does not abide by singular definitions. In advancing a perspective of public as a network of relationships, I seek not to circumscribe its meaning but to illuminate the advantages of focusing on relationships—which give publics their energy, dynamism, and productive force—for understanding practice and bolstering theory and analysis. A focus on relationships directs scholarly inquiry from approaching publics as abstractions—spheres that mark social space—to publics as practices sustained by human action.[15] In this way, scholars may complicate frameworks that draw clear demarcations among multiple publics and firm distinctions between public and private, political and economic, collective and individual.

Scholars have recognized the constitutive power of relationships for publics. Hannah Arendt observes in *The Human Condition* that people enact their agency as they appear publicly in a "web of human relationships." Relationships reveal an "in-between" quality of public lives, which "consists of deeds and words," and "is no less real than the world of things we visibly have in common."[16] In this way, relationships among individuals, and not individuals as self-contained beings, constitute one's public self. Public selves do not rest at network nodes; they emerge and move across relationships.

And these public selves vary depending on different interactions within and across networks. Gerard Hauser articulates a *"reticulate* structure" to the contemporary public sphere that takes shape as "a web of discursive arenas, spread across society."[17] This networked constitution explains how particular encounters may participate in larger social structures and processes. Moreover, both specific interactions and wider networks engage other social institutions and practices, like education, that shape publics and, in turn, may be shaped by publics.

Networks of relationships illuminate the fluidity of publics as individuals may engage different sets of relationships. These relationships carry transformative power, as people may learn and think differently when interacting with others. Further, developing one's perspective constitutes an ongoing process of human interaction and learning. Iris Marion Young invokes relationality to conceptualize the variety of individual and group perspectives that circulate in diverse societies: "Since individuals are multiply positioned in complexly structured societies, individuals interpret the society from a multiplicity of social group perspectives."[18] In varying degrees, these relationships shape people's values and beliefs, interests and desires. Moreover, relationships fundamentally shape people's sense of individual and collective agency, mediating the I and the we of public life. As mediating forces, relationships resist the collapse of the individual into the collective and the dispersion of the collective into aggregable individuals. Even as relationships exert considerable constitutive force, people may take relationships for granted, engaging in public life without reflection on their connections with others, and they may act purposefully to build new relationships and revise existing relationships. As I explain in this book, both democratic and market-oriented visions of education may exhibit taken-for-granted and purposefully engaged relationship networks.

As my reference to alternative visions suggests, people may organize relationships on different bases to enable different practices and serve different ends. Relationship networks, in and of themselves, do not necessarily serve empowering or emancipatory functions for the individuals and groups who participate in these networks. Humans must construct relationships with others actively to affirm particular values, processes, and principles and to achieve specific goals. Believing that the importance of a particular end justifies any and all means may lead people to pursue methods that undermine or gainsay the goal they seek. On the other hand, asserting the applicability of a particular means for achieving innumerable ends risks obscuring and erasing distinctive goals pursued by diverse actors and institutions.

Relationship-building invites participants to consider means and ends in regard to each other, reflecting on the legitimacy of processes and outcomes. With regard to democratically oriented action, Dewey insisted that "democratic ends demand democratic methods for their realization."[19] He warned of public figures who assert their superiority and infallibility in relation to various publics when advocating for political outcomes.

Dewey sometimes invoked the example of the robber band to demonstrate how relationships can be beneficial and harmful both for active participants in a set of relationships as well as others who suffer the consequences of their actions.[20] A robber band presumably facilitates the individual enrichment of its members. The cost to others from the band's activity seems clear—loss of property and the experience of personal trauma from having suffered a crime. Indirectly, these costs circulate outward from perpetrators and victims as the material and social costs of crime may elicit wider attention and resources. Yet the robbers suffer costs, too, insofar as the maintenance of their criminal enterprise requires them to disavow potentially diverse, multiple connections with others that could engender fuller perspectives and empathy. To justify their actions, the robbers must deny themselves varied, rich modes of human solidarity. As this example suggests, relationships may promote equality and inequality, justice and injustice, inclusion and exclusion, belonging and alienation, diversity and homogeneity. People may tend to relationships in different degrees, make them more or less open to revision and reconceptualization, envision them more or less capaciously.

In this context, as I argue in this book, I value democratic relationships. I regard democratic relationships both as a normative framework for analyzing practice and as a description of human interactions that engage diverse perspectives and build inclusive and reflective communities. Signaling active processes, democratic relationships require regular tending, which entails conscious effort, care, continuity, consideration of future growth and development. Tending need not constitute a full-time endeavor, since explicit attention to the quality of relationships may recede as people coordinate their activities to pursue particular tasks and achieve mutually valued goals, yet democratic relationships should encourage explicit reflection, discussion, and judgment in terms of mutually shared values and goals. In specific relationships, participants determine values and goals in terms of their needs and interests. More generally, democratic relationships should orient themselves toward values of equality, freedom, and justice. Along these lines, Wendy Brown argues that democratic concerns with justice, freedom, and equality demand vibrant and varied engagement. Efforts to fix and narrow

these values, exemplified in efforts to remake public institutions and practices in market terms, weaken their normative force.[21] For Dewey, democratic
values circulate as "hopeless abstractions" when dissociated from human
relationships.[22] While scholarship cannot specify the content of these values as applied to all potential public engagements, scholars may underscore
their mutual determination—each should be understood in relation to the
others—and the need for inclusive judgments about the comportment of
these values with existing relationships.

While all human relationships mediate the individual and the collective,
democratic relationships regard this mediation as critically generative to public engagement and productive of vibrant practices and modes of publicity.
As I argue, market relationships seek to obscure individuals' dependence on
others, tripping over the nurturing and developmental roles of families, in
particular. In contrast, democratic relationships embrace engagements of I
and we, appreciating human agency as multiform and affirming the value
of collective agency to secure ameliorative social change. Rhetorical scholars
have understood the importance of discourse as a mediating mode. Celeste
Condit explains that "it is precisely the practice of public rhetoric that converts
individual desires into something more—something carrying *moral* import,
which can anchor the will of the community."[23] A multiple public sphere
extends discursive mediation from what Condit characterizes as the "duality
of communication" to networks of publics and counterpublics. From different
nodes and linkages in these networks, individuals may affiliate with multiple
communities. Further, engagements among publics and counterpublics may
illuminate relations of power. More specifically, I argue that analyzing and
engaging democratic relationships with the insights of contemporary public
sphere theory and advocacy may raise awareness of and mitigate exclusions
and inequities.

When cultivated to raise awareness of mutual implication and standing,
foster consideration of shared interests and goals, and facilitate coordinated
action that empowers individuals and groups while respecting diverse affiliations, democratic relationships constitute a public good. In this way, a public
good appears not in a desired object, value, or goal as such, but in people's
relationships to each other as they seek to live purposeful, empowering, and
ameliorative public lives. From this perspective, a public good circulates as a
relational good. A relational public good does not refer to specific, bounded
content, nor does it demand shared experiences or aim for consensus. Rather,
by drawing on mutually sustained and valued relationships, this public good

invites people to specify its content across multiple articulations. Specifications require inclusive, participatory engagement as individuals and communities invoke contextualized notions of a public good to achieve varied ends. Public education may support the realization of articulations of a public good by developing students' capacities and modeling reflective, diverse, and inclusive communities.

Generative of publics, relationships also play crucial roles in processes of democratic education. Dewey regarded the quality of school relationships as a crucial factor for distinguishing unidirectional, passive, formal instruction from multidirectional, participatory learning that engages teacher and student. Formal education, like all education, establishes relationships, but Dewey argued that formal education does not craft relationships that engender student agency. Conversely, he held that relationships developed through education can enable students to direct the course of their education in classrooms and elsewhere.[24] As current and former students and (in many cases) teachers, readers of this book may reflect on their own educational experiences to recognize the centrality of relationships and learning—teachers and peers who inspired inquiry, supported growth, and bolstered one's agency, or, conversely, alienating settings that deadened ostensibly lively material. As I argue, through their communicative engagement, contemporary local advocates exemplify how relationships outside of school may influence classroom relationships.

Enacted through communication, democratic relationships may strengthen and extend practices of communication. As means of communication, democratic relationships do not serve as neutral conductors of information. The values that orient these relationships also invite democratically aligned communication. Of course, actually existing communication practices undertaken in the name of democracy, even when engaged through forthright and sustained efforts, may exhibit inequalities and exclusions. At the level of scholarship, Ralph Cintron urges scholars to resist the idea that "democracy is on a teleological trajectory"—regularly making improvements over prior iterations, arising as the resolution of prior troubles.[25] Against the idealization of democracy as a final stage of history, democratic relationships offer a locally accessible alternative to market publics and their anti-deliberative and restricted views of communication. Democratic relationships offer an orientation for working toward a vibrant, egalitarian, and just networked public sphere. The local advocates we interviewed shared inspiring yet honest perspectives on strengths and limits of their communicative engagements. Even when they experienced the exclusionary efforts of others, they recommitted to critically engaging key terms like community, fairness, and justice. The communicative dimensions of democratic relationships thus support practices of advocacy and frameworks for analysis.

Market Relationships, Publics, and Education

Contemporary market relationships operate in a wider market regime of governance that rhetorical scholars and others have referred to as neoliberalism. This term originally described the efforts of a group of North American and European intellectuals, including Milton Friedman, who came together in the years after World War II to defend what they regarded as individualism and freedom under threat by expanding social welfare states.[26] In *Capitalism and Freedom*, the Friedmans identified the preferred term for their project as "liberalism," gesturing back to what they regarded as the absolute sovereignty of individual freedom in classical liberalism.[27] However, the Friedmans held that twentieth-century social policy had usurped and corrupted the meaning of this term. A neoliberalism, then, would do more than dismantle the welfare state and elevate the individual: it would articulate a bold normative project of reimagining human relationships. In this spirit, Rebecca Dingo, Rachel Riedner, and Jennifer Wingard observe that "neoliberal discourses are often rhetorically framed in absolutist terms, as beyond debate and common sense."[28] These discourses articulate a convergence of economic, political, and social developments that have propagated interrelated formations of ideology, policy, and subjectivity.[29] Drawing on market-oriented values and beliefs, neoliberal policies like education vouchers seek to enlist the state in the creation and maintenance of markets. These policies, in turn, affirm particular values and beliefs, like the superiority of individual choice over other means of organizing school systems. Both ideology and policy work to shape individual behavior through a market lens, as, for example, by encouraging parents to see themselves as education consumers and not members of neighborhood school communities. Parental behavior, in turn, serves as evidence for the appropriateness of market ideologies and policies.[30]

In their normative vision, market relationships form the basis of market publics as voluntary, informed, and mutually advantageous exchanges among free, choosing individuals. Emphasizing freedom and autonomy, market relationships suggest that the relationships that people maintain are the relationships they choose. Individuals determine when and with whom to begin and end relationships. Individuals determine the character of the relationships in which they participate. In the absence of coercion—which, in normative visions, arises from outside of markets themselves—individuals have no connections, entailments, or obligations that they do not want. This is the ethical lesson conveyed in the advice offered by the administrator at the Community Christian School: individuals need not consider the implications of their actions for their neighbors and potentially affected others; they need only worry about themselves and other individuals whom they choose. Expressing distrust, skepticism, and fear of collective agency, market relationships support market publics as aggregations of individuals, networks of exchange. Exhibiting the confidence identified by Dingo, Riedner, and Wingard, market relationships assert their universality. As part of a regime of market governance, as Wendy Brown notes, they facilitate the dissemination of "the *model of the market* to all domains and activities—even where money is not at issue."[31] As part of a normative vision, market relationships insist that there is no alternative.

Yet the vision of market relationships and publics stands in contradiction to many of the practices of neoliberal advocates who seek changes in education policy and other areas. As I argue, market relationships express a paucity of imagination—including limited views of human connection, knowledge, motivation, and aspiration—that generates limited resources for advocating for the social change necessary to fulfill a market vision. Human relationships offer people more than opportunities for exchange. People value relationships with others in noninstrumental ways. Desiring community, people want to work together to achieve shared goals. Indeed, neoliberal advocates have done just this. Historical collaborations among intellectuals, funders, and politicians enabled the development and circulation of market models.[32] Contemporary collaborations have expanded the reach of these models. In Wisconsin, groups like the American Federation for Children, which Betsy DeVos chaired, have spent millions of dollars to elect pro-voucher state legislators. These legislators have worked with lobbyists from organizations like School Choice Wisconsin to advance voucher legislation. Influential policy-oriented law firms like the Wisconsin Institute for Law and Liberty have made vouchers and other market reforms a policy priority.[33] All of these coordinated activities contrast with the legitimating discourses of markets that highlight individual action as the mode of public engagement. Market advocates work collectively to achieve their goals while demanding individual responsibility from others and devaluing community connections.

This contradiction between a normative vision and common practices of advocacy intimates how market publics form through people's use of varied activities and assets—plans and goals for public engagement, symbolic and material resources to support public engagement, and potential collaborators and antagonists to engage publicly. While the Friedmans regarded markets as noncoercive networks for coordinating individual action, their perspective presents a partial and misleading account of the dynamics of coordination. Historian Philip Mirowski discerns a "multilevel, multiphase, multisector" network among the different actors who have promoted markets as a mode of governance, including international societies, select academic departments at universities, foundations, think tanks, news organizations, venture capitalists, and more. This structure has served "to amplify and distribute the voice of any one member throughout a series of seemingly different organizations, personas, and broadcast settings."[34] In these ways, the prominent and influential advocacy of particular individuals often has reached larger, multiple audiences through the collective efforts of others.

Advocates have sought to leverage moral exhortation, economic insecurity, and coercion to enact market-oriented change. Representing individuals as rational actors, explains Crystal Colombini, market discourses nevertheless "balance the rational-actor subjectivity against the ongoing moralization, discipline, and regulation of needful behavior."[35] From this vantage point, freeing individual agency appears as insufficient for individual choice to produce proper market activity. Individuals need regular lessons, encouragement, and admonishment on how they should behave. Colombini analyzes how, during the US housing crisis of the late 2000s, media commentators and policymakers lectured home mortgagors to stay current on their loans regardless of their financial situation or the current market value of their property. Beyond self-interest, a principle of "obligation" applied: borrowers carried obligations "to financial institutions and agreements, but also more deeply to the correction and restoration of a foundering market."[36] Market survival depended on individuals' connections to people and larger forces they did not choose directly. Moving from moral suasion to demand, Jodi Dean characterizes the current era as driven by "commanded individuality": "The 'do-it-yourself' injunction is so unceasing that 'taking care of oneself' appears as politically significant instead of as a symptom of collective failure—we let the social safety net unravel."[37] Insistence on individual responsibility functions as a veiled threat, since an unraveled net will not catch anyone who falls. By weakening or eliminating some options and directing people toward others, policy change also may compel individuals to abide by market directives. Neglect of and disinvestment from public schools have compelled some parents to locate whatever options they can find—both inside and outside of public school systems—in desperate attempts to provide their children with a quality education. To be clear, policy change does not affect all public schools equally, as wealthier communities may have the resources to withstand state-level cuts.[38] But market-based education policy induces all parents to act as market actors, whether or not they would choose this mode of engagement.

Promoting individualism while obfuscating differences in background, experience, and identity among individuals, market relationships assert a universal human motivation in self-interest while assuming equitable treatment of different individuals in markets. Since individuals only seek exchanges that serve their self-interest, differences among individuals with regard to race, gender, ethnicity, religion, class, sexuality, and more do not matter. As the Friedmans insisted, market relationships dissipate the influence of identity on human interaction: "There is an economic incentive in a free market to separate economic efficiency from other characteristics of the individual."[39] Moreover, they held that discriminators only harm themselves by limiting their options for exchange. On this basis, market publics threaten to render inequality invisible, censuring those who seek to call attention to racism, sexism, and other forms of discrimination. On racism, for instance, Darrel Wanzer-Serrano characterizes a market public as operating through "an active suppression of 'race' as a legitimate topic or term of public discourse and public policy."[40] Bradley Jones and Roopali Mukherjee hold that a market public presents a "socially progressive politics by articulating a colorblind, cosmopolitan, post-race subject, while characterizing as 'backwards' or 'racist' those who invoke racial claims."[41] In this spirit, as I argue, market advocates see racism as an individual practice—"taste," according to the Friedmans— neglecting the role of larger social forces and institutions in sustaining racism. Circumscribing the force of racism, market advocates equate its practice with efforts to call attention to its practice. Jones and Mukherjee explain that market advocates often cast charges of racism as excuse-making that serves to justify personal failures. By depoliticizing and privatizing difference, "culture becomes a matter of individual choice."[42] Market relations offer no structural basis to consider such challenges as racism, sexism, and more.[43]

Consistent with their antipathy toward collective agency, market relationships privilege one-to-one modes of communication over group communication, like deliberation, and flatten communication as information exchange. For pro-market intellectuals like the Friedmans, human communication finds a model in the price system. According to this view, prices circulate information about market activity and exchanges far beyond an individual's direct experiences. An individual, in turn, may use this information to make decisions about their exchanges with others. As the Friedmans maintained, the price system scales up individual action to create larger publics "without central direction."[44] Yet this model betrays a highly circumscribed view of the dynamics and function of communication. Focusing on Milton Friedman, Catherine Chaput explains that he dismissed efforts to learn about actual human motivation and aspiration since, in his view, an ascription of self-interest sufficiently explains market activity. Whether through conscious reflection or habituation, market actors respond to information uniformly.[45]

This imagined dynamic assumes that information constitutes the core of communication and that different people will have the same understanding of information. Christopher Duerringer addresses these points in relation to what he terms "rhetorical arbitrage." In economic theory, arbitrage refers to the practice of simultaneously buying and selling the same items in different markets to profit from price differences. Rhetorical arbitrage suggests that market action does not depend on information as such, but the meanings that different actors associate with information: "If economic actors are possessed of vastly different interpretations of a given piece of information, it is possible for one to buy that asset cheaply and sell it quite dearly."[46] Duerringer cites the case of Uber, which sells itself to customers as a highly convenient taxi service, but, when faced with calls from public officials to recognize its drivers as employees and abide by regulations governing taxis, presents itself as a private ride-sharing service. These differences in meaning, and the ability of market actors to exploit them, reveal the limits of market communication generally. People do not only receive information and act on it. Rather, communication engages human understanding, imagination, judgment. Individuals may share understandings and they may misunderstand; they may ascribe similar and different meanings to actions; they may judge shared experiences differently. As rhetorical scholars know, human communication is anything but a uniform and predictable process. These varying possibilities demonstrate the need for the very modes of communication—participatory, deliberative, collective—that market relationships dismiss.

A market education supports the goals of promoting societal stability, such that markets can operate without the threats of upheaval or interference, and teaching market competency, such that students know and value their roles as market actors. In *Capitalism and Freedom*, the Friedmans cast this project as inculcating "some common set of values."[47] They did not specify these values when discussing the role of education, but their arguments in this book and elsewhere suggest such values as freedom, autonomy, respect, and more.

Contemporary advocates have stressed a need to prepare students to compete in a global marketplace. Yet, as I argue, even on these terms, the limits of market relationships raise questions for a vision of market education, since the societal stability that secures competition intimates shared belief and coordinated action. Nevertheless, making comparisons to the technology sector, Betsy DeVos called on entrepreneurs and reformers to develop educational innovations. Similarly, Wisconsin legislators foresaw more efficient delivery of education and improved student outcomes in expanded markets.

Countering Education Markets with Local Democratic Community

Expanding education markets represent both a triumph of public policy as well as a change in political culture. When the Friedmans' *Capitalism and Freedom* appeared in 1962, their arguments occupied a marginal position in relation to increasing public investments in education in the 1960s, as evidenced in the 1965 Elementary and Secondary Education Act. In contrast, contemporary market advocates operate in a political culture much more hospitable to their claims. In *School Choice and the Betrayal of Democracy*, I seek to represent these political and policy changes in my case studies. My chapters on Dewey and the Friedmans serve both as case studies as well as critical frameworks for illuminating the policy developments and community engagement I address in subsequent chapters. This book does not constitute a complete account—each presidential administration of the past few decades and every state with school vouchers could tell its own story—but my cases offer important insights and lessons for realizing a more vibrant democratic public education.

I start with John Dewey in chapter 1 to illuminate the historical resonance and contemporary urgency of visions of democratic relationships and education. Defining democracy as a way of life, Dewey argued that democracy cannot serve as an ameliorative force without direct and regular human engagement. Since democratic relations do not arise naturally, education serves an indispensable role in cultivating relevant skills in students. However, I argue that we need to reread Dewey's project rhetorically in light of contemporary scholarship on a multiple public sphere. Against Dewey's invocation of scientific inquiry as a model for democratic practice in his later writings, I maintain that a rhetorical approach sustains his communicative contributions, while the insights of scholarship on a multiple public sphere draw attention to dynamics of power, race, and difference.

In chapter 2, I turn to the Friedmans' vision of market relationships and education, which, over the course of their career, moved from the policy margins to the mainstream. Underscoring the normative force of their work, the Friedmans effectively articulated a vision of markets as a way of life. Recognizing the necessity of relationships in society, the Friedmans imagined these relationships as established by autonomous, free individuals exercising unfettered choice. They held that education, too, needs to reflect these fundamental values, both in the classroom and in organization of schooling. I argue that the Friedmans' vision of relationships obscures the structural advantages and disadvantages faced by different people in unequal societies, perpetuates a false equivalency of choice with regard to consumerism and basic issues of justice, and ignores the influence of economic coercion in people's lives.

Moving from intellectual realms to direct policy advocacy, in chapter 3 I analyze Betsy DeVos's campaign for expanding education markets as US secretary of education. Joining neoliberal arguments with a technology-infused vision of the future, DeVos cast public education as a monopoly and urged disruptive innovation from education entrepreneurs and reformers. In her discourse, DeVos presented herself as an outsider to an "education establishment." Protests against her public appearances, in her view, only confirmed the establishment's fear of meaningful change. DeVos identified fit as the basic problem of education: every child, no matter the excellence of their neighborhood public school, needs a good educational fit. Betraying an individualist orientation, fit serves as the proper diagnosis for a range of educational issues, including challenges of race and racism in education.

In chapter 4, I consider the statewide expansion of vouchers in Wisconsin. In 2013, with the support of Governor Scott Walker, the Joint Finance Committee, the budget-writing committee of the state legislature composed of Assembly and Senate members, voted to establish a statewide voucher program. Two years later, the Joint Finance Committee eased income requirements for the program and approved a gradual elimination of enrollment caps. Drawing on speeches from Walker and Joint Finance Committee hearings, I analyze how policymakers articulated an education marketplace in Wisconsin. I foreground the roles of power, money, and race in shaping the ostensibly neutral creation of this marketplace. Further, I explore how the legislature employed antidemocratic means toward the securing of market ends, most notably passing statewide voucher legislation literally in the middle of the night.

Shifting sites from state to local and positions from pro-voucher to pro-public schooling, in chapter 5 I consider community-based advocacy for public education in Wisconsin. Placing Dewey in dialogue with contemporary advocates, I develop a conception of community as a process of relationship-building and a means for realizing visions of democracy as a way of life. My analysis focuses on the interviews that Kelly Jensen and I conducted in the summer of 2019. Interviewees expressed a capacious perspective of public education as connecting schools and communities. They actively engaged in community-building even as they recognized the limits of actually existing communities. Recognizing resource disparities across districts and the influence of structural racism within and across districts, these advocates critically engaged local practices of community and democracy toward ameliorative ends.

In the conclusion, I draw together the different advocates discussed in this book to illuminate the implications of market and democratic visions for education. I argue that articulating an empowering and efficacious vision of education for our contemporary era requires aligning means with the ends we wish to achieve. On this score, the limits of market relationships engender stunted visions of education that disavow and obscure the very connections on which human development depends. A democratic vision of education may foster individual and collective growth and fulfillment, but only if we discuss honestly the exclusions and limitations of existing democratic practices and institutions and public schools. While public schools need democratic communities, and democratic communities need public schools, their mutual engagement represents an ongoing process of critical reflection and advocacy.

I

DEMOCRACY AS A WAY OF LIFE: JOHN DEWEY'S VISION
FOR INDIVIDUALS AND THEIR RELATIONSHIPS

As the Great Depression lingered in the United States and war began in Europe, John Dewey addressed the present crisis of democracy in his 1939 essay "Creative Democracy." He explained that this crisis arose, in part, because "we acted as if our democracy were something that perpetuated itself automatically; as if our ancestors had succeeded in setting up a machine that solved the problem of perpetual motion in politics."[1] But democracy does not operate as a machine; it does not include an on-off switch, nor does democracy contain an internal motor. By themselves, institutions cannot sustain democracy; neither can laws, nor founding texts, nor enumerated rights. The perpetuation of democracy requires regular human engagement. Democracy does not exist apart from human action but arises through human action, even as humans sometimes formalize their actions through institutions, laws, texts, and rights. Democracy names a particular vision of human relationships. In this spirit, Dewey defined democracy as "a *personal* way of individual life; . . . it signifies the possession and continual use of certain attitudes, forming personal character and determining desire and purpose in all the relations of life."[2] Democracy connotes movement, informing diverse relationships as people pursue individual and collective goals. Democracy may foster particular institutions, but these institutions warrant continual assessment in light of people's needs, interests, hopes, and desires. As an organized public, for example, "a state is ever something to be scrutinized, investigated, searched for."[3] The movement of democracy represents an ameliorative force.

Eighty years after Dewey's exhortation for a creative democracy, its search continues amid a new set of challenges. Democratic societies may not be confronting a world war and global economic upheaval, but a collective spirit, commitment to coordinated action, and recognition of public goods necessary to address large-scale crises and maintain everyday democratic practices appear to have receded from view, at least in prominent public fora.

Neoliberal regimes of governance treat these social resources as representative of an outmoded naïveté or, worse, as a cover for personal ambition and control. Democracy as a way of life appears foolish or dangerous. Individuals may achieve more for themselves while facilitating opportunities for others when they pursue their self-interests through voluntary relationships with similarly motivated others. Education, which Dewey regarded as a crucial force for cultivating democratic relationships, also has been reconstructed through a neoliberal framework. In this guise, education serves students and society best when schools teach specific, instrumental skills and goals. The organization of education, too, works best when structured by market models. Some commentators lament that "enactments of education, democracy, and a public that bear any resemblance to Dewey's vision are only spectral presences in contemporary American culture."[4] While these observations may prompt despair among advocates of democracy, we should recognize that Dewey himself seemingly spent as much time detailing threats to democracy as he did singing its praises. Nevertheless, Dewey retained a faith in democracy, and he urged a recommitment to this faith: "The present need is vigorous reassertion of this faith, developed in relevant ideas and manifested in practical attitudes."[5] A reassertion of faith does not entail a retreat from reality, but a renewed effort to realize democratic values and practices.

Dedicated to democracy, Dewey regularly underscored the significance of communication, persuasion, deliberation, and debate. In "Creative Democracy," for example, he held that "the heart and final guarantee of democracy is in free gatherings of neighbors on the street corner to discuss back and forth what is read in uncensored news of the day, and in gatherings of friends in the living rooms of houses and apartments to converse freely with one another."[6] Elucidating this aspect of Dewey's philosophy, scholars of rhetoric and communication have discovered extensive, diverse resources in Dewey's work. Some see in Dewey a recognition of the contingency that characterizes public life, and the articulation of a mode of individual and collective judgment that resonates with rhetorical models of decision-making.[7] Others highlight how Dewey's notion of judgment informs his approach to analysis, suggesting that scholars may find in Dewey implicit perspectives for rhetorical criticism.[8] Still others underscore the value of Dewey's ideas about education for rhetoric and communication pedagogy, tracing historical resonances in the discipline and illuminating the pedagogical potential of continued engagement with Dewey's theories of education.[9] However, while Dewey regularly referenced various modes of communication, he rarely discussed rhetoric directly. Indeed, Nathan Crick explains that "the most explicit and thoughtful reference to rhetoric in all of Dewey's writings" occurred in a biographical essay that he had written about a rhetoric professor while at the University of Michigan.[10] Moving from Dewey's scholarship to his pedagogy, William Keith discerns a link to rhetoric in suggesting that Dewey likely taught some future professors of rhetoric and communication, including A. Craig Baird of the University of Iowa, while on the faculty at Columbia University in New York.[11]

Considering Dewey's work from a rhetorical perspective remains relevant today. In this book and in my other scholarship, I have approached Dewey with an interest in critical publicity and the contemporary public sphere. From this perspective, as I have argued elsewhere, drawing on Dewey enables rhetoric and communication scholars to avoid some of the problems that arise in trying to update Jürgen Habermas's early research on the public sphere, namely, his strict separation of public and private and his primary focus on the discourse of the bourgeoisie.[12] Moreover, Dewey's vision of a renewed spirit of public engagement manifest in a Great Community—effectively a network of diverse local communities—anticipates contemporary scholarly interest in multiple publics and the networks that connect them.[13] In this vision, democratic relationships constitute and energize these local publics and their networked connections. In our contemporary era, we may glean insights from noninstitutional models of democracy, as extant political institutions—bolstered by market-based logics that equate money and speech—replicate the inequalities that governments supposedly legitimated by the voice of the people should guard against.[14] In his own era, Dewey diagnosed a "money culture" that aptly describes our contemporary era, too.[15] To some degree, perhaps to a significant degree, sustained political change requires changing political institutions, including the people who populate them as well as the values, procedures, and aims to which these institutions subscribe. But political institutions also operate in specific cultural contexts. Without attending to this culture, changed institutions may reproduce current problems. In this situation, the expansiveness conveyed by democracy as a way of life may serve us well. .

Although he may serve as an inspiration, Dewey does not offer a complete answer for scholars of rhetoric and communication. We need to approach Dewey as a resource to "rhetoricize." While scholars have brought Dewey to rhetoric, we also need to bring rhetoric to Dewey.[16] As I argue in this chapter, we need to resist Dewey's call for a "scientific democracy." Even if we understand science in the capacious manner in which Dewey understood the term, science will not act as a helpful heuristic for the contemporary challenges we face. Further, while Dewey recognized multiple publics, we need to engage his views on democracy and education in terms of the contemporary public sphere. Drawing on Dewey, we need to emphasize more explicitly issues of inclusion and exclusion, equality and inequality. We need to attend to the dynamics of power and difference to illuminate the opportunities and constraints, advantages and disadvantages of diverse participants within and among multiple publics and counterpublics.

Pursuing these claims in this chapter, I begin with a discussion of how Dewey conceived of individual and collective as mutually informative aspects of human relationships. I then consider the implications of Dewey's views of relationships for publics and democracy. Dewey regarded democracy as developed, in part, through education, and this relationship is the focus of the next section. After explicating the relationship of democracy and education, I turn to what I judge as Dewey's unhelpful identification of science as an orientation for democracy. After noting the limits of this approach, in the final major section of this chapter I reread Deweyan relationality in terms of contemporary scholarship on publics and counterpublics.

Individuals and Collectives

Individual and collective represent for Dewey two dimensions of the same vitality of human relationships. Individuals do not grow and mature in isolation, nor do collectives dissolve individuality. Both individuality and collectivity arise as people engage in networks of relationships to pursue diverse interests and ends. In *Individualism, Old and New*, Dewey maintained that society consists of "the relations of individuals to one another in this form and that." Engaging people in various ways, these relationships strengthen individuals' agency and sense of self while bolstering their connections to others. Relationships entail "the give and take of participation, of a sharing that increases, that expands and deepens, the capacity and significance of the interacting factors." While neoliberal theorists like Friedrich Hayek and the Friedmans discerned the threat of conformity in a collective, Dewey countered that "conformity is a name for the absence of vital interplay; the arrest and benumbing of communication."[17] Cultivating vital, participatory, lively relationships would ensure that individuality and collectivity productively inform each other, enabling people to make meaningful their interactions with others and purposefully direct their activities.

Mutually informative, individual and collective both play key roles in Dewey's vision of democracy. Individual and collective do not signal two distinct approaches to democracy but constitute democracy's dynamics through their interaction. Dewey explained that "from the standpoint of the individual, [democracy] consists in having a responsible share according to capacity in forming and directing the activities of the groups to which one belongs and in participating according to need in the values which the groups sustain." Likewise, "from the standpoint of the groups, it demands liberation of the potentialities of the members of a group in harmony with the interests and goods which are in common."[18] In democratic relationships, individuals enact their agency when they participate in groups, while groups provide individuals with resources for pursuing interests they share with others. While Dewey defined these two standpoints distinctly on a conceptual level, in practice they inform democratic relationships jointly. Moreover, since individuals participate in many groups, individual and collective do not merge into a singular perspective among members of a particular group. Indeed, democratic relationships demand that "different groups interact flexibly and fully in connection with other groups."[19] Any group that denies these connections disavows democratic aspirations.

Even as he articulated individual and collective qualities of human relationships, Dewey recognized that individuals confronted serious challenges in building democratic relationships with others. He explained that a "money culture" had reshaped American public life, undermining professed public commitments to individual flourishing and democratic values of freedom, equality, and civic engagement. Instead, this money culture instantiated a kind of economic determinism that controlled people's lives, disconnecting them from their employment and denying people meaningful understandings of their daily activities. Corporate dominance increasingly had characterized economic and political life, and business models proliferated, including their adoption by "colleges [that] only follow the movement of the day when they make athletics an organized business." A money culture reconfigured public engagement in market terms, as "buying becomes an economic 'duty'": "The individual is told that by indulging in the enjoyment of free purchasing he performs his economic duty, transferring his surplus income to the corporate store where it can be most effectively used."[20] Buying constituted an individual's contribution to a public good, transferring resources to business executives who, after taking their profits, used some of these resources to create more opportunities for buying. Yet, Dewey retorted, profits did not fulfill human potentiality—even for those who profited most. A money culture only produced alienation, denying people the opportunities to realize themselves as individuals in relationships with others.

Denied in people's daily lives, an ideology of individualism circulated in public discourse as a defense of the status quo. Dewey traced this ideology to the continuing influence of an earlier individualism, which progressively had argued for such values as liberty and free speech in the eighteenth and nineteenth centuries but had since calcified as a reactionary worldview. He maintained that even as classical liberalism contributed to movements toward democracy, classical liberals themselves lacked a historical perspective. They argued for their values and principles in timeless terms, which "blinded the eyes of liberals to the fact that their own special interpretations of liberty, individuality and intelligence were themselves historically conditioned." As liberals had transformed politics in Great Britain and the United States by the middle of the nineteenth century, "they had become in turn the vested interest, and their doctrines, especially in the form of *laissez faire* liberalism, now provided the intellectual justification of the *status quo*." Having succeeded the established interests they previously challenged, classical liberals did not reject social change, but they insisted that positive social change could occur only through private enterprise. Dewey observed that a classical liberalism continued to hold sway as its champions invoked a "rugged individualism" to gainsay "all new social policies."[21] Classical liberals, like the neoliberals who have celebrated them, did not recognize how the concentration of wealth and economic control could operate as coercively as the tyrannical state.

Current conditions necessitated a new individuality, "a composed, effective and creative individuality."[22] Drawing on the technological, scientific, and artistic advances of society, this new individuality would recover agency, responding to the dictates of a money culture by facilitating individuals' ability to articulate their own needs and interests. Society had developed the tools necessary for the emergence of a new individualism, but these tools were harnessed for strictly pecuniary ends. A new individualism would effectively democratize social progress, resisting the concentrated control of a money culture. It would reclaim the moral import of equality and freedom in the growth of individualism "through personal participation in the development of a shared culture."[23] As this quote suggests, a new individuality would instantiate the qualities of democratic relationships. Individuals would not realize their selves apart from others, but in interacting with others on significant shared concerns. A new individuality required collective associations for its emergence, just as collectives needed individuals. These interactions would not overwhelm individuality because a new individuality would represent, for every individual, "a unique manner of acting in and with a world of objects and persons."[24] Democratic relationships would bolster individuality by refusing a uniform set of attributes as characterizing the individual as such. Instead, people would pursue their individuality through networks of relationships presenting innumerable, diverse opportunities. No two individuals would cultivate exactly the same sets of relationships.

A new individuality would not dispense with classical liberalism's democratic values, especially its steadfast commitment to freedom and liberty, but would reinterpret these values to address present conditions. Dewey explained that the classical liberals struggled to reconcile their ideas about freedom with the need for coordinated action amid rising social complexity. A notion of freedom that stipulated particular forms of economic and political organization could not account adequately for social change, as, for example, with the shift in the United States from an agrarian to an industrial economy. The earlier liberals did not recognize the possibility for economic coercion because they held firm to ideas about how economies operate that had become antiquated with the progress of industrialization and the rise of corporations. While the classical liberals feared the baneful effects of concentrated political control, "they had no glimpse of the fact that private control of the new forces of production, forces which affect the life of every one, would operate in the same way as private unchecked control of political power."[25] Under these conditions, notions of freedom and liberty could not stand still. Without connecting theory and practice, values of freedom and liberty would not free and liberate individuals. Effective articulation of liberty meant "liberation from material insecurity and from the coercions and repressions that prevent multitudes from participation in the vast cultural resources that are at hand."[26] If a new individuality demanded the freedom to participate on equal terms in the formation of a shared culture and other concerns, then this individuality could not be exercised without an "effective liberty" that required restructuring both economic and political conditions to resist coercion, subjugation, and exploitation in their many forms.[27]

Publics and Relationships

In *The Public and Its Problems*, John Dewey maintained that human action holds the key to the formation of publics. He explained that all human action produces consequences, but these consequences vary. Sometimes, the consequences of human action affect only the people participating in the action, as, for example, with the decisions of members of a neighborhood garden about which varieties of tomatoes to plant in an upcoming growing season. Other times, the consequences of human action affect people who do not participate in the action itself, as, for instance, with the decision of a farmer whose land abuts a river to use chemical fertilizers on crops. Private actions affect only those directly involved, whereas public actions implicate others: "The public consists of all those who are affected by the indirect consequences of transactions to such an extent that it is deemed necessary to have those consequences systematically cared for."[28] In focusing on consequences, Dewey resisted a priori distinctions that regard particular topics, places, or people as holding intrinsic public significance. Depending on its context, a conversation about gardening could carry public import, regardless of where the conversation takes place or who participates. Consequences present the conditions for public formation, namely, that our actions in the world—whether we like it or not—implicate others. Consequences signal the unavoidability of human relationships.

Yet consequences alone do not create publics. People need to perceive their mutual implication in the consequences of human action; they need to recognize that they share interests and can act on them in coordination with others. Dewey held that "the consequences of conjoint action take on a new value when they are observed. For the notice of the effects of connected action forces [people] to reflect upon the connection itself; it makes it an object of attention and interest. Each acts, in so far as the connection is known, in view of the connection."[29] Public formation constitutes an active process that involves people's perception and purposeful effort. Publics arise through the cultivation of human relationships. And individuals do not have to wait for consequences to unfold to construct public relationships. Employing foresight, individuals can anticipate consequences and build public relationships to pursue shared needs, interests, and goals.[30] Actively constructed, publics exhibit fluidity, multiplicity, and variety. Public interest and focus shift as perceptions shift, giving advocates the opportunities to fight for progressive social change. On this score, Dewey observed that political institutions seem to "persist of their own momentum," thereby potentially restricting social change. For this reason, "to form itself, the public has to break existing political forms."[31]

As perception and purpose enable publics to express and enact their agency, an absence of perception and purpose places publics in eclipse. In his (in)famous diagnosis of the eclipse of the public, Dewey located the source of the problem in perception itself. Consequences abounded that warranted people's attention and action, but individuals could not perceive their implication in these consequences: "An inchoate public is capable of organization only when indirect consequences are perceived. . . . At present, many consequences are felt rather than perceived; they are suffered, but they cannot be said to be known."[32] People experienced the turbulence of economic and political transformation and social complexity; they sensed the unsettling that these developments provoked, but they had not sufficiently surveyed the relationships produced by these changes. Without active engagement, publics could not form, but active engagement—fueled by critical inquiry and communication and manifest in the cultivation of relationships—could remedy the public's problems.

Democracy constitutes a critical formation of public relationships. As Dewey suggested in his rebuke of a passive approach that relies on supposedly automatic operations, democracy requires active relationship-building. Democratic relationships harness the mutually productive force of individual and collective: "'We' and 'our' exist only when the consequences of combined action are perceived and become an object of desire and effort, just as 'I' and 'mine' appear on the scene only when a distinctive share in mutual action is consciously asserted or claimed."[33] Desire, effort, conscious assertion—these terms signal the ways that individuals exert their agency in democratic relationships to achieve shared goals and to empower themselves by drawing on the collective resources of others. Moreover, democratic relationships align means and ends. While nondemocratic regimes like authoritarianism promise followers material and spiritual well-being if only they subordinate their agency to a superior actor, democracy proceeds through "day by day adoption and contagious diffusion in every phase of our common life of methods that are identical with the ends to be reached."[34] In this way, democracy envisions a radical public practice, since "nothing [is] more radical than insistence upon democratic methods as the means by which radical social changes be affected."[35] In a money culture, democracy sustains the radical idea of individual fulfillment in coordination with others.

Informing relationships, democracy exerts a normative force that sustains a critical tension between theory and practice by which people may critique specific relationships and larger networks of relationships. Because public relationships and institutions, organized as a state, warrant continual reflection and assessment, and because individuals construct varied and changing relationships over time, democratic relationships exhibit movement and fluidity. They do not delineate specific starting points and end points but illuminate an ongoing process of living purposefully with others. Democracy promises no apotheosis. Even as they cultivate relationships, people should not rest satisfied with existing practices. As this view suggests, Dewey believed that democracy carries a strong moral dimension. In "Creative Democracy," he held that "democracy is a moral ideal and so far as it becomes a fact is a moral fact."[36] As an ideal and a practice, democracy expresses its morality in a commitment to human potential and a resolve to make meliorative change: "Democracy has always professed belief in the potentialities of every human being, and all the need for providing conditions that will enable these potentialities to come to realization."[37] Democracy's professed belief demands faith. But this is not an otherworldly faith, nor does this democratic faith constitute political quietism. Dewey located his democratic faith in history. Noting that he had been accused of utopian thinking, he retorted that "I acquired [this faith] from my surroundings as far as those surroundings were animated by the democratic spirit."[38] Democracy requires faith because the action it entails and the regular threats it faces cannot be known fully in advance of any particular relationship. Democratic relationships unfold in contexts of contingency; they enable people to interact purposefully in a contingent world, but they cannot remove contingency. Without faith, a person could not act democratically, as a lack of faith would signal that one has resigned themselves to the fortunes of an arbitrary world or has insisted on certainty as the basis of action.

Individuals may practice democracy as a way of life by building relationships with others. When these relationships bring individuals together in collectives, they enable the creation of communities. Community thus represents the embodied practice of organizing public relationships democratically. If democracy consists of ongoing activity among people, community gives this activity a particular shape. At times, Dewey appeared to use the terms democracy and community as synonyms. In *The Public and Its Problems*, he wrote that democracy "is the idea of community life itself." He reiterated that "the clear consciousness of a communal life, in all its implications, constitutes the idea of democracy."[39] Still, especially in his vision of a Great Community, Dewey sketched an outline for community that he did not address with democracy. If the values of democracy too often circulate in political culture as abstractions, community gives them a tangible meaning: "Fraternity, liberty and equality isolated from communal life are hopeless abstractions."[40] Participating in communities, individuals could coordinate their actions in specific ways, and community members could convey their needs, interests, and perspectives to each other directly. Yet these differences in specification are based on the close connection between democracy and community. Both carry normative force; both require people's active engagement; both materialize in relationships.

A Great Community constitutes Dewey's clearest vision of a renewed public energized by democratic relations. A Great Community could redress the problem of a Great Society (great in scale, not quality) that placed a public in eclipse. Diagnosing this eclipse, Dewey wrote that "there are too many publics and too much of public concern for our existing resources to cope with."[41] This diagnosis did not represent a rebuke of multiple publics but focused on their (lack of) relationships. Isolated publics could not respond adequately to present needs—only consciously connected publics could engage the necessary individual and collective effort. Arguing this position, Dewey invoked "integration" as a key term: "The meaning of the Great Society" lay in the circumstance "that it exists, and it is not integrated." An efficacious response required relationships: "The need is that the nonpolitical forces organize themselves to transform existing political structures: that the divided and troubled publics integrate."[42] In this process, multiple publics would not combine into a larger, single public; rather, they would form a network of local publics. And the movement facilitated by this network would lend a dynamic quality to these local publics: "Mobility in the end may supply the means by which the spoils of remote and indirect interaction and interdependence flow back into local life, keeping it flexible, preventing the stagnancy which has attended stability in the past, and furnishing it with the elements of a variegated and many-hued experience."[43] Mobility suggests movement of people, ideas, values, perspectives, and experiences as individuals may interact with many groups and across different local publics.

As this sketch suggests, and as scholars have noted, Dewey placed considerable value on the ideas and practices of local communities.[44] According to Axel Honneth, Dewey approached local community as "a form of prepolitical association [that] must be presupposed, such as those that originally existed only in the small, easily observed communities of American townships: Society's members must have been able to see in advance that, through their cooperative actions, they are pursuing a common goal."[45] Honneth's characterization of community as pre-political does not fit with Dewey's strong association of community with democracy, but his reference to identifying successful practices points to Dewey's historical justification of his democratic faith.[46] The potential for local communities to sustain vibrant publics arises not through philosophical speculation, but with reference to a historical (albeit mixed) record of achievement. Indeed, Dewey was explicit about his historical invocation of local community; he appreciated that "we have inherited, in short, local town-meeting practices and ideas. But we live and act and have our being in a continental national state."[47] Even as he looked to local communities as a model, Dewey did not simply take them as he found them. As his reference to "stagnancy" indicates, he recognized the provincialism and prejudice that has characterized some local communities. Serving a critical purpose of reimagining local communities, a Great Community would "manifest a fullness, variety and freedom of possession and enjoyment of meanings and goods unknown in contiguous associations of the past."[48] Further, in *Freedom and Culture*, Dewey expressed a willingness to reimagine forms of local community, suggesting that even as the "development of local agencies of communication and cooperation" remain important, "groups having a functional basis will probably have to replace those based on physical contiguity."[49] A static idea of local community will not respond to changing economic and political contexts.

I address my concerns with Dewey's formulation of local community below, but here I want to discuss briefly what Dewey saw as its benefits. As democracy as a way of life requires people's active participation, a network of local communities addresses the issue of scalability by enabling widespread participation even as Americans live in a "continental national state." Further, local communities enable a balance of stability and change, rest and movement. Dewey discerned a creative energy in the innumerable, diverse relationships of a Great Community: "Its larger relationships will provide an inexhaustible and flowing fund of meanings upon which to draw."[50] Yet even as individuals form new relationships and encounter new perspectives, they need a place to stand, if only for particular moments. For meaning to become meaningful, for people to exercise judgment, they need to situate themselves within larger networks of relationships. Local communities offer individuals a sense of belonging. Dewey held that "there is no substitute for the vitality and depth of close and direct intercourse and attachment."[51] In building relationships and coming to know their interlocutors, members of local communities can practice public engagement through familiar experiences. Because of the regularity of these relationships, community members can approach public engagement through a process of trial and error; they can reflect on past experiences, learn from what they regard as mistakes, and adjust their future interactions accordingly. Public engagement in local communities develops people's competence, confidence, and perspective.

In its various modes, enabling democratic relationships, communication offers the means and materials for the development of a Great Community. In this project, Dewey ascribed a distinct capacity to communication: "Communication can alone create a great community."[52] Communication functions both instrumentally and constitutively, revealing both pragmatic and aesthetic qualities. As a tool, communication facilitates problem-solving. In their inter-actions, individuals can weigh perspectives, evaluating the potential advantages and disadvantages of proposed responses to shared concerns. To solve problems collectively, individuals do not need to possess the knowledge of experts; rather, they need to exercise judgment: "The essential need, in other words, is the improvement of the methods and conditions of debate, discussion and persuasion. That is *the* problem of the public."[53] Communication also functions constitutively in making meaningful people's experiences and circulating shared meanings. Problem-solving invokes a "we" that does not exist independently of efforts to create and sustain it. To create community, individuals need to appreciate their relationships, committing themselves to "an energetic desire and effort to sustain it in being just because it is a good shared by all." As this quote suggests, through communication, communities satisfy desires for affiliation. Further, as he called for a program of critical social inquiry, Dewey underscored the artistic dimensions of communication. He held that "presentation is fundamentally important, and presentation is a question of art."[54] An approach to communication that foregrounds its instrumental function at the expense of its aesthetic force would only reproduce the divisions and dissociations that placed the public in eclipse.[55]

Democracy and Education

In *Democracy and Education*, which was published eleven years before *The Public and Its Problems*, Dewey positioned communication as the central link between democracy and education.[56] In the opening pages of the book, he underscored the constitutive role of communication in education. "In its broadest sense," he explained, education represents "the means of [the] social continuity of life." If human relationships require active attention, then adults could not assume that children would automatically develop fulfilling relationships without instruction. They could learn relationship practices through "communication of habits of doing, thinking, and feeling from the older to the younger."[57] Through these intergenerational interactions, children could learn to build communities; communication could enable them to understand how "they come to possess things in common" and to develop "similar emotional and intellectual dispositions."[58] While Dewey's reference to "habits of doing, thinking, and feeling" intimated the substance of communication, he also affirmed the educational value of the communicative experience: "All communication (and hence all genuine social life) is educative. To be a recipient of communication is to have an enlarged and changed experience."[59] In this educative experience, children and adults may enact qualities of democratic relationships.

Like democracy, education unfolds through relationships. Dewey criticized traditional pedagogical practices because they fail to build relationships in the classroom. He did not reject the traditionalist view that the teacher holds knowledge that could benefit students—indeed, in *Experience and Education*, he bemoaned the "either-or" philosophies that characterized debates about pedagogy—but he maintained that the development of knowledge requires the active involvement of teachers and students.[60] Learning would not develop if students sit passively as their teacher lectures on topics, effectively treating knowledge as discrete content that could be transferred among human minds. By cultivating classroom relationships, teachers could facilitate students' experience of progress in learning as a desired activity: learning represents "a *joint* activity, as a means of setting up an active connection between the child and a grownup."[61] On this basis, Dewey distinguished between learning and training. Training elicits particular behaviors from trainees without generating understanding. Training does not enable people to participate purposefully in activities; training does not develop individual agency. Only by developing relationships in the classroom could students learn to cultivate democratic relationships and build communities: "Community life does not organize itself in an enduring way purely spontaneously. It requires thought and planning ahead."[62] In the classroom, both teacher and student contribute importantly to this project.

Conceiving of education as a reconstruction of experience, Dewey articulated a perspective that resonates with democracy as a way of life. He observed that "we never educate directly, but indirectly by means of the environment."[63] In this elliptical sentence, he intimated that an adult could not force a child to learn. Through threats and rewards, an adult could train a child to engage in particular behaviors, as in correctly answering questions on a standardized test. But learning requires interest and attention, and the teacher bears responsibility for engendering these qualities. Dewey's reference to the "means of the environment" suggests two key tasks for the teacher. First, the teacher needs to craft an environment conducive to fostering relationships. In a successful classroom, students see learning as an activity in which they can participate. Rather than distancing students from the curriculum, successful classroom environments express relationships between the curriculum and students' agency and actions in the world. Second, the teacher serves a critical role in directing students' interactions with their environments, facilitating understanding of and giving meaning to students' experiences with others. Drawing on their knowledge and experience, the teacher may guide students in the classroom to develop their own agency. In this way, the teacher remains an authority figure, yet in constructing a classroom environment their "planning must be flexible enough to permit free play for individuality of experience and yet firm enough to give direction towards continuous development of power."[64] Educating indirectly by means of the environment recasts education as a coordinated activity that ascribes individual and collective roles to everyone in the classroom.

Dewey presented a "technical definition" of education as the "reconstruction or reorganization of experience which adds to the meaning of experience, and which increases ability to direct the course of subsequent experience."[65] Although this definition appeared prior to his diagnosis of a public in eclipse, we can discern a consistency in how Dewey regarded the value of education for fostering efficacious public engagement. He explained that his reference to added meaning indicates "the increased perception of the connections and continuities of the activities in which we are engaged."[66] An eclipsed public feels its implication in the consequences of human affairs but does not perceive the relationships necessary to identify and act on these consequences. Education benefits publics by increasing understanding, enabling individuals and groups to locate themselves in networks of relationships. Relatedly, in developing perception, education bolsters people's abilities to direct their experiences. Education gives people the tools and ability to act purposefully, to identify and pursue needs, interests, and aims. Moreover, because education (unlike training) connects action with understanding, education enables publics to respond not only to present consequences but to act confidently in the future, anticipating new situations and experiences and cultivating new relationships. In this way, education does not lead to a fixed end but constitutes "its own end." Education represents the "continuous reconstruction of experience."[67] As individuals construct democratic relationships, they continue to learn and grow.

Just as education serves democracy, democracy serves education by providing a critical framework for the cultivation of relationships. Dewey noted that participation in a group educates its members, but the quality of this education differs according to group interests and aims. In light of these possibilities, education requires standards for judging relationships and the communities they may form. Dewey identified these standards as the presence of "many interests consciously communicated and shared" and "varied and free points of contact with other modes of association."[68] Representing the virtues of democratic communities, these criteria facilitate the development of coordinated action while respecting the distinctiveness and varied interactions of individual members. In the classroom, these criteria model diverse, fluid relationships that bolster individual and collective agency, cultivating shared interests among students while valuing their differences.[69] To the extent that classroom relationships create community, they should not obscure students' differences. Rather, these differences and the wider networks of relationships they represent may energize a classroom community, offering the important lesson that no community should demand unqualified allegiance, nor could any single community fully account for the complex needs, interests, identities, and aspirations of diverse individuals.

Democracy also provides a critical framework for education by demonstrating that schools should not ignore the societies in which they operate, especially as societal inequalities shape students' experiences inside the classroom and their prospects outside the classroom. On this point, education as the continuous reconstruction of experience holds no magic power. Redress requires resources: "School facilities must be secured of such amplitude and efficiency as will in fact and not simply in name discount the effects of economic inequalities, and secure to all the wards of the nation equality of equipment for their future careers."[70] Achieving this outcome entails attention to school facilities, family finances, and traditional ideas about the appropriate education for members of different classes. Of course, schools could not wait for these changes. Even under unequal conditions, schools could contribute to change by developing in students "the type of intellectual and emotional disposition" that would seek "the improvement of those conditions."[71] By practicing democratic relationships in a classroom community, students might commit themselves to building these relationships in the other areas of their lives, and their commitment could foster a wider resolve to make change.

In concluding this section, I turn briefly to Dewey's ideas about vocational education, which illustrate his commitments to democracy and education. Unlike contemporary programs of vocational education that constitute a narrow, instrumental track for noncollege-bound students, Dewey discerned in vocational education important qualities of individual fulfillment and valued relationships with others that should inform education generally. An expansive understanding of vocation grounds this vision. Dewey conceived of vocation as "a direction of life activities as renders them perceptibly significant to a person, because of the consequences they accomplish, and also useful to [one's] associates."[72] Believing that every individual could develop a variety of interests and life paths, Dewey nevertheless emphasized that "the dominant vocation of all human beings at all times is living—intellectual and moral growth."[73] On this basis, he rejected views of education as preparing children for predetermined occupations, which stunts their growth. Instead, the classroom environment enables students to pursue a variety of callings as they learn to make meaningful and purposefully direct their activities. A fully realized vocational education would not segregate students according to an adult's determination of their future prospects. Rather, it would build a productive relationship of school and society, reconfiguring "school materials and methods so as to utilize various forms of occupation typifying social callings, and to bring out their intellectual and moral content."[74] Against a money culture, this form of vocational education would combat alienation in society; it would give meaning to people's daily activities.

Dewey recognized that schools could not enact a productive program of vocational education without changes to the economic and political conditions of an unequal society that left masses of people to toil in mind-numbing and dehumanizing employment. He held that "any scheme for vocational education which takes its point of departure from the industrial régime that now exists" would become an instrument for perpetuating "the feudal dogma of social predestination." While Dewey regarded all education as potentially vocational, since all successful education enables students to discover and develop life paths, he appreciated that the inequalities of industrial society would lead to a narrow vocational education as "trade education" that prepared some students for futures of subservience to others. Dewey envisioned an alternative, a transformed society "in which every person shall be occupied in something which makes the lives of others better worth living, and which accordingly makes the ties that bind people together more perceptible."[75] As this quote suggests, Dewey's vision of vocational education made him susceptible to charges of utopian thinking. Along these lines, Robert Westbrook argues that the lack of "anything resembling a *political* strategy for the redistribution of power" limits the radical potential of Dewey's reimagining of industrial employment.[76] For his part, Dewey believed that schools could transform students' perceptions, modeling the types of societies they wished to realize.[77]

Scientific Democracy

As scholars have noted, Dewey regularly invoked science in his writings, but he did not subscribe to a conventional understanding of science. Robert Westbrook discerns in Dewey's references to science a "methodological conception": "Science in its most important sense was not the body of knowledge accumulated by the special sciences but the common method by which this knowledge had been produced."[78] Articulating a rhetorically friendly notion of Deweyan science, William Keith and Robert Danisch explain that Dewey regarded science as "a refinement of the ordinary procedures for reflexive and practical problem solving by a community." Keith and Danisch urge rhetorical scholars not to dismiss Dewey's references to science, arguing instead that such references illuminate its role in rhetoric and suggest "an ethical project of scientific-minded, community-based deliberation."[79] Suggesting similar rhetorical implications, Don Burks holds that a Deweyan "scientific method, when applied to the problems of [people], implies a democratic situation, a shared community of inquirers."[80] Although I share these interpretations, as I explain in this section, Dewey's interest in scientific democracy grew in problematic ways in his later works, and scientific democracy stands in tension with other aspects of his democratic views. Perhaps most important, in a neoliberal era, scientific democracy is not the normative framework we need now.

In my view, Dewey's linkage of science and democracy became stronger and more direct as he moved from *The Public and Its Problems* to *Liberalism and Social Action* and *Freedom and Culture*. In *The Public and Its Problems*, Dewey discerned a clear role for science in the revitalization of publics as part of a project of critical social inquiry. He criticized current scientific practice as disconnected from the concerns of most people: "At present, the application of physical science is rather *to* human concerns than *in* them." Science appeared "external" to most people's daily lives, its application "made in the interests of its consequences for a possessing and acquisitive class." As part of a project of critical inquiry, "application *in* life" would reconfigure science as "the instrumentality of that common understanding and thorough communication which is the precondition of the existence of a genuine and effective public."[81] Reflecting the methodological interpretations of Westbrook, Keith and Danisch, and others, this sentence articulates a reconfigured science as a tool for improved communication and engaged publics. Moreover, Dewey argued that science alone does not constitute knowledge, as "knowledge is communication as well as understanding." In rhetorically resonant language, he explained that knowledge requires judgment, as determining future plans involves a contingent situation that belies popular connotations of knowledge as settled fact.[82] While he endorsed an "experimental" approach to public affairs, he strongly rejected any suggestions of expert rule. Expertise does not appear in "framing and executing policies, but in discovering and making known the facts upon which the former depend." Through education, members of publics may develop "the ability to judge of the bearing of the knowledge supplied by others upon common concerns."[83] In *The Public and Its Problems*, publicity, democracy, and community function as Dewey's organizing terms. Science plays an important role in the public's reemergence, but the democratic relationships of a Great Community determine this role.

In *Freedom and Culture*, Dewey tied the prospect of democracy to the propagation of science, holding that "the future of democracy is allied with spread of the scientific attitude." He called for the "democratic extension of the scientific morale till it is part of the ordinary equipment of the ordinary individual."[84] What, then, is this scientific morale? In answering this question, Dewey enumerated qualities familiar to scholars of rhetoric and deliberation.[85] He explained that the scientific morale involves a willingness to suspend belief until obtaining appropriate evidence, a willingness to follow compelling evidence rather than a predetermined position, a willingness to test ideas rather than assert them dogmatically, and a satisfaction in exploring new questions and addressing new problems.[86] In these qualities, we may discern a rebuke of extremism and absolute authority. Writing in the late 1930s, Dewey recognized the danger of global figures who asserted an absolute truth impervious to evidence and testing. On an interpersonal level, insisting on one's infallibility does not facilitate the perspective-taking entailed in democratic relationships. Engaging difference means opening oneself up to new ideas, experiences, and perspectives, and risking changes to one's values, beliefs, and sense of self in the process. Dewey saw in science a welcoming of diverse opinions and viewpoints and a readiness to pursue solutions to shared problems cooperatively. Further, in testing ideas and revising them in light of evidence, science represents the reciprocal engagement of theory and practice. In these ways, a scientific morale compares favorably to the conduct of politics by manipulating individuals through propaganda.

Espousing the virtues of a scientific morale, Dewey at times appeared to advance a broader notion of science that would exert influence beyond the boundaries of method. He wondered if the spread of a scientific attitude could reshape culture and, in turn, reshape human desire and purpose. He saw some cause for optimism in the expression of "new desires and new ends" in some people who had already adopted a scientific morale, indicating that "science is capable of developing a distinctive type of disposition and purpose."[87] Desires, ends, disposition, purpose—these potential achievements of a scientific morale move beyond the methodological view of science that some commentators have attributed to Dewey. These terms suggest that, at times, Dewey believed that science holds the power to refashion subjects. He did not represent this power ominously as a threat to individual freedom, but as a hopeful possibility for inculcating cultural and personal qualities that would help individuals resist their subjugation.

In *Liberalism and Social Action*, Dewey downplayed the roles of discussion and persuasion in enacting progressive social change. Addressing pressing social problems required the organized social intelligence exemplified in the scientific method. Dewey held that the historical growth and proliferation of public discussion represented an important advance over arbitrary rule, shining the bright light of publicity on previously unexamined ideas. Discussion encourages individuals to engage public affairs: "But discussion and dialectic, however indispensable they are to the elaboration of ideas and policies after ideas are once put forth, are weak reeds to depend upon for systematic origination of comprehensive plans, the plans that are required if the problem of social organization is to be met."[88] In this passage, we can discern two limits to discussion. First, discussion does not discover new ideas. Discussion may elaborate ideas that have been put forth, but discussion itself does not generate these ideas. Second, discussion does not facilitate planning and organization, which necessitate a more experimental approach that tests ideas in practice and revises them accordingly. On both counts, discussion cannot provide the social intelligence that should guide reform.

Discussion appeared to be limited to Dewey because discussion, when understood through the lens of contemporary political practice, elevated an individual notion of intelligence over a social practice. He maintained that "our system of popular suffrage, immensely valuable as it is in comparison with what preceded it, exhibits the idea that intelligence is an individualistic possession, at best enlarged by public discussion." Treating individuals as quantifiable units, current political practice exhibited a belief that "intelligence is an individual possession to be reached by means of verbal persuasion."[89] In contrast, science practiced a "procedure of organized cooperative inquiry" that held the potential for the widespread circulation of a new social intelligence. The crisis in democracy would not be resolved by relying on existing forms and institutionalizations of knowledge, but by substituting "the intelligence that is exemplified in scientific procedure for the kind of intelligence that is now accepted."[90] In this process, discussion would need to defer to the directives of science. And the circulation of a new social intelligence could not wait. The rise of fascism and other threats presented fundamental challenges to democracy. Dewey held that "democracy has been a fighting faith," and a new social intelligence would provide it with the tools necessary to win this fight. The question of whether Americans could develop and enact a plan to realize democracy "cannot be answered by argument. Experimental method means experiment, and the question can be answered only by trying, by organized effort."[91] In this passage, Dewey insinuated a distinction between argument and action, and social change demanded action.

I have explicated Dewey's advocacy of science and concerns with discussion and persuasion in *Freedom and Culture* and *Liberalism and Social Action* not to suggest that Dewey disavowed his commitments to communication but to reveal tensions in his writings and to indicate the need for conceptualizing democratic relationships more fully from a rhetorical perspective. Indeed, in *Freedom and Culture*, Dewey declared that "democracy is a way of life."[92] And "Creative Democracy," which located "the heart and final guarantee of democracy" in discussion and conversation, was published the same year as *Freedom and Culture*. Moreover, I believe that Dewey's concerns partially reflected his assessment of the ongoing political situation. As he articulated the limits of discussion and persuasion in *Liberalism and Social Action*, he noted the increasing influence of "propaganda," in which "words not only take the place of realities but are themselves debauched."[93] He attributed its rise to party politics, which valued advantage and expedience over insight and inquiry; the development of mass media, which expanded the audiences for political manipulation; and the failings of education. In these circumstances, Dewey sought out alternative resources for progressive social change.

Even with this historical contextualization, and even if we recognize Dewey's idiosyncratic, capacious use of the term, science does not serve as a useful orientation for democratic relationships. Other orientations hold greater promise. Indeed, Dewey himself ascribed to communication the virtues he saw in science. For instance, in his explication of communication in *Experience and Nature*, in which he declared that "of all affairs, communication is the most wonderful," Dewey discerned in communication qualities of discovery, cooperation, sociality, and intelligence.[94] Communication enables thought because it adds a reflective dimension to immediate experience that engenders conceptualization and meaning. In thought, communication facilitates an "inner experimentation" through the imaginative re-creation of people's experiences. While past philosophers had believed that mind consisted of an independent realm of ideas prior to language, Dewey characterized thought as an internal soliloquy: "Through speech a person dramatically identifies [oneself] with potential acts and deeds. . . . Thus mind emerges." Nor does mind emerge in isolation as an achievement of individual discovery.

Rather, "soliloquy is the product and reflex of converse with others; social communication not an effect of soliloquy."[95] As a social practice, communication itself unfolds as a cooperative activity: communication consists of "the establishment of cooperation in an activity in which there are partners, and in which the activity of each is modified and regulated by partnership."[96] In these ways, communication constitutes a cooperative social intelligence; communication creates diverse relationships.

As an analogue for democratic practice, the scientific method does not translate well. To be useful for contemporary theory and practice, scientific method requires a lot of reconstructive work to avoid narrow, technical connotations. And yet, even with this reconstructive work, the term still suggests a purification of politics. Further, taking a scientific view of democracy from Dewey distracts from other aspects of his writings on democracy that warrant emphasis, including the influence of contingency as an ongoing aspect of public life and the need for individual and collective judgment on public affairs. Moreover, Dewey stressed the need for regular democratic innovation, both as a means of reviving a public in eclipse and as a way of sustaining active public engagement. He imagined an art of communication that would connect people to issues in insightful ways, holding that "the function of art has always been to break through the crust of conventionalized and routine consciousness."[97] And Dewey insisted that democracy requires faith—a historically grounded, practically oriented faith. Faith underscores that democracy does not operate according to a formula; it requires people's active engagement.

Rhetoric and Democratic Relationships

Dewey's vision of democracy as a way of life and the democratic relationships that sustain it provide resources and inspiration for rhetorical scholars committed to meliorative, inclusive, and just democratic practices, but we need to rhetoricize his perspective more fully. Following Dewey's own method of reconsidering concepts to illuminate different historical situations, we need to consider relationality in our own time, in the context of the conceptual model and practices of a multiple public sphere and the prospects for democracy. Dewey directly and indirectly discussed multiplicity across his writings, as, for example, in the culturally and historically varied forms of the state as an organized public, in the affirmation of individuals' interactions within and across different groups, in the network of local communities that would constitute a Great Community, in the varied relationships of I and we, and elsewhere. Perhaps the most explicit difference between Dewey's approach to multiple publics and contemporary scholarship appears in the rise of "counterpublic" as a framework for understanding the engagement of people who perceive themselves excluded from and/or oppressed by wider publics and resolve to develop alternative interpretations of their needs, interests, and identities and to reengage wider publics.[98] Dewey did not use the term "counterpublic," which is unsurprising, since it first appeared in print two decades after his death. Further, in mentioning this term, I do not seek to frame the difference between Dewey and contemporary scholarship as a technical matter of lexicology; rather, I reference it to signal the wider critical developments that the term exemplifies. Considering relationality in our own time requires contemporary scholars to investigate the entailments and implications of a multiple public sphere consisting of publics and counterpublics, which include power, cooperation and contestation, inclusion and exclusion, and equality and inequality.

As I have argued elsewhere, counterpublic illuminates power relationships among differently situated participants in public spheres.[99] In their practices, publics may ignore the contributions of some participants, or they may actively prevent people from participating, or they may prescribe participation on particular grounds that advantage some people and disadvantage others. Publics may articulate norms and values that ostensibly appear as disinterested standards of judgment but implicitly reflect cultural privilege, racial and other biases, and economic entrenchment; they may circulate disparaging and disempowering stereotypes of marginalized individuals and groups that make it harder for people to enact their agency.[100] Counterpublics respond to these and other manifestations of power through a dialectic of inward-outward movement. In their inward-facing moments, they generate understandings of their needs and desires, devise strategies for engaging wider publics, and consider widely circulating discourses relevant to their interests.[101] In their outward orientation, counterpublics engage wider publics to expand their agendas and reconsider their priorities and to urge these publics to recognize their relationships to people and publics they may discount.[102] These nuanced relationships suggest that "when public dialogues reflect a multi-faceted negotiation of power, it is particularly important to recognize the complexity of various public spheres."[103] Highlighting the influence of power, counterpublic casts public sphere theory as critical theory.

In his own writings, Dewey did not highlight power as a key term. In part, we may trace the absence of a developed concept of power to historical context, as "power was not a central concern among philosophers during his life-time."[104] Nevertheless, the absence of a developed conception of power reveals something about Dewey's perspective on democratic relationships. Even as he denounced economic exploitation and various forms of prejudice, even as he decried the manipulative effects of propaganda, when discussing relation-ships Dewey tended to focus on their dynamic and creative energies. In this way, he operated with an implicit theory of power that resonates with Hannah Arendt's view of power, which she characterized as a force that "springs up between [people] when they act together and vanishes the moment they dis-perse."[105] Sympathetic commentators have drawn on pertinent concepts and ideas in Dewey's writings to reconstruct more elaborate Deweyan notions of power. Beginning with a basic conception of "power as the capacity to execute desired ends," R. W. Hildreth turns to Dewey's ideas about inquiry, experi-ence, habit, and social custom to complicate this straightforward notion of agentive power.[106] Inquiry associates power and knowledge, while experience situates agency within a field of possibility and constraint that reflects wider, systemic distributions of power. Power thus appears as "capacity *in relation* to a complex transactional field."[107] Habit and social custom indicate how power may operate beyond the perceptions of individuals and groups, informing people's interests and desires as well as the social environments in which they interact. Relatedly, Joel Wolfe argues that Dewey explicitly and implic-itly articulated direct and indirect operations of power. Direct power operates through social institutions, material inequalities, laws and procedures, and other forces that compel behaviors. Indirect power appears in the shaping of the social environment for coordinated action.[108] While these reconstructions emphasize inquiry and people's environments, scholars of rhetoric and com-munication need to consider how power may shape relationships within and across publics.

Focusing too closely on inquiry as the central activity of democratic rela-tionships may foreground cooperation at the expense of contestation. Indeed, part of Dewey's attraction to science arose because he regarded science as an exemplary cooperative activity. In contrast, contemporary rhetorical schol-arship has elucidated the democratic significance of both cooperation and contestation. In this spirit, Robert Ivie has advanced a rhetorical model of democracy that affirms "rowdy" deliberation. Refusing to bracket or mask relations of power, a rhetorical conception of deliberation in a pluralistic polity forwards a "positive expectation of political advocacy, dissent, and disagreement," recognizing deliberation as a "rowdy affair."[109] From this per-spective, contestation does not serve as a dialectical vehicle for transcendence;

disagreement does not indicate error. Contestation contributes productively to democratic relationships. Contestation may generate ideas; it may foster awareness of differences; it may enable people, especially those who have been marginalized, to assert their voices, even if others disagree with them. Further, to the degree to which individual and collective inform networks of relationships, contestation need not sunder communities. Ivie identifies dissent as a particular practice of contestation that encourages communities to revise self-understandings and refashion common sense, revealing that dissenters may express "sharp differences with prevailing attitudes and policies" while affirming "points of mutual dependency" between themselves and the publics they engage.[110] Chantal Mouffe expresses this interdependence in stressing the need for democratic public engagement to recast those with whom one disagrees from enemy to adversary. Representing a political opponent as an adversary, "somebody whose ideas we combat but whose right to defend those ideas we do not put into question," recognizes that we maintain "some common ground" in disagreement.[111] According to Raymie McKerrow, contestation implies an acceptance of difference, which recognizes alternative voices articulating different modes of public engagement.[112] Too great an emphasis on cooperation may privilege consensus as an exclusive orientation for public engagement, which may effectively stultify the very relationships that Dewey sought to revive in a Great Community.[113]

The dynamics of inclusion and exclusion within and across publics and counterpublics has become a key concern for contemporary scholarship. While Dewey advocated strongly for widespread inclusion in public life, he did not extensively consider the implications of exclusion. Advocating inclusion, Dewey held that faith in democracy "means faith in the potentialities of human nature as that nature is exhibited in every human being irrespective of race, color, sex, birth and family, of material or cultural wealth." In comparison to the universalizing tendencies of other foundational theories of the public sphere, notably Arendt's *Human Condition* and Habermas's *Structural Transformation of the Public Sphere*, this statement indicates attention (albeit underdeveloped) to difference. Further, Dewey did not express this faith as an idle wish; he employed it as critique. In the sentences that follow, he pointed to the insincerity of American denunciations of the intolerance, cruelty, and hatred of Nazism that overlook the everyday occurrence of "racial, color or other class prejudice" at home.[114] Yet Dewey did not investigate the public implications of these everyday prejudices. I have argued that exclusion operates directly and indirectly in public. Direct exclusions expressly prohibit particular individuals and groups from participating in publics, as, for example, with historical conventions regarding women's domesticity.[115] Indirect exclusions formally expand access to publics but restrict participation by prescribing particular modes of engagement that discount or disqualify the perspectives and experiences of previously excluded individuals and groups, as, for example, with the disciplinary power of contemporary circulating stereotypes of women, especially poor women of color, that place excessive and competing demands on women's agency.[116]

Explicating the dynamics and implications of exclusion, Eric Watts places Dewey in dialogue with W. E. B. Du Bois, a contemporary with whom Dewey did not engage in his writings but who articulated a mode of publicity for marginalized Black publics that resonates strongly with Dewey's vision of a Great Community. Envisioning this Great Community, Dewey associated the local communities comprising it with locales. He held that "community must always remain a matter of face-to-face intercourse," which suggests a geographically bounded community.[117] But this delimitation does not answer the question of what constitutes a local community. Even for a particular locale, we may ask, which community? Dewey and Du Bois lived in New York City at the same time, but they did not appear to participate in the same local community. Indeed, as Watts explains, Dewey underscored the importance of face-to-face community "without acknowledging any black face or community."[118]

As he engaged Black and white people to advance civil rights, Du Bois employed distinctive resources to cultivate Black publics. Whereas Dewey's local community invoked the image of a New England town hall meeting, Du Bois drew on the African village as an ancient and contemporary model of human relationships. Recreating the African village in rich texture in his writing, Du Bois reformulated village life as "the birthplace of the New Negro and as an alternative modernity." Interacting with its environment, remaining flexible while sustaining important values and practices, the African village exhibits "order, peace, work, commerce, and faith." The village experience integrates "art, religion, and education." Fostering individual development and cultivating collective affiliations, the African village exemplifies the mutually informative roles of individual and collective in energizing human relationships: "What emerges is a human being with self-respect and reverence for the village."[119] Du Bois's invocation of the African village illuminates the different ways that people may create local community. In a Great Community, local communities may find inspiration in New England, Africa, and elsewhere. Moreover, Du Bois's vision demonstrates that locale cannot exclusively define local. As with any public, a local public requires active engagement to emerge. And participation itself will be limited by social conditions like racism, even as publics may seek to change social conditions.

Noting that Dewey enables scholars to avoid exclusions associated with universalist theories of publics, Eddie Glaude, Jr., holds that Dewey's neglect of the dynamics of racism on the constitution of publics may perpetuate other exclusions.[120] With regard to fostering inclusive, diverse publics, Glaude maintains that Dewey's approach facilitates recognition of differences among interlocutors "and that, in some cases, individuals are treated differently because of [their] identities." Against universalist approaches, Dewey contextualized the emergence of publics historically, appreciating the interactions of "multiple publics that challenge restricted conceptions of the common good. For Dewey, this does not undermine democratic life but, instead, is a reflection of its vibrancy." To address the issue of racism for contemporary Black publics, Glaude reads Dewey in conjunction with the insights of African American writers like Toni Morrison and James Baldwin. He discerns a shared sensibility across their perspectives that appreciates how the contingency of public life underscores the value of sustained public engagement and creative problem-solving. Writers like Morrison and Baldwin have explained how the persistent racism conditioning these activities warrants recognition but not resignation: "Always we must know it, but act anyway."[121] In this struggle, African Americans may develop innovative modes of Black publicity that "break existing political forms." Participating in a Great Community, contemporary Black publics may exemplify "deep commitments to expanding democratic life and enlarging the possibilities for individual self-development."[122] Like Watts, Glaude demonstrates the value of engaging a Deweyan perspective on publics with contemporary conceptual developments and reformulations.

Scholarship on Dewey, race, and racism also reveals how equality and inequality function as forces that shape and are shaped by publics. For example, Du Bois did not have access to the same opportunities and resources as Dewey. Although he lived to the age of ninety-five, Du Bois would not live long enough to see the first Black professor tenured in 1969 at Columbia University.[123] Considering the ways that multiple Black publics confront economic and political marginalization and subordination, Catherine Squires observes that "different public spheres will have access to different resources and will forge different relationships to the state and dominant publics."[124] As Squires suggests, inequality shapes relationships in various ways, including people's opportunities to create relationships as well as the qualities and conduct of the relationships they create. Inequality also may place publics in relationships that they do not seek, as Squires explains in her analysis of state surveillance and intimidation of the Black press in the United States in the first half of the twentieth century.[125]

Investigating how inequality informs public relationships involves considering different dimensions of inequality and the conditions in which individuals and groups create and sustain relationships. Addressing its generative potential, Daniel Brouwer holds that counterpublic *requires recognition of resource disparities among social actors.*[126] These disparities may entail symbolic and material aspects. Differences in social status and cultural authority may ascribe a "common sense" to the perspectives and practices of some individuals and groups, sustaining relative advantages and disadvantages in public engagement. Material resources such as financial and physical well-being also may influence public engagement and foster particular outcomes. A mutually informative relationship augments the symbolic and material aspects of inequality: greater economic wealth and institutional authority may confer higher social status, and higher social status may entrench greater economic wealth and institutional authority.

Unpacking these complex forces involves attention to the identities and social positions that people bring to public relationships. In her critique of Habermas's account of the bourgeois public sphere, Nancy Fraser argues that he did not attend to the bourgeoisie's claim to bracket status in public, suggesting that interlocutors discounted differences in their interactions. Expressing skepticism toward this claim, Fraser retorts that "in most cases it would be more appropriate to *unbracket* inequalities in the sense of explicitly thematizing them."[127] To redress inequalities, interlocutors must address them. Counterpublic actors have addressed inequality in a wide variety of ways, including contesting the agendas of wider publics to challenge a priori distinctions of public and private, contesting established notions of expertise, employing their bodies as sites and strategies for protest, and more.[128] To invoke a Deweyan spirit of engaging theory and practice in our present day, scholars need to consider diverse public practices and relationships that sustain and contest inequality.

Conclusion

Explicating and rhetoricizing John Dewey's views of individuals and their relationships, I have developed an underemphasized perspective of democratic relationships, at least in relation to national and state-level discourses on US public education. Over the next three chapters, as I turn to the Friedmans' market-based vision of relationships and efforts to realize this vision at the federal level and in the Wisconsin state legislature, Dewey's vision recedes from view as a prominent theme in these discourses. Nevertheless, it circulates across these chapters as a normative and historical alternative that resonates with the ways that Americans have understood their connections to one another, even as Americans also have understood themselves as market actors and participants in market publics. Moreover, this vision informs my analysis as a critical framework that illuminates the limitations of treating market-based relationships as the model for all human relationships. As I explain with regard to the Friedmans, a market-based model cannot account for the affinities and affiliations that people feel for one another, and the ways that these perceived connections motivate and facilitate coordinated action. A market-based model simplifies human subjectivity and agency, disregarding the individual and collective components elucidated by Dewey and contemporary scholars. Advancing a limited view of a human, a market model advances a limited view of the curriculum and organization of public education. When particular perspectives appear to overwhelm public life, meliorative change requires that we remember that alternatives exist. In chapter 5, as I turn to the efforts of local advocates in Wisconsin fighting for public education, the perspective on democratic relationships developed in this chapter shifts from critical counterpoint to complementary framework. These local advocates have envisioned alternatives that reconstruct public education in democratic ways.

2

MARKETS AS A WAY OF LIFE: THE FRIEDMANS' VISION
FOR INDIVIDUALS AND THEIR RELATIONSHIPS

Economists often present themselves as seers of reality. Breaking through the bounds of convention and clarifying the colorations of language, economists purport to describe the world as it actually is. Through this lens, their public positions and prescriptions appear independently of political ideology, outlining an objective course of action for partisans of varying political stripes. Economists, explains James Aune, adopt as their default rhetoric a realist style that "works by radically separating power and textuality, constructing the political realm as a state of nature, and by depicting its opponents as prisoners of verbal illusions."[1] As their opponents advance arguments and perspectives, economists articulate fundamental truths. In their self-presentation, the Friedmans were no exception. They located the primary motivation for human interaction in self-interest, "one of the strongest and most creative forces known to man."[2] Their characterization of self-interest as a powerful force ascribed to this source of human motivation an energy and drive of its own: self-interest does not arise as a social construct that varies across time and culture. Rather, self-interest stands outside of history to shape its course. Elsewhere, the Friedmans observed that government intervention in the marketplace fails because it confronts "scientific laws. [The market] obeys forces and goes in directions that may have little relationship to the intentions or desires of its initiators or supporters."[3] Policymakers cannot direct the economy because they cannot control autonomous forces.

Even as they participated in the realist style of economics, the Friedmans articulated a normative perspective on markets. From this approach, markets both express values and protect values. Markets model exemplary behaviors and appropriate interactions. The Friedmans did not encrypt a normative framework within their explicit realist style, nor do I maintain that this framework arose unbeknownst to them, despite their explicit arguments. Rather, this normative orientation appears alongside their economic realism in their writings, interviews, and public statements. Drawing on the normative framework of the market, they articulated a powerful vision for living one's life with others. The normative force of this vision appears, for example, in the Friedmans' refusal to accept what is and to argue instead for what could be. In his keynote address to the 1988 meeting of the Mont Pèlerin Society, Milton Friedman decried "an inevitable tendency to regard what is as somehow the appropriate base, the appropriate starting point" for change.[4] He countered that theorists need to illuminate possibilities independently of what he and Rose Friedman referred to as the "tyranny of the status quo."[5] Further, the Friedmans defended their market model against the contrary practices of actually existing markets. To the extent that actual markets exhibited flaws, these shortcomings arose because some actors did not abide by proper market norms. In a series of papers and speeches in the 1970s and 1980s, Milton Friedman identified "businessmen" (alongside intellectuals) as one of the primary threats to freedom. Whereas intellectuals desired freedom only for themselves, businessmen, through their monopolistic practices and lobbying efforts, favored "freedom" for others but protection for themselves. In a 1974 interview with *Reason* magazine, Milton Friedman asserted that a free enterprise system is the "only system that will keep capitalists from having too much power."[6] As this quote suggests, the Friedmans deployed their normative market model to critique existing markets. A model of the market promises to protect freedom against a world that constantly attacks freedom.

Unlike Dewey, who famously aligned his view of democracy with a way of life, the Friedmans offered no parallel maxim for markets. But their writings do evidence an expansive approach to markets as a way of life. On this point, the Friedmans anticipated and influenced a wider neoliberal perspective that has treated markets not as a demarcated realm of society but as a general framework that can be applied to any activity.[7] In *Free to Choose*, the Friedmans situated market relationships at the basis of society. They contended that "a society's values, its culture, its social conventions—all these develop in the same way, through voluntary exchange, spontaneous cooperation, the evolution of a complex structure through trial and error, acceptance and rejection."[8] As I explain in this chapter, the Friedmans celebrated voluntary, informed, and mutually beneficial relationships as constitutive and distinctive market relationships. Identifying these relationships as the means for building society, culture, and convention demonstrates the productive power, when freed from coercion, of engaging markets as a way of life. Of particular concern to democratic relationships, the Friedmans characterized economics and politics as two different types of markets, and, not surprisingly, extolled the advantages of the former.

Viewing the atomistic individual as the primary market actor, the Friedmans nevertheless recognized that the individual acts in relationships. They appreciated the inevitability of relationships, as social complexity and the division of labor require individuals to coordinate activities. In *Capitalism and Freedom*, they acknowledged that "the challenge to the believer in liberty is to reconcile this widespread interdependence with individual freedom."[9] A market model does not remove the individual from relationships but underscores the need to enable particular types of relationships among individuals. Moreover, the Friedmans understood their core value of freedom as relational. They held that "freedom as a value in this sense has to do with interrelations among people; it has no meaning whatsoever to a Robinson Crusoe on an isolated island."[10] A person separated from other humans may, to the extent that the conditions of their existence permit, decide for themselves how to live, but their life could not be regarded as free.

Taken together, the Friedmans' commitments to individuals, freedom, and market-inspired relationships outline a model of publicity and a policy agenda that has attracted attention from scholars, policymakers, and laypeople alike.[11] Their focus on the individual names the agent of this model public, denying, at least in theory, the possibility of collective judgment and the formation of a collective "we" comprising people working together to redress commonly recognized problems and achieve shared goals. Freedom orients this public as an ultimate value that elevates individual choice above all while obscuring structural advantages and disadvantages afforded to differently situated people in diverse and unequal societies. Transferring the normative qualities of market relationships to publics, this model treats these relationships as free of coercion and the uneven influence of power. In this way, differences between parties to a relationship do not matter in terms of shaping the dynamics of their relationship.

Articulating a model that delineates key qualities of a market public, the Friedmans recognized the important role of education in developing the individuals, values, and relationships they championed. The Friedmans believed that education could impart the skills and capacities of the market actors they valorized, and they wished to see market relations practiced in educational settings. Toward this end, they introduced into public discourse what may be the most consequential market-based education reform the United States has ever seen: vouchers. In the Friedmans' vision, vouchers would redirect tax dollars to parents, who, considering a range of public and private educational enterprises, would decide where to send their children to school. The contemporary school choice movement received its start with the introduction of vouchers.[12] Like Dewey, the Friedmans regarded education as absolutely essential to realizing their vision of human relationships, but they fundamentally disagreed about the nature of these relationships and the educational institutions necessary to achieve them.

In this chapter, I engage the key components and consequences of the Friedmans' normative vision. First, I explicate critical tensions in their views of the individual. Turning to their core value of freedom, in the next section I argue that their conception of freedom promotes an equivalency of choice that obscures constraint and relies on a common set of values. Exploring relationships in the third section, I explain how the Friedmans failed to recognize the possibility of economic coercion as an infringement on ostensibly voluntary relationships. I then explore their implicit theory of persuasion and decision-making. In the fifth section, I consider the roles that the Friedmans ascribed to education in helping to realize their vision.

The Atomistic Individual

At the beginning of *Capitalism and Freedom*, the Friedmans unequivocally committed themselves to the individual actor over the collective. Quoting President John F. Kennedy's famous statement from his inaugural address that Americans should "ask not what your country can do for you—ask what you can do for your country," the Friedmans rebuked the appeals to national unity and shared purpose conveyed in Kennedy's exhortation. They chided the sentiment as unworthy of "the ideals of free men in a free society." A nation could not act, nor should individuals subordinate themselves to a nation by deferring their own interests and needs for some putative broader purpose. The very idea of a collective subject pursuing a shared purpose serves as a chimera disguising the coercive actions of a government seeking to usurp individual agency. The Friedmans countered that "to the free man, the country is the collection of individuals who compose it, not something over and above them. . . . He recognizes no national purpose except as it is the consensus of the purposes for which the citizens severally strive."[13] Cast as a call to cultivate the bonds of community, President Kennedy's reformulated question raised the specter of a supra-individual agent standing "over and above" individuals. In contrast, a nation properly understood provides individuals with the opportunity for voluntary exchange without attempting to transform their interests and aspirations.

The Friedmans' atomistic individual appears as a universal subject driven by an innate human motivation of self-interest and yet capable of choosing different activities and ends in life. Representing self-interest as a force outside of history, the Friedmans positioned it as the unadulterated origin of human action. When enabled, self-interest realizes personal fulfillment and financial gain. Conversely, efforts to constrain self-interest lead to personal alienation and perverse economic outcomes. On both dimensions, normative and material, the Friedmans critiqued contemporary concerns with equality. In the United States, contemporary arguments for equality distorted the vision of the nation's founders, who advocated an equality of opportunity that regarded every individual as "an end in himself" and "his own ruler." The founders' view of equality demanded the removal of "arbitrary obstacles" that prevented people "from achieving those positions for which their talents fit them and which their values lead them to seek."[14] In contrast, contemporary reformers sought an equality of outcomes that deprived people of the just rewards for their efforts. Given the standing of self-interest as "one of the most basic instincts of all human beings," the Friedmans asked, if equality of outcome became the new standard for action, then "what incentive is there to work and produce?"[15] At the level of policy, the welfare state represented an ongoing failure to refashion self-interest as its other. The welfare state had sought to contravene the imperative of self-interest by redirecting individual earnings (through tax revenues) toward purposes that individuals did not directly oversee or approve in the name of a "rhetoric of the general interest."[16] Yet this rhetoric only masked the true, self-interested aims of government actors to increase the resources they control.

While all individuals act on self-interest, every individual chooses for themselves the interests they wish to pursue. In this way, the universal motivational structure of the atomistic individual facilitates specific differences and respects diversity. Pursuing different interests, individuals follow different life paths. A person seeking a high salary might build a career in banking, while another person interested in youth may find their vocation in teaching. For the Friedmans, these and other differences among individuals, ranging from serious issues like parenthood to more lighthearted topics like favorite sports teams, warrant celebration and respect; they underscore the vibrancy and richness of humanity. In his *Reason* interview, Milton Friedman held that "in a free society each individual will have to formulate, and act in accordance with, his own personal values and beliefs and ethics."[17] Allowing individuals to act as individuals underscores the Friedmans' normative vision of agency that asserts that individuals, on their own terms, may live fulfilling lives. Moreover, individual fulfillment produces larger gains, as individual creativity and innovation—through the likes of heroic figures such as Isaac Newton, Thomas Edison, and others—facilitate progress. Efforts to cultivate collective agency squash diversity and ingenuity. Institutionalized through government, efforts to foster progress only produce stagnation: "Government can never duplicate the variety and diversity of individual action."[18] In these ways, the Friedmans contrasted individual diversity with collective conformity.

The universality of self-interest accommodates individual differences in part because the Friedmans defined self-interest expansively. In their terms, self-interest, in effect, subsumes all interests beyond the collective and government. In *Free to Choose*, the Friedmans challenged perspectives that equate self-interest with selfishness. Instead, they argued that self-interest "is whatever it is that interests the participants, whatever they value, whatever goals they pursue." To underscore this point, they offered the examples of the scientist searching for discoveries, the missionary seeking converts, and the philanthropist aiding the poor. "All are pursuing their interests, as they see them, as they judge them by their own values."[19] This definition of self-interest is a tautology—self-interest is the interest of the self—but this tautology illuminates the Friedmans' perspective. First, this definition underscores their strict separation of the individual and the collective. Any activity an individual willingly pursues is a self-interest, whereas other interest, or collective interest (as institutionalized in government), comes from outside the self. And any interest originating outside the self constitutes an imposition. Second, this definition suggests that actions reveal interests. The banker, by virtue of their career, expresses an interest in a high salary. No banker experiences alienation in their employment but nevertheless continues in this path, say, to pay off student loans. Similarly, no teacher chooses their profession because, in some historical moments and cultures, teaching may be more open to people of a particular gender than banking. Third, this definition insinuates a theory of knowledge that places it in direct connection with one's immediate activities. A banker knows banking and a teacher knows teaching, but neither could perform the job of the other. More generally, each individual knows their own interests, but individuals overstep when they claim to know others' interests. This fundamental problem frustrates claims to represent a general interest or form a collective subject. As I explain in a subsequent section, this theory of knowledge shapes the Friedmans' views of persuasion, deliberation, and decision-making.

Constitutive of the nation, driven by an instinct for self-interest, the individual appears as the irreducible element of the Friedmans' vision of human relationships. However, they equivocated when discussing the individual and the operative units of a market society. In particular, they encountered two difficulties. First, individuals (even the recluse) do not live alone their entire lives. All individuals are born into relations. Second, these individuals are not born as ready-made individuals, in the Friedmans' sense. Recently born individuals can only pursue their self-interest after a period of development, which often includes education. To address these concerns, the Friedmans turned to the family, which seemingly offered a means of resolving potential conflicts between independence and dependence. They explained that "the ultimate operative unit in our society is the family, not the individual." The Friedmans conceded that this formulation rests on "expediency rather than principle."[20] Nevertheless, it ostensibly preserves their normative vision of human relationships while accounting for human development. Children, they explained, are not fully mature individuals but "responsible individuals in embryo."[21] Children possess ultimate rights even as they depend on familial relations for their development.

Far from resolving their problems with the individual, the Friedmans' turn to the family reveals the particular, gendered character of their supposedly universal individual. Over the years, the Friedmans argued with greater enthusiasm for the role of the family as an integrative social institution. By the 1983 publication of *Tyranny of the Status Quo*, they held out hope that a turn away from "big government" would promote a "strengthening of the family and reestablishing its traditional role in instilling values in the young."[22] However, in none of their major co-authored books did they inquire into the socially prescribed roles for the different members of the (heterosexual) family. They did not ask which family member bears the primary responsibility for children's development. Perhaps the answer seemed obvious to them. Yet if women have been construed socially as caregivers of children, the individualist basis of this obligation does not appear clearly. Do women pursue their self-interest in childrearing? An affirmative answer would need to explain the pervasiveness and persistence of gender roles within the family in light of the Friedmans' repeated references to individual diversity. Does childrearing fulfill a natural women's role? If natural, gender roles presumably exist outside of the motivation of self-interest, which suggests the limits of the Friedmans' individual and *his* relationships. Whichever the answer, the family effectively sustains relationships of dependence and subordination.[23] The gendered relations of the heterosexual, two-parent family suggest that only one family member can act as an individual in the Freidmans' sense. Women's domestic duties facilitate the individuality of the male breadwinner.[24] Families that do not mirror this two-parent ideal confront even greater constraints on independence. In single-parent families, the responsibilities of childrearing cannot be delegated to a specific individual.

Although they did not identify its gender, the Friedmans acknowledged that they reserved the independent status of the individual for "responsible individuals." They held that "freedom is a tenable objective only for responsible individuals. . . . Paternalism is inescapable for those whom we designate as not responsible."[25] They explicitly named as irresponsible "madmen and children," although the latter, through women's caregiving, presumably would develop as responsible adults. However, the very invocation of responsibility as a delimiting quality of the individual carries with it the historical exclusions of the term that have constructed some people as independent and others as dependent through nonbehavioral markers such as gender, race, and class.[26] In the United States, public understandings of independence and dependence historically have shifted as different groups of Americans have experienced economic, cultural, and familial transformations and have sought to participate in public programs designed to assist targeted populations. Behaviors regarded as unremarkable when practiced by white women, for example, have appeared as problematic when undertaken by Black women.

In the first half of the twentieth century, through state-based programs and the federal Aid to Families with Dependent Children (AFDC) program, single-parent families, mostly headed by white women, received with little controversy pensions to account for the absence of a male breadwinner.[27] However, as these programs expanded in the 1960s to include higher proportions of urban single-parent families headed by Black women, public concern about "welfare dependency" arose. The federal AFDC program, which by this time had subsumed separate state pensions, had not significantly changed its benefit model, but the color of the families receiving benefits had shifted, and an emergent discourse of "personal responsibility" began to dominate policy discussions of poverty programs.[28] Indeed, the Friedmans themselves attributed to the 1960s a troubling shift in emphasis from "individual to societal responsibility." This change suggested that "people are the creatures of their environment and should not be held responsible for their behavior."[29] In particular, the Friedmans pointed to the environments of poor, urban, single-parent families, reproducing the particularizations (including racialization) of responsibility that historically have attended these discussions.[30]

Freedom

A possession of the individual, freedom enables one's autonomy. Freedom means that individual choice reigns supreme. So long as an individual does not harm others or create unwanted costs for others, which the Friedmans addressed as "neighborhood effects," freedom positions the individual as the absolute authority on their choices. Any effort to compel an individual to pursue a specific action or to prevent them from acting—any decision that arises from outside the atomistic individual—constitutes coercion. Coercion represents the other of freedom by which freedom, as a strictly negative liberty, takes shape. The Friedmans held that freedom "means the absence of coercion of a man by his fellow men, be it in the hands of a monarch, a dictator, an oligarchy, or a momentary majority."[31] As the enumerated examples suggest, coercion does not limit itself by type of government.

Consistent with their normative framework, the Friedmans advanced a moral argument for freedom emphasizing dignity and respect. Even as freedom operates through individual choice, its maintenance requires reciprocal commitments among individuals. Milton Friedman explained that "moral values have to do with what each of us separately believes and holds to be true." Yet freedom retains its relational dynamic insofar as ensuring one's own freedom requires recognizing others as full moral agents. Freedom obligates individuals not to treat "others as objects to be manipulated for our own purposes or in accordance with our values but as persons with their own rights and their own values."[32] The morality of freedom as a practice arises not in determining ends but in safeguarding the means for the exercise of individual choice. The Friedmans held that "freedom has nothing to say about what an individual does with his freedom."[33] Apart from proscribing coercion, freedom, on this view, offers an individual no basis for judging the morality of another's choices. Yet, such freedom is not amoral; its morality resides precisely in the willingness to respect the autonomy of the other. This includes the recognition that actions have consequences, and that individuals alone must face the consequences of their actions. Believing in freedom means believing in "the freedom of individuals to make their own mistakes."[34] Individuals who do not save money in their youth, for example, bear the responsibility for impoverishment in their old age. From this perspective, efforts to ameliorate this condition would constitute immoral actions.

Respecting the dignity of individuals, the relational practice of freedom also underscores the limits of one's own knowledge. In his *Reason* interview, Milton Friedman explained that his commitment to freedom "derives fundamentally from a belief in the limitations of our knowledge—from a belief in the idea that nobody can be sure that what he believes is right, is *really* right."[35] In the absence of certainty, individuals need to proceed cautiously in their relations with others, so that the possibility of individual error would not harm the self-interest of another. Milton Friedman rejected a nihilistic orientation that renders human action meaningless, but he foregrounded freedom over other values like equality because it places "the least weight on personal views about what's right or wrong. . . . It says that every other man has just as much right to his opinions as I have."[36] In this way, a commitment to freedom suggests an ethical stance of humility. In their relationships with others, individuals should not place themselves above others, disparaging or dismissing opinions that differ from their own. The Friedmans contended that "humility is the distinguishing virtue of the believer in freedom; arrogance, of the paternalist."[37] They ascribed arrogance to the social reformer because the social reformer asserts that they know better than the individual the proper course of the individual's life.

While the Friedmans effectively viewed markets as a way of life, they discerned an economic basis to diverse practices of freedom. Across their writings, the Friedmans held that "economic freedom is an essential prerequisite for political freedom."[38] Economic freedom could not guarantee political freedom, but the latter could not arise in the absence of the former. The Friedmans believed that markets disperse power among individuals, thereby ensuring that no one individual could override the autonomy of others. Markets present individuals with multiple, diverse opportunities to satisfy their self-interests. If a market actor attempts to coerce another, the other market actor simply may make a different choice with someone else. In contrast, politics, which the Friedmans treated as synonymous with government, concentrates power. In politics, choice does not occur across individuals but takes place through central actors and institutions. Whereas markets function productively to create new opportunities for individuals to pursue freedom, politics/government operates as a closed system that controls a finite amount of resources. The Friedmans maintained that "there seems to be something like a fixed total of political power to be distributed."[39] Dispersing freedom and power, markets counteract the political tendency to concentrate power. But markets do not provide a guarantee against tyranny. Radical political change could upend existing market structures and threaten everyone's freedom.

Even as the Friedmans associated their vision of freedom with the values of dignity, respect, and autonomy, they created an equivalency of choice by insisting on the sovereignty of individual choice and the inability of one individual to judge the choices of another. From this perspective, all choices, no matter the subject, carry the same moral weight. The Friedmans illustrated the operation of freedom with reference to a staple of menswear: the necktie. They explained that government decision-making coerces citizens who disagree with a decision and, in turn, enforces conformity. In contrast, the free operation of markets promotes individual diversity. Indeed, markets better serve citizens as a system of proportional representation than do governments: "Each man can vote, as it were, for the color of tie he wants and get it; he does not have to see what color the majority wants and then, if he is in the minority, submit."[40] A reader of *Capitalism and Freedom* (and this chapter, too) likely would struggle to identify a real-world instance in which a government has sought to implement a uniform necktie color policy through a democratic vote. Nevertheless, this example demonstrates the moral inviolability that the Friedmans ascribed to choice, which always warrants careful attention.

An equivalency of choice becomes clear as the Friedmans broached more serious subjects, like racial discrimination. Indeed, they defined discrimination as a choice, "a 'taste' of others that one does not share."[41] Discrimination as taste—one white person hates Black people, while another white person does not hate Black people. One man prefers blue neckties, while another man prefers red neckties. For many readers of this chapter, this may appear as a strange and offensive definition, since contemporary analyses of race and discrimination often address both individual actions and structural forces.[42] Yet the Friedmans' unwavering commitments to the individual and freedom required them to see discrimination exclusively as an individual act. Acknowledging a social or structural dimension to discrimination would have threatened these commitments. As they offered this definition, the Friedmans insisted that they believed that "a man should be judged by what he is and what he does and not by these external characteristics [i.e., skin color]."[43] Further, they reasoned that the racist only harms themselves by denying themselves the services and products of a competent market actor.

Despite these protestations, their equation of discrimination with choice undermines the practice of freedom for all individuals, not just the racist. In an encounter between two individuals, one who discriminates and the other who is discriminated against, the choice to discriminate does not affect them equally. The discriminator is free to choose; they do not feel their agency as circumscribed by their choice. In contrast, the person discriminated against experiences their own freedom as constrained. Discrimination as choice thus privileges the status quo. Moreover, by denying freedom to some individuals, discrimination as choice undermines the Friedmans' arguments for dignity, respect, and autonomy. Indeed, the choice to discriminate (or not discriminate) reveals the entailments of all choice. Choice functions as a relational practice not just in the need to respect the choices of others but in the consequences—sometimes positive, sometimes negative—that one choice carries for others.

A key value, freedom nonetheless evinces fragility, requiring a stable society for its effective operation. The Friedmans characterized freedom as "a rare and delicate plant."[44] Properly cultivated, freedom would bloom for all individuals, but harsh environments could kill freedom. In his *Reason* interview, Milton Friedman argued that "a free society is fundamentally unstable." A survey of history revealed that free societies tend to emerge for brief periods of time then disappear. Whereas the authoritarian achieves stability through a "monopoly of power and authority," free societies permit the open inquiry—including collectivist inquiry—that portends their downfalls. Advocates of freedom need "to ask ourselves how we can introduce a greater degree of stability."[45] The Friedmans discerned multiple paths toward this end. One path consists of the development and maintenance of shared values. Even as self-interest leads individuals to pursue different life paths, safeguarding freedom requires some agreement about a basic set of values regarding the institutions, laws, and norms that facilitate freedom. As I explain in more detail below, the Friedmans supported public education for this reason, as schooling may inculcate "some common set of values."[46] In *Capitalism and Freedom*, they associated stability and democracy. However, elsewhere Milton Friedman suggested that "a wide variety of political structures have proved consistent with open societies."[47] Freedom does not necessarily require democratic governments. With respect to the US government, the Friedmans sought to establish particular limits that would protect freedom against political coercion. They advocated for a variety of amendments to the US Constitution to constrain the federal government, including balanced budgets, spending limits, a line-item veto, a flat-rate tax, and more.[48]

Relationships

Free individuals engage in relationships voluntarily. They do so with clear understandings of the ways that the relationships they enter into will advance their self-interests. In choosing which relationships to initiate, individuals possess sufficient information about their advantages and disadvantages, as well as the opportunities and responsibilities they entail. Under these conditions, the individual parties to a relationship will find the relationship mutually beneficial. If not always realized in practice, this ideal informs the Friedmans' view of how people should interact in society, even in complex and diverse societies. No matter the scale, the relationship qualities of voluntary, informed, and mutually beneficial should prevail. The Friedmans recognized that specialization and the division of labor of contemporary societies requires larger enterprises than the household. Nevertheless, even in complex forms, market-based relationships display the dynamics of "simple exchange": "As in that simple model, so in the complex enterprise and money-exchange economy, co-operation is strictly individual and voluntary."[49] To the extent that their relationships evidence these qualities, contemporary societies and publics could enable the practice of freedom.

Properly practiced relationships extend the reach of the individual while respecting their autonomy. Interacting through freely chosen relationships, individuals pursue their self-interests without sacrificing their selves. Yet, in discussing human relationships, the Friedmans presented their audiences with a stark, either-or choice. They insisted that "there are only two ways of co-ordinating the economic activities of millions. One is central direction involving the use of coercion. . . . The other is voluntary co-operation of individuals."[50] From the complex back to the simple, from the economy as a societal arena to markets as a normative frame, all human relationships confront this binary. On this basis, in a 1976 essay, Milton Friedman contrasted what he regarded as the economic and the political markets. Foregrounding a normative judgment, he asserted that "the economic market is a freer, more democratic market than the political marketplace."[51] While the economic market disperses power among actors, in politics some actors exert undue influence over outcomes. Because they pay particular attention to their pet issues and curry favor with relevant politicians, special interests control politics, while individuals act in economic markets. In economic markets, individuals can discern a clear connection among their interests, actions, and outcomes. In politics, third-party actors (special interests, bureaucrats, and self-serving politicians) stand between individuals and their preferred actions. Politics presents individuals with limited choice, whereas economic markets foster a full range of choices. The Friedmans summed up these contrasts with their contention that "the ballot box produces conformity without unanimity; the marketplace, unanimity without conformity."[52] Market-modeled relationships enable individuals to satisfy their interests while bolstering the "common set of values" on which freedom depends.[53] In contrast, politics mandates a sameness that satisfies no one.

Locating politics entirely within government, the Friedmans ascribed a minimal role to government as an "umpire" that facilitates the creation and enforcement of a clear set of rules. As with umpires in sports, governments should adopt a neutral stance with regard to different actors. They also need to apply rules consistently rather than arbitrarily.[54] The role of umpire suggests three basic functions for government: providing forums for the modification of rules, mediating differences in the interpretation of rules, and enforcing compliance with rules. Enumerating these functions, the Friedmans conceded that their view of government serves as an accommodation to reality. Pure freedom does not exist; an institutional actor needs to intervene when individuals cannot resolve their disagreements on their own. Yet government warrants no commendation—virtue rests with individuals engaged in market relationships and the publics they constitute. Further, in recognizing the necessary roles of government and law, the Friedmans rejected the idea of individual rights as natural. They cited property rights as an example of the "complex social creations" that ensure voluntary and mutually beneficial relationships.[55]

Although the Friedmans frequently warned of the baneful consequences of concentrated government power, they discerned no potential for concentrated power in markets. Markets may not be natural formations, but they appear to disperse power almost naturally. Stressing the mutually beneficial quality of market relationships, Milton Friedman contended that "in the marketplace, individuals do not have the power to coerce other individuals."[56] Presumably, individuals who perceive coercion in a particular relationship will exit this relationship and fulfill their self-interest by forming a new relationship with another individual. However, as a descriptive claim, this assertion is false. Individuals may endure low-paying and/or hostile work environments because they cannot lose the health insurance that accompanies their employment. A powerful market actor may pressure another individual into selling an item below a prevailing price because a bad relationship with this buyer could have wider repercussions. These examples and others suggest that individuals in markets frequently encounter one another from unequal positions of power. Only a tautological definition of self-interest can excuse these relationships as noncoercive. As a normative statement, Friedman's claim also fails to model productive relational dynamics. Interpreted normatively, this statement suggests that relationships function most effectively when participants approach their interactions through a narrowly instrumental orientation. Considering differences in identities, access to resources, social standing, and other factors that may enable and constrain individual agency only obscures a proper focus on the mutual satisfaction of interests. As such, this statement perpetuates what public sphere scholars have critiqued as status bracketing—the assumption by powerful and privileged publics that successful interactions proceed without attention to differences among interlocutors.[57] Rather than ignoring important differences, on this account, interlocutors may thematize difference as a dynamic informing their relationships.

Dissociating relationships and identity, the Friedmans regarded market relationships as anonymous in their aggregate operation. Individuals may know the identities of the people with whom they relate directly, but self-interest and mutual benefit orient the individual toward oneself and away from extended engagement with the other. Beyond their direct encounters, individuals cannot know all the other relationships of the specific individuals with whom they relate, or the relations of their relations. At the level of the network, prices permit individuals to interact anonymously. Prices serve as a form of communication, conveying the interests of dispersed market actors and enabling individuals to exercise choice beyond their immediate environments. Prices circulate information uniformly and widely—each market actor receives the same information about prices. Individuals do not need to depend on special knowledge or favored standing with others. Instead, they can consult prices to assess the comparative benefits of entering into relationships with others.

Facilitated by the price system, the anonymity of market relations offers individuals the normative benefit of preventing discrimination. If prices effectively bracket the status of specific producers and consumers, if market-based relationships do not consider identity, then historical patterns of discrimination cannot prevail. The Friedmans explained that "when you buy your pencil or your daily bread, you don't know whether the pencil was made or the wheat was grown by a white man or a black man." These identity markers appear irrelevant to market relationships. Instead, "the price system enables people to cooperate peacefully in one phase of their life while each one goes about his own business in respect of everything else."[58] Individuals ostensibly interact with others to satisfy their own interests, not to constrain the choices of others. Yet, in a direct relationship, or a direct potential relationship, an individual might know the identity of the prospective relationship partner, and on this basis the racist consumer might refuse to shop at the stationery store owned by the African American businessperson. Even with indirect relationships, individuals might act to marginalize others on the basis of identity, as, for example, with a racist wholesale pencil distributor, who might charge higher prices to the African American store owner than their white peers. In this case, consumers acting on price alone would be supporting the distributor's discriminatory behavior with their pencil purchases. To prevent discrimination, people must be aware of discrimination, which gainsays the suggestion that identities do not matter in relationships.

Persuasion and Decision-Making

The Friedmans doubted the motivations and efficacy of social reformers, but they did not deny the need to change some beliefs and practices while upholding others. Ever vigilant to the possibility of coercion, they turned instead to persuasion and free discussion as the means for encouraging the racist to disavow their prejudice. On this issue and others, the Friedmans filled their writings with praise for persuasion. They valued social stability as exemplified in "an ideal of unanimity among responsible individuals achieved on the basis of free and full discussion." Rejecting the idea of self-evident limits to proper government activity, they countered that "we must rely on our fallible judgment and, having reached a judgment, on our ability to persuade our fellow men that it is a correct judgment, or their ability to persuade us to modify our views." On desegregating schools, they urged individuals to "try through behavior and speech to foster the growth of attitudes and opinions that would lead mixed schools to become the rule and segregated schools to become the rare exception." On compulsory retirement savings, they rebuked Social Security, offering that "we may argue with [the spendthrift], seek to persuade him that he is wrong," but individuals and government could not compel an individual to plan for their future.[59] As these examples suggest, the Friedmans valued persuasion as a means of change that comports with their vision of human relationships.

Indeed, the very possibility of freedom, at crucial moments, appeared to depend on persuasion. The Friedmans worried about the eagerness of the social reformer, "impatient with the slowness of persuasion," and anxious to

effect grand change. Preserving freedom in the face of the growth of government and its centralization of power would happen "only if we persuade our
fellow men that free institutions offer a surer, if perhaps at times slower,
route to the ends they seek than the coercive power of the state."[60] For the
Friedmans, since coercion operates as a capacity of government while markets disperse power, market relationships could not counteract government
coercion in kind. If force alone determined the fate of individuals, freedom
would lose. Advocates of freedom had no alternative but to employ persuasion to secure their values in "the beliefs, understanding, and character of the
people."[61] Against the physical force of government, market relations could
only respond with discursive power.

Crucial for the preservation of freedom, persuasion nevertheless represents a potentially dangerous activity. This danger arises in part from the
ambiguous character of relationships involving persuasion. Unlike an ideal
market relationship, a persuasive relationship suggests that at least one
party, and perhaps both, does not know fully their self-interest. If the racist's
views on difference constitute an appropriate object for persuasion, and the
Friedmans emphasized the value of trying to persuade the racist to change,
then the racist presumably does not understand their self-interest accurately.
Properly functionally self-interest should require no change; instead, individuals could enter into relationships with other individuals to satisfy their
separate self-interests. Further, the ambiguous standing of persuasive relationships suggests that persuasion may also operate politically. Acknowledging the necessity of government, the Friedmans recognized the need to reach
agreements with others about its activities. Yet this need raises the potential
for persuasion to disrupt the social stability on which freedom depends, as
"every extension of the range of issues for which explicit agreement is sought
strains further the delicate threads that hold society together." Persuasion
both maintains freedom and threatens freedom. The Friedmans held that
"the fewer the issues on which agreement is necessary, the greater is the likelihood of getting agreement while maintaining a free society."[62] Considering
the threat of coercion by government, advocates of freedom have no other
choice; persuasion appears as a compulsory activity for advocates hoping to
avoid compulsion.

Across different media, the Friedmans demonstrated a commitment to
persuasion as they extolled the virtues of market relationships and publics.
Citing regular magazine columns, newspaper op-eds, and television appearances, Jamie Peck argues that Milton Friedman "fabricated a new form
of public economics."[63] Together, as they explained in the preface of *Free*

to Choose, the Friedmans developed a television series of the same name that originally aired on the Public Broadcasting Service (PBS) in 1980. The Friedmans agreed to the television series after being approached by Robert Chitester, president of the PBS station in Erie, Pennsylvania, and an enthusiastic convert to the Friedmans' vision after having read *Capitalism and Freedom*.[64] Appreciating the qualities of television as a medium and displaying his speaking skills, Milton Friedman cultivated a compelling persona as the on-camera advocate for market relationships. He explained market dynamics in everyday terms that could resonate with viewers, expressed excitement for the ideas he shared, and presented himself as a relatable person while also drawing on his authority as a Nobel Prize–winning economist.[65]

Across their persuasive efforts, the Friedmans engaged diverse relationship networks that intimated the tension between their championing of individual agency and the coordinated efforts they undertook to realize their vision as well as the differential material resources that publics may utilize in their engagement. An adroit PBS executive, Chitester conducted a robust private fundraising campaign to pay for the production of the *Free to Choose* series without any assistance from the Corporation for Public Broadcasting. His knowledge of the industry and PBS sponsorship rules enabled corporate and foundation sponsors to participate without running afoul of relevant regulations and laws. Chitester successfully pitched the show to other PBS executives as balancing the viewpoints of other programs while providing objective economic ideas.[66] Funders not only supported the television program but facilitated its wider distribution to high schools, colleges, and other audiences. In these ways, the Friedmans "could rely on a network of allied institutions to provide the forms of support that this new era of advocacy required."[67] As such, the Friedmans' persuasive campaigns constituted innovative modes of publicity.

If persuasion represents a necessary, powerful, and potentially destructive tool, what kind of persuasion did the Friedmans favor? From one perspective, this may appear as an unanswerable question. Their contrary claims about individual interest, humility, and respect may suggest that they held no coherent view of persuasion, tactically delimiting its use to argue for their preferred policy positions and visions of publics. However, seeking an answer to this question, while acknowledging irresolvable tensions, offers potential insights into historical and contemporary neoliberal opposition to political movements and public policies that address societal inequalities and injustices. Some of this neoliberal resistance may rest importantly on the perceived nature, dynamics, and domain of persuasion itself. For their part, the Friedmans favored persuasion as a private individual practice rather than a public group effort.

I characterize a "Friedmanian" theory of persuasion as explicating an individual-to-individual mode of communication that appeals to people in their roles as direct decision-makers and carries implications for notions of knowledge and contingency. On this basis, persuasion must proceed as a cumulative process by which an individual has to successfully persuade anyone affected by a change. When concerned with an individual's belief, persuading the individual alone meets the obligations of this theory. Any wider change that affects more than one individual would require multiple instances of persuasion. For instance, the passage of laws prohibiting racial discrimination in hiring, which the Friedmans themselves opposed, would require persuading everyone affected by the law, rather than just a majority of legislators. This theory recognizes the possibility of one-to-many persuasion, as represented in the traditional rhetorical situation, but in these cases, audiences would operate not as collective agents but as functional collections of individuals. Indeed, as Catherine Chaput explains, Milton Friedman's on-camera persona in the *Free to Choose* television series exemplified an individual orientation to persuasion. Noting Friedman's positive energy as host, Chaput maintains that the program owed its popularity in part to "his ability to harness this intangible, affective quality within the television medium, making it feel like the audience is receiving that one-to-one personal value production."[68] Chaput suggests that Friedman did not lecture to viewers as a mass but conversed with viewers as individuals.

In this way, a Friedmanian theory of persuasion makes a radically empirical demand of efforts to conceptualize ethical decision-making as a social process. In his essay on discourse ethics, Jürgen Habermas argues that all ethical theories that recognize the possibility of evaluating competing ethical claims carry some degree of generalizability. Values and principles warrant our assent only if we (not just I or you) would abide by them. Ethical theories vary in the generalizability they demand: some seek universal adherence, while others recognize differences across cultures and other distinctions. Any single-case ethical claim, from this perspective, would not permit people to assess its merits in comparison to other ethical claims. Generalizability suggests that the knowledge relevant to persuasion is sharable and scalable. Addressing the possibility of ethical decision-making in large, complex societies, Habermas locates the discovery of sound ethical claims in their ability to secure the agreement of diverse interlocutors in *potential* dialogic encounters.[69] Insisting on the *actual* agreement of everyone potentially affected would effectively disqualify the ethical basis of any public effort to advance ameliorative change. Yet this is exactly what a Friedmanian theory of persuasion would demand from advocates, who could act only as individuals in direct exchange with other individuals.

A Friedmanian theory of persuasion draws on a conception of knowledge as arising from direct experience. In discussing the relational practice of freedom, I explain that it carries an ethical stance of humility that corresponds with an awareness of the limits of one's knowledge. The limits of one's knowledge also outline the basis for persuasion. Most of the time, individual choice would signal the non-adjudication of competing claims and views. Since no individual could judge the self-interest of another, there would be no reason for individuals to make comparative judgments about self-interests. Persuasion presumably would arise in those circumstances where an individual identifies their self-interest in engaging someone else's views. By proceeding at an individual-to-individual level, persuasion would operate on the basis of self-knowledge. As suggested by the example of the individual seeking to persuade the racist, persuasion would unsettle the certainty of self-interest, but the dyadic character of a persuasive relationship would ensure that any uncertainty must be resolved by the assent of the participants themselves. If the racist decides to renounce their discriminatory views, then they would do so in their self-interest. If the racist refuses, then their continued commitment to bigotry would remain in their self-interest, even if their interlocutor disagrees with this view.

Persuasion veers off-course when individuals address topics that they do not know, namely, others' self-interests. From a Friedmanian perspective, we can imagine a case of off-course persuasion when two individuals compare proposals to address another person's racism. If, for example, these two individuals debate the best means for achieving passage of a law that bars discriminatory considerations in hiring decisions, they improperly infringe on the self-interest of the employer to utilize their own preferred hiring criteria. The Friedmans insisted that majority-rule decision-making necessarily commits this error. In seeking to address some "general" interest, majority rule places people in the position of making decisions about someone else's interest without permitting the other to determine for themselves whether the decision reflects their self-interest. This is why the "the ballot box produces conformity without unanimity."[70] The Friedmans identified unanimity as their ideal because it avoids the coercion entailed in majority-based decision-making. In this spirit, the Friedmans offered a distillation of their implicit theory of persuasion in holding that "the only person who can truly persuade you is yourself."[71] Only the individual really knows their self-interest. With the issue of racism, perhaps, a Friedmanian theory would locate persuasion not in the interactions of interlocutors, but with the holder of the racist views.

The conception of knowledge underlying the Friedmans' implicit theory of persuasion resonated with the views of their like-minded intellectual contemporaries. In *The Phantom Public*, Walter Lippmann questioned the capacity of people to participate actively in public affairs. According to Lippmann, democratic faith in the power of the public rests on a "false ideal" of an "omnicompetent, sovereign citizen."[72] Against this view, Lippmann proposed a sharply circumscribed alternative for public action based on a distinction between specific, direct opinion and general, indirect opinion. In their daily lives, individuals regularly make decisions regarding the specific activities in which they participate directly, as, for example, bankers or teachers. Lippmann observed that "the work of the world is carried on by men in their executive capacity, by an infinite number of concrete acts."[73] These concrete acts cultivate sound opinions that draw on a firm foundation of experience. In contrast, the democratic vision of public engagement depends on the uncertain character of general opinion, which exceeds individuals' experiences and demands a wider knowledge. Yet, "modern society is not visible to anybody, nor intelligible continuously and as a whole."[74] Publics lack the knowledge to act as publics. The best public opinion can do is to arise in times of crisis to support political actors who may resolve the crisis.

Inspired by Lippmann, in his foundational book *The Road to Serfdom* Friedrich Hayek also articulated a perspective tying decision-making to direct experience. While Hayek developed his conceptual framework independently, he found in Lippmann's *The Good Society* a positive argument for freedom and the threat it faces from central planning.[75] Both authors argued that collective decision-making relies on uncertain knowledge. Hayek held that the philosophy of individualism stands on the basic recognition that "it is impossible for any man to survey more than a limited field, to be aware of the urgency of more than a limited number of needs." Like the Friedmans, who found their own inspiration in *The Road to Serfdom*, Hayek underscored individual diversity. Different values and interests motivate different individuals, suggesting innumerable life paths and means of personal fulfillment. Warranting respect for the uniqueness of every individual, diversity positions "the individual as the ultimate judge of his ends."[76] Individuals pursuing their own interests make decisions on a sound base of knowledge, and they coordinate their activities with others when their interests align. In contrast, the invocation of a "general interest" lacks a "sufficiently definite meaning" and facilitates no "particular course of action."[77] Individuals cannot act on what they do not know.

The implicit theory of persuasion outlined by the Friedmans and the attendant model of decision-making they shared with Lippmann and Hayek constitute an effort to contain contingency. Living in a world of unique individuals presents an endless array of opportunities. Market-based relationships do not involve coercion because any interest unavailable through one particular relationship could be satisfied through another. Yet this world also underscores an individual's modest place in an infinite network of human relationships. This wider network demands humility and, perhaps, awe and fear. The unknown represented by contingency implies potential energy and excitement as well as caution and danger. Basing persuasion and decision-making on direct experience and knowledge offers a surer path through an uncertain world. Along these lines, the Friedmans, Lippmann, and Hayek all called attention to what they regarded as the vagueness and ambiguity connoted in such phrases as the "general interest" and the "common good." Urging action on these bases would only risk the more ominous consequences of contingency. We may compare this approach with the way rhetorical scholarship has contended with contingency. In contrast to this self-proclaimed individualism, a rhetorical framework has sought the wisdom of the collective. Because decision-making addresses uncertainty, individuals should interact to articulate and evaluate different perspectives, identifying potential strengths and weaknesses on grounds that participants themselves may accept.[78] From a rhetorical perspective, far from being a problem, collective decision-making has represented an efficacious solution for dealing with contingency.

Education

The Friedmans recognized that their vision of human relationships would not materialize automatically. Indeed, they regularly expressed a fear that existing societies were moving in the opposite direction, toward more centralized control and less individual autonomy. In this context, to save freedom, the societal institutions of the family and schools had to play critical roles. As I explain above, families (or, more accurately, particular family members) needed to nurture children and foster their growth from irresponsible individuals into responsible adults who could exercise choice. Schools needed to teach children how to build proper relationships that would embody self-interest, freedom, dignity, and respect. This charge, importantly, consisted of inculcating among students a common set of values that would secure the social stability necessary for the practice of freedom. Ideally, families and schools could work together, which the Friedmans identified as a benefit of their highly influential voucher proposal.[79]

Addressing the topic of education across their writings, the Friedmans articulated a consistent normative framework while modifying their justification for vouchers and their policy positions on education. Throughout their work, their commitments to the individual and freedom did not waver. Nor did they retreat from a view of schooling as an important vehicle for teaching values. When the Friedmans first began to discuss vouchers, they did so, in Milton Friedman's words, as an expression of "the philosophy of a free society." Themselves graduates of public schools, the Friedmans did not devalue their experiences: "Both my wife and I were satisfied with the public schools we had attended."[80] Instead, they wished to see the organization of education exemplify the values that schools should teach. However, in the 1980s, participating in wider public discourses about problems with public education, they diagnosed a dramatic decline in the performance of public schools. Even as publics devoted more resources to schools, students learned less. Accompanying this changed justification for vouchers, they also shifted their positions on education financing and compulsory school attendance laws.[81]

Education could promote stability for market publics by teaching students a minimum degree of literacy and knowledge and a common set of values. Yet the Friedmans resisted a detailed account of the values that education could instill: "Drawing a line between providing for the common social values required for a stable society, on the one hand, and indoctrination inhibiting freedom of thought and belief, on the other is another one of those vague boundaries that is easier to mention than to define."[82] Nevertheless, we may discern the contours of these values from the Friedmans' normative vision. From this perspective, stability requires instruction in the qualities of market-modeled relationships, including the enactment of freedom through choice, as well as the need for tolerance of diversity and respect for the dignity and autonomy of individuals. A pedagogy of common values would also consider the duties and obligations of these relationships, such as a willingness to represent one's interests honestly and to deliver promised goods and services. Because stability would need to extend from human relationships to the societal institutions facilitating these relationships, instruction would address such values as the inviolability of property rights and the enforceability of contracts.[83] Teaching these as shared values, education would benefit all members of a society.

In their early, "philosophical" case for vouchers, as they recognized the essential contributions of education to their normative vision of human relationships, the Friedmans distinguished between a "general education for citizenship" warranting taxpayer support and a specific vocational and professional education warranting no such support. A general education, oriented toward the relationships and values I have explicated, benefits everyone in a society by securing a climate conductive to freedom. Education enables individuals to anticipate the actions of others, thereby informing choice. Individuals can pursue their self-interests in relationships with others knowing that other individuals will act similarly. In contrast, vocational and professional education only benefit the individuals seeking this education. The Friedmans regarded this training as an investment in human capital analogous to investments in machinery, buildings, or other assets. While individuals pursuing this training reap rewards through higher salaries, other individuals receive no benefit. Therefore, the Friedmans concluded, the individuals benefiting from vocational and professional education should bear the full cost.

On this point, even as vouchers have become a primary mechanism for contemporary neoliberal education reforms, advocates and policymakers have not maintained the Friedmans' distinction among types of education. To the contrary, contemporary neoliberal reforms have focused on STEM education and job training at the expense of any general education for citizenship. For instance, in a 2012 speech, Wisconsin governor Scott Walker held that his administration would evaluate higher education by considering whether "young people [are] getting degrees in jobs that are open and needed today."[84] As this quote suggests, many contemporary policymakers see widespread benefits in vocational and professional education while they question the value of civic education.

With particular values and relationships shaping school curricula, vouchers offer the meta-value of restructuring educational institutions and systems to align with market visions of human relationships. Most directly, a widespread system of vouchers would enable all parents and guardians to exercise their "own choice" in selecting educational options for their children from a range of public and private enterprises.[85] Parents and guardians presumably would choose schools on the basis of what they regard as the most appropriate option for their children, but choice would not serve only as a means to this end. Choice would constitute the practice of freedom. Celebrating the fiftieth anniversary of Milton Friedman's original 1955 voucher essay, Abigail Thernstrom identified "the freedom of individuals to make choices" as "central to the American creed."[86] The exercise of choice enacts individual and cultural identities. In choosing, Americans assert their agency and autonomy. In making educational choices, then, parents would model for their children the identity of independent agent.[87] Denying choice fosters alienation by placing both parents and children in dependent positions.

Enabling choice, vouchers promote practices of public engagement that resist political conformity and facilitate the formation of market publics that embrace individual diversity. On this basis, vouchers facilitate individual agency in education: "Parents could express their views about schools directly by withdrawing their children from one school and sending them to another." This withdrawal, or market exit, itself constitutes a direct form of communication. Parents' choices convey information, and they do so without requiring the intervention of others. Without vouchers, wealthy parents possess the means to send their children to private schools, but other parents may "express their views only through cumbrous political channels."[88] Politics disrespects individuality, forcing people to reach a common judgment as a basis for action. Removing unnecessary layers of talk, markets express a communicative energy that speaks directly to experience and enables diverse action. Moreover, this decisive action communicates to other market actors who may not be aware of particular options. In his argument for privatizing public education, Mark Pennington holds that "freedom of exit" does not "simply let parents impart their own values to their children but [allows] the broader community of children and parents alike to benefit from whatever wisdom may be contained therein."[89] From this perspective, market exit represents a form of public reasoning based in experience. In contrast, traditional public schooling depends on methods of majoritarian reasoning that "stifle the processes of public learning that occur when people can observe the results of a polycentric process" as exemplified in markets.[90] Rooted in practice, market exit enacts the individual-to-individual mode of persuasion that the Friedmans preferred.

Over time, the Friedmans' case for vouchers shifted from emphasizing their fit with market relationships to their capacity to redress pressing educational problems. The virtues of vouchers did not disappear, but the Friedmans reformulated their argument to meet a changing public context.[91] Noting widespread concerns with the quality of schools, which were exacerbated in part by the National Commission on Excellence in Education's scathing 1982 report A Nation at Risk, the Friedmans located the problems with the "increasing centralization and bureaucratization of schools."[92] Since the 1960s, the federal government had consolidated its control over education, usurping the proper authority of parents and local communities. On this point, in *Free to Choose*, the Friedmans approvingly quoted Walter Lippmann to rebuke the arrogance of federal education officials who believed that "there are no limits to man's capacity to govern others."[93] Federal officials stood between teachers and parents, pursuing their own self-interest in obtaining more power over the interests of children. As Mark Hlavacik explains, the Friedmans blamed the "bureaucrats" for damaging public education. Denying parents their independent agency, federal bureaucrats believed that they made better decisions. Hlavacik observes that, from the Friedmans' perspective, "the bureaucrats, by definition, collectivize what should be decision making driven by individual agents."[94] Bureaucratization had reduced choice, imposed conformity, and worsened educational outcomes.

Bureaucratization had failed education because bureaucrats lacked a sound basis of knowledge for their decision-making. They had no direct experience with the children for whom they expressed concern. This experience resided with parents: "Parents generally have both greater interest in their children's schooling and more intimate knowledge of their capacities and needs than anyone else."[95] Preventing the rightful application of parental knowledge, consolidation of power at the federal level had dissociated experience and decision-making. Illustrating the circulation of this theory of knowledge and decision-making among contemporary supporters of market-based education reform, Pennington holds that policies promoting parental choice rest "on the proposition that no authority or majority has sufficient knowledge to coordinate educational provision *on a society-wide basis.*"[96] This theory denies the wisdom that rhetorical scholars have associated with group deliberation and collective judgment. Only by returning decision-making to parents as individuals may schools improve. Further, choice would spur competition among schools, promoting a wide variety of options addressing the interests of diverse students. In this context, "only schools that satisfy their customers will survive."[97] Successful schools in a voucher system would emulate the practices of individual market actors; they would fulfill a self-interest of survival in relationships with parents and guardians exercising their self-interests.

A Vision and a Vehicle

The Friedmans took full advantage of the realist style of economics. Especially when they criticized what they regarded as the folly of government officials,

they wrote with the confidence and authoritativeness of individuals possessing the special insight of unyielding truths. From the Friedmans' perspective, their confidence did not replicate the arrogance of the social reformer
because they appreciated the power of self-interest. They knew that no one—
not even economists—could decide what is best for everyone. Pursuing their
self-interest, individuals alone should chart their life paths. Of course, no
individual operates in isolation, but their relationships with others properly
take shape with consideration for what each individual hopes to accomplish.
Relating to others this way, individuals may enact their freedom, which warrants respect to protect everyone's freedom.

As this characterization of the Friedmans' views of individuals and their
relationships suggests, they articulated a powerful normative vision, which
they did not attempt to conceal in realist prose. Markets solve problems,
certainly, but the relationships that markets model enable a fundamental
realization of one's humanity. Through market relationships, individuals
can realize themselves as free and independent actors. Breaking from constraint, they can renounce dependency and conformity and pursue what
they really want. In this way, the Friedmans reversed the long-standing
tendency among rhetorical scholars to locate freedom in public engagement. To the contrary, the Friedmans saw politics as a ruse for shackling
individuals. Their forceful normative vision has circulated as a capacious
vision. Not every contemporary neoliberal advocate draws inspiration from
the Friedmans, but the Friedmans' elucidation of free human relationships
accommodates multiple neoliberalisms. Advocates have defended various
market-based policies under the banner of freedom. They have justified
calls to lower taxes and repeal regulations by invoking a release of individual
energy and innovation. They have identified competition as the means to
revive sluggish bureaucracies and solve pressing problems. And individuals
have been instructed to enable their self-improvement by following their
self-interests.

Vouchers, and the larger movement for school choice they have spurred,
have provided the vehicle to realize the Friedmans' vision. If self-interest represents an instinctual force, self-interest does not determine its own content.
Indeed, the Friedmans' definition of self-interest includes a seemingly innumerable set of life paths as distinctive as the individuals who may pursue
them. Individuals, then, need to learn how to discover their self-interests.
Moreover, they need to learn how to relate to others in ways that advance
their freedom while respecting the freedom of others. This requires shared
values, as well as practices and institutions that may sustain a wider climate

of freedom. All of this requires education. Vouchers promise to orient curricula around proper values and relationships while restructuring educational institutions on market terms. Vouchers represent one approach in neoliberal reforms of public education, but they embody the fundamental framework driving these reforms.

3

COMPETITION AND INNOVATION IN
THE EDUCATION INDUSTRY: BETSY DEVOS'S
CAMPAIGN FOR SCHOOL CHOICE

The US federal government substantively entered the realm of K–12 education policy in 1965 under the banner of "opportunity."[1] In a January message to Congress that previewed the parameters of the Elementary and Secondary Education Act (ESEA), President Lyndon Baines Johnson urged policymakers to join him in declaring "a national goal of *Full Educational Opportunity*."[2] He observed that since its founding the nation had compiled an admirable record of educational advancement. However, not all Americans benefited from these accomplishments. Divergent educational outcomes had revealed two school systems: the first system successfully served the needs and interests of a majority of schoolchildren, their families, and the nation, while the second system failed the mostly poor students and families it served. The problems of this second system did not arise because educators lacked sufficient commitment or competence. Instead, insufficient resources hampered poor families inside and outside the classroom. President Johnson linked "ignorance" and poverty: "Just as ignorance breeds poverty, poverty all too often breeds ignorance in the next generation." Since the concentration of poor families in particular urban and rural areas created uneven burdens for the nation's local school districts, the adequate distribution of resources across the country constituted a "national problem."[3]

Johnson emphasized the economic value of education, but he did so differently from contemporary market-oriented advocates like Betsy DeVos. Johnson focused on education itself as a collective good, without distinguishing public and private modes of providing this good. Further, Johnson situated economic value among the multiple benefits of education. He held that "nothing matters more to the future of our country: not our military preparedness—for armed might is worthless if we lack the brain power to build a world of peace; not our productive economy—for we cannot sustain growth without trained manpower; not our democratic system of government—for freedom is fragile if citizens are ignorant."[4] Moreover, while economics functioned as a powerful appeal in his congressional message, Johnson contextualized this appeal amid relationships of inequality, mutuality, and responsibility. He articulated the primary purpose of the ESEA as bringing the successes of education to all students, including poor students. Redressing disparities entailed pooling resources at the national level and then redistributing them through the federal government. Even though their children received a good education, middle-class and wealthier Americans could not remain complacent about a substandard education for the poor. Inequality ultimately harmed everyone.[5]

By the time Betsy DeVos took office as the eleventh US secretary of education, public discourse on education reform had shifted dramatically to highlight themes of accountability, competition, and choice. Both Democratic and Republican presidents linked the quality of the nation's schools primarily to its economic health and international competitiveness. In his advocacy for the No Child Left Behind Act, President George W. Bush identified accountability as "the cornerstone of reform," and he articulated a business framework in referring to school principals as "the CEO of a school."[6] Illuminating the competitive advantages of excellent schools, President Barack Obama stressed that nations "that outeducate us today will outcompete us tomorrow," which evidenced the centrality of education in determining "the quality of our future as a nation and the lives our children will lead."[7] Education served as an irreplaceable economic asset and potent international weapon.

As these quotes from Presidents Bush and Obama suggest, we cannot understand the shifts in education discourses from the 1960s through the contemporary era strictly in terms of partisanship. Beyond party affiliation, broader economic, political, and cultural changes—which neoliberalism names—have directed the attention of policymakers and citizens to the market as the means of efficacious social change. When Johnson sent his message to Congress, the United States was in the midst of a post-WWII economic boom that doubled household incomes between 1948 and 1972, and Americans expressed great trust in government and other societal institutions. A series of crises, ranging from the Vietnam War and Watergate to gas shortages and double-digit inflation, subsequently weakened the economy and reduced trust in government.[8] When the Friedmans wrote *Capitalism and Freedom*, which was published only three years before the ESEA, they articulated a marginal perspective. By the 1970s and 1980s, their neoliberal framework attracted mainstream and powerful adherents like British prime minister Margaret Thatcher and US president Ronald Reagan. These diverse developments promoted a commonsense view of the superiority of markets over governments.[9] In an especially prominent example, in his first inaugural address, President Reagan asserted, "In this present crisis, government is not the solution to our problem; government is the problem."[10] In this statement, Reagan realigned the capacities and responsibilities of government and markets. He rejected the role of government as a counterweight to markets. Instead, Reagan advanced markets as a corrective to and heuristic for government, thereby subjecting society, in Michel Foucault's terms, to the "dynamic of competition" and engendering "an enterprise society."[11]

Betsy DeVos built her own reputation as a promoter of markets and a champion of school choice. Prior to her selection as education secretary, she gained attention as a sharp critic of the public schools and government-based reforms. In a 2015 speech to the South by Southwest Education Conference, which has portrayed itself as a venue for discussion of leading-edge education reforms, DeVos declared flatly that "government really sucks." Favoring "one-size-fits-all solutions," government "stifle[s] innovation and it abhors improvisation." She called on her business-savvy audience to work with her to "open up the education industry—and let's not kid ourselves that it isn't an industry—we must open it up to entrepreneurs and innovators." The current education system operates as "a closed system, a closed industry, a closed market. It's a monopoly. It's a dead end. And the best and brightest innovators and risk-takers steer way clear of it."[12] Competition would bring business talent to education. Guided by their ingenuity, these leaders would generate technological advances and bountiful choices for the education consumer, who has grown accustomed to choice in other industries.

As education secretary, Betsy DeVos presented herself as an astute businesswoman with a forward-thinking view of the potential for technology to reanimate an antiquated system. Positioning herself outside of the "education establishment," DeVos aligned herself with the interests of students as individuals who should exercise choice, through their families, to find the right educational fit. As this characterization intimates, DeVos's advocacy of market-based reform combined familiar themes articulated by the Friedmans with a contemporary embrace of technology as a reliably transformative force. Her advocacy exemplified a "technoliberalism," which Damien Smith Pfister has invoked to illuminate technologically inflected visions of market-based societies. Pfister explains that technoliberalism sustains the neoliberal focus on the atomistic, self-interested individual as the universal subject while recontextualizing this actor in a digital world. In this setting, innovation operates as a key term. Yet calls for innovation betray a "circular logic" as "innovation for innovation's sake," without any assurances that particular innovations will constitute progress. An especially prized form of transformation arises from "disruptive innovation." As Pfister explains, "'disruptive innovation' refers to a kind of innovation that creates brand new markets for products and destabilizes, or even eliminates, markets for older products."[13] In looking to open up the education industry, in working to break the monopoly of the education establishment, Betsy DeVos sought to disrupt public education in the name of competition, choice, and freedom.

Establishing a context for my analysis, I begin by discussing the pronounced economic shift in federal education policy discourse in recent decades. I then explain how DeVos's public persona both drew attention to her market-based advocacy and frustrated her reform goals. In the following section, I address how DeVos sought to capitalize on her notoriety through the bully pulpit of her cabinet post. Turning to my analysis, in the subsequent sections I examine key themes that emerged in DeVos's public advocacy: a call to innovate educational delivery systems, a self-presentation as an outsider, an identification of "fit" as the basic problem with education, an affirmation of parental knowledge, and an individualistic approach to race and racism.

Emphasizing Economics in Education Policy

The 1982 publication of *A Nation at Risk*, prepared by the National Commission on Excellence in Education, both reflected and precipitated changes in state and federal education policy. By the early 1980s, policymakers had abandoned the expansive vision of Johnson's Great Society. Stagflation—simultaneous economic stagnation and inflation—frustrated the widely accepted approaches that policymakers used to manage the economy. In a July 15, 1979, nationally televised address, President Jimmy Carter diagnosed a "crisis of confidence" that "strikes at the very heart and soul and spirit of our national will." This crisis had engendered "growing doubt about the meaning of our lives" and instigated "the loss of a unity of purpose for our nation."[14] In more educationally specific terms, crises over court-mandated busing for the purposes of racial integration cast doubt on the relationships of mutuality and the principle of equality that informed Johnson's message to Congress. Further, rising public concerns about school performance dampened the sense of accomplishment articulated in Johnson's message.[15] Yet the late 1970s and early 1980s sent conflicting signals over the direction of federal education policy. In 1979, Congress and President Carter created the US Department of Education, which began operating in May 1980. Over the same period, Republican presidential candidate Ronald Reagan denounced the move, and after his November 1980 electoral victory, President Reagan continued to call for the department's elimination.[16]

An enormously influential report, A Nation at Risk precipitated fundamental change in state and federal education policy. A rarity among government publications, copies of the report circulated like a best-selling novel.[17] A Nation at Risk facilitated a paradigm shift in US education policy, defining new problems for educators, policymakers, and citizens, and changing the terms of debate over education reform. The report successfully focused public attention on the supposedly deteriorating quality of education as a pressing national problem.[18] Holly McIntush argues that A Nation at Risk "set the agenda for education policy" by shifting "the focus of education discourse from education as a means of social and political equalization to education as a means to economic prosperity."[19] In this vein, to aid individuals and the nation, policymakers privileged the economic value of education.

The report itself adopted an alarmist tone. In its opening paragraph, A Nation at Risk insisted that "the educational foundations of our society are presently being eroded by a rising tide of mediocrity that threatens our very future as a Nation and a people." Identifying an immediate crisis, the commission suspected that "if an unfriendly foreign power had attempted to impose on America the mediocre educational performance that exists today, we might well have viewed it as an act of war. As it stands, we have allowed this to happen to ourselves." This self-inflicted injury carried enormous consequences: "We live among determined, well-educated, and strongly motivated competitors. We compete with them for international standing and markets."[20] This association of education, economics, competition, and war did not appear to be coincidental. The United States simply could not ignore the economic planning of other nations, as these combatants strategized for comparative advantage. The United States had to compete, and education constituted an irreplaceable component in its arsenal. The stakes of this competition were paramount: losing threatened the viability of the nation.

Hearing the alarm bell of A Nation at Risk, state and federal policymakers pursued various education reforms centered on standards and accountability. In the 1980s, state-level policymakers, especially governors, initiated policy reforms, while federal policymakers largely supported their actions.[21] These efforts culminated in the 1989 Charlottesville Education Summit, which President George H. W. Bush convened to discuss education reform with the nation's governors.[22] At the conclusion of the summit, the president and governors issued a joint communiqué declaring their agreement that "a better educated citizenry is the key to the continued growth and prosperity of the United States." Recalling the urgency of A Nation at Risk, they asserted that "as a Nation we must have an educated workforce, second to none, in order to succeed in an increasingly competitive world economy."[23] During the summit, the governors expressed support for voluntary national education goals. Although Congress rejected President Bush's proposal for such standards, some governors continued to advocate for reform. In his foreword to a 1990 book on education reform, Arkansas governor Bill Clinton, who had led the nation's governors on education issues, warned of the baneful consequences of losing an international competition: "We have to measure ourselves by international standards. By those standards, we're not doing very well. Unless we do better, our ability to compete in the world economy will be severely damaged." Comparing schools to "modern corporations," Governor Clinton called for (among other reforms) reducing "bureaucracy, paperwork, and unnecessary layers of management."[24] A few years after his victorious presidential campaign, in 1994, President Clinton secured congressional passage of Goals 2000, which sought the development of voluntary national standards and offered grants to states to support these efforts.[25]

The No Child Left Behind Act of 2001 (NCLB), signed into law by President George W. Bush in early 2002, strengthened the federal role in K–12 education policy by shifting from voluntary to mandatory standards and testing and by imposing penalties for failures to meet benchmarks.[26] As a condition of federal funding, NCLB prescribed annual testing of students in core subject areas. To avoid sanctions, schools needed to demonstrate "adequate yearly progress" toward a goal of 100 percent student proficiency in 2014. Increasingly strict penalties, including the potential replacement of instructional staff and school restructuring, could apply to schools that did not exhibit "adequate yearly progress." NCLB moved through Congress as a bipartisan piece of legislation, with key contributions from Democrats at critical junctures and overwhelming bipartisan support for the conference report in the House and Senate.[27]

From A Nation at Risk to NCLB, calls for accountability, standards, and testing effectively served as movement toward establishing the conditions for dynamic education markets, even as Democrats and Republicans disagreed about whether choice in these markets should be pursued through charter schools or vouchers.[28] Although it did not support vouchers, the Obama administration's Race to the Top program offered competitive grants to states for educational innovations, including performance-based teacher evaluations and the expansion of charter schools.[29] In a bipartisan manner, accountability and standards functioned analogously to the roles of central banks and other regulatory market institutions in establishing common measures of educational value and exchange. Various actors, from state education officers to individual families, could participate in educational markets confident that they could exchange with others through commensurable means. Testing and test scores served as market valuations and currency. Individual schools, local districts, and states could market themselves to individual and institutional investors as sound opportunities.[30] Test scores also provided market actors with the information they needed to make comparative choices among various education providers.[31]

While the primacy of markets did not lessen, impatience with testing and frustration with federal mandates grew after NCLB. From the start, the law stipulated its own shortcomings, insofar as substantial progress toward a goal of 100 percent proficiency would have required fundamental, structural social changes inside and outside of schools that policymakers historically have been unwilling to pursue.[32] Even so, the prominence of testing in the NCLB era engendered public resistance. News accounts described an "opt-out" movement across local communities in the United States, in which parents removed their children from testing. "It's an act of civil disobedience," remarked one Wisconsin parent.[33] As he advocated for his own education reforms, President Obama remained committed to standards and testing, but he retorted that "this is not about the kind of testing that has mushroomed under No Child Left Behind. This is not about more tests. . . . It is about finally getting testing right, about developing thoughtful assessments that lead to better results."[34] Nevertheless, President Obama and Congress could not agree on a strong federal role for K–12 education policy. Instead, on December 10, 2015, President Obama signed the Every Student Succeeds Act (ESSA), which returned much of the federal authority claimed in NCLB back to the states.[35] In his speech at the signing ceremony for ESSA, President Obama affirmed the goals of NCLB but critiqued its "cookie-cutter reforms." This new legislation, he promised, would "consider the specific needs of each community."[36] In the subsequent administration, Betsy DeVos would refocus educational needs from the community level to each individual, and her plan consisted of more choice.[37]

Unqualified and Incompetent: The Challenging Public
Persona of Betsy DeVos

The Senate confirmed Betsy DeVos as the US secretary of education only
after Vice President Mike Pence entered its chamber to cast a tie-breaking
vote in her favor, the first time a vice president had done so for a cabinet
nominee. Hailed by conservative activists for school choice, DeVos encountered adamant opposition elsewhere. Two Republican senators broke ranks
with their party to force the tie, after receiving "thousands of messages" from
home-state constituents to reject the nomination.[38] In the weeks before her
confirmation, news accounts portrayed DeVos as a questionable choice. *Education Week* reported that DeVos would be the first secretary of education
never to have attended a public school or sent a child to a public school.
A commentator in the *New Yorker* characterized DeVos as an exemplary "representative of the 'donor class.'"[39] The *Washington Post* represented DeVos as
"a billionaire Republican power broker with no professional experience in
schools" who had spent "millions of dollars in a successful push to expand
voucher programs." The *New York Times* reported that DeVos's advocacy had
"focused little on existing public schools, and almost entirely on establishing newer, more entrepreneurial models to compete with traditional schools
for students and money."[40] A coalition of thirty-three civil and human rights
groups issued a public statement asserting that DeVos's nomination called
into question "core principles of fairness, equality and a commitment to education."[41] As education secretary, DeVos attracted a lot of attention, but much
of it was negative: detractors and news media often represented her as a
wealthy dilettante with a tendentious agenda and a questionable commitment to civil rights. Public missteps in congressional testimony and media
interviews reinforced an image of incompetence.

During DeVos's confirmation hearing, Democratic senators repeatedly
referenced her wealth and potential conflicts of interest. In her opening
statement, Senator Patty Murray, the ranking member of the Health, Education, Labor, and Pensions Committee, argued that citizens deserved an education secretary "free of conflicts of interest" and someone who would "put
families and workers first and not millionaires, billionaires, or big corporations." Her colleague Senator Chris Murphy explored potential conflicts of
interest related to the DeVos family's involvement with K12 Inc., an operator
of for-profit online charter schools. Noting the seven-figure salary of the CEO
and the millions of dollars in K12 corporate profit, Senator Murphy asked,
"Do you support companies and individuals profiting from public education

dollars that is essentially taking money away from students to pay salaries for CEOs in return for investors?" In response, DeVos invoked a theme that, as I explain in my analysis, constituted a key component of her market advocacy: she distinguished the content of education from its "delivery." For now, I cite Murphy's question to illustrate the persistent oppositional portrayal of DeVos as a wealthy profiteer. Advancing this image even more directly, Senator Bernie Sanders asked, "Do you think that if you were not a multibillionaire, if your family has not made hundreds of millions of dollars in contributions to the Republican Party, that you would be sitting here today?"[42] Unsurprisingly, DeVos resisted the association.

While DeVos could not rewrite her personal or family histories, missteps before congressional committees and in prominent interviews as well as evasiveness in answering questions reinforced negative representations. During her confirmation hearing, in response to a senator's question about student assessment, DeVos confused proficiency and growth-based measures of achievement; the former set a specific threshold for identifying student achievement, while growth-based measures track student improvement over time. Preferring growth-based approaches, many educators and researchers have criticized proficiency standards as proxies for socioeconomic status.[43] On a different topic, when asked about the appropriateness of guns on school grounds, DeVos referenced an earlier exchange to respond that "there's probably a gun in the school to protect from grizzlies."[44] Satirizing this statement, a guns-against-grizzly-bears meme, which included images of Winnie the Pooh and Smokey Bear, quickly circulated on social media. One month into her tenure as education secretary, in preparation for a speech to the leaders of the nation's historically Black colleges and universities (HBCUs), DeVos issued a public statement praising HBCUs as "real pioneers when it comes to school choice." Predictably, online commentators also skewered this historically ignorant comment by, for example, posting images of segregated drinking fountains and labeling them pioneers of "beverage options."[45] One year later, in a heavily promoted 60 Minutes interview, Secretary DeVos seemed unprepared to explain the poor performance of schools in her home state of Michigan. Interviewer Lesley Stahl asked DeVos, "Have you seen the really bad schools? Maybe try to figure out what they're doing?" DeVos replied that she had "not intentionally visited schools that are underperforming." Stahl suggested that "maybe you should." DeVos concurred: "Maybe I should." Later in the interview, when Stahl asked her why she had become "the most hated cabinet secretary," DeVos explained that "I'm more misunderstood than anything."[46] Amid these and other struggles, DeVos received no public statement of support from the person who appointed her. Indeed, a "tell-all" book from a former White House staffer disclosed that President Trump referred to his education secretary in private as "Ditzy DeVos."[47]

When asked challenging questions during congressional testimony, Secretary DeVos undermined her own self-presentation by often appearing evasive, especially in response to questions about the potential for discrimination by private schools that may receive government funding. For instance, during a hearing regarding the Department of Education's fiscal year 2018 budget request, Senator Jeff Merkley asked DeVos to ensure that private schools, which "generally set their own admissions policies," would "not be allowed to discriminate against LGBTQ students." She responded that "schools that receive federal funds must follow federal law." Merkley noted the ambiguity of federal law on this issue, but DeVos did not provide an unambiguous assurance. As Merkley pursued the point, DeVos continued to offer a variation of her statement on federal law. Later in the hearing, when Senator Jack Reed asked about discrimination on the basis of disability, DeVos repeatedly returned to this stock response.[48]

Perhaps the most notable instance of evasion occurred in response to Representative Katherine Clark, across two hearings separated by ten months. In a House hearing on the Department of Education fiscal year 2018 budget request, Representative Clark cited the example of a Christian school in Indiana that received state voucher funds but denied admission to students from LGBTQ families. Clark asked DeVos whether a federal voucher program, for which the secretary had sought funding, would prohibit such discrimination. DeVos began with a general reference to school choice, but Clark cut her off. Clark then expanded her question to ask about any form of discrimination. DeVos still would not answer, affirming instead the wisdom of parental choices. The two continued in this vein until the representative's time ran out.[49] Ten months later, at the hearing for the fiscal year 2019 budget request, Representative Clark resumed her questioning. This time, after another prolonged exchange in which Secretary DeVos offered her "federal dollars, federal law" response more than a half dozen times in a sixty-second span, she finally, exasperatedly, answered "yes," she would include nondiscrimination language in any federal program. Clark, expressing the same level of irritation, retorted, "Took a year."[50]

With the prominent counterexample of her statement on pioneering HBCUs, DeVos tended to struggle more during interactive formats, whether in congressional appearances or media interviews, during her first two years as education secretary. She appeared flustered by tough questions, or, conversely, too determined to stick mechanically to her talking points. In speechmaking situations DeVos had greater autonomy to employ the power of the bully pulpit. In her speeches, DeVos developed a more consistent message that expressed technology-friendly, market-inspired themes.

A Cabinet Secretary's Bully Pulpit

Nine months into her tenure, Secretary DeVos conducted a six-state "Rethink School" tour to highlight schools that had tapped the power of choice to serve their students. DeVos hoped that by drawing attention to what she regarded as innovative, outside-the-box thinking, she could persuade parents, administrators, and educators to support school choice. This tour depended on visibility; DeVos did not announce new policy initiatives, nor did she propose new rewards and sanctions to compel schools to act.[51] Instead, she planned to use her visibility as "arguably the best-known and most controversial secretary in the [Education] department's 30-plus-year history" to engender wider conversations about market-based reform.[52] On the one hand, employing the bully pulpit resonated with the inclinations of an education secretary who rebuked top-down, "one-size-fits-all" policymaking. On the other, Congress rejected her request for new funding for a federal voucher program.

In this effort, DeVos had comparatively greater freedom than some of her peers in the cabinet. During the campaign and after his election, Donald Trump did not address the topic of education very often. While his administration highlighted issues of immigration and trade, for example, education policy appeared to occupy a subordinate role. In its first two years, the Trump administration's most substantial K–12 education policy contribution consisted of a relatively modest provision in a December 2017 tax law that permitted withdrawals for primary and secondary educational expenses from education savings accounts typically directed toward college expenses.[53] Because the administration did not prioritize education, DeVos did not have to align her statements with those of her unpredictable boss, and she did not face the prospect of public censure, via Twitter or some other medium, if her statements contradicted the often-changing positions of the president. However, as a consequence, DeVos could not rely on the greater visibility of the presidential bully pulpit to reinforce her message.[54]

Neither could DeVos rely on some of the tools available to her immediate predecessors in the Bush and Obama administrations, as the ESSA reduced the authority of the secretary of education to modify or demand changes to state education plans. Under the ESSA, states still needed to test students once a year in grades 3–8 and once during high school. States also needed to develop standards, evaluation criteria, and reporting systems. The ESSA required states to submit to the Department of Education plans outlining their standards, assessments, learning goals, and other aspects of accountability. However, the law prohibited the secretary from demanding changes in state standards, education goals, assessment methods, accountability indicators, and other items.[55] DeVos recognized these limitations in a speech to state chiefs of education, as she rebuked "overreach" from past administrations and pledged that "every plan I sign is a commitment to that, and only that—the plan meets the requirements of the law." Nevertheless, while DeVos pledged to follow the letter of the law, she exhorted the state chiefs to adopt a new spirit. She insisted that "just because a plan complies with the law doesn't mean it does what's best for students." DeVos appealed to her audience to go beyond "the bare minimum required by the law." She maintained that the ESSA has given states flexibility, but few states have seized it. In particular, DeVos called on state chiefs to expand choices available to students, because accountability ultimately mattered for their sake. She also challenged her audience to "rethink school" and "question everything," asking, "What are you doing to rethink education in your state?"[56] Clearly, Secretary DeVos did not envision rethinking as an amorphous process—she had some strong ideas about education reform that she wanted the state chiefs to adopt. Unable to compel particular reforms, she hoped that some "tough love," as DeVos characterized her approach, would generate the authority that the ESSA formally removed.

Through the first two years of her term, DeVos embraced the bully pulpit to campaign regularly for school choice. Like a candidate for elected office, she gave stump speeches that repeated slogans, stock phrases, and familiar anecdotes. Even after her "Rethink School" tour, she frequently urged audiences to "question everything" about existing schools in the pursuit of innovation. She often shared the success stories of the same individuals, including Denisha Merriweather, who effectively became DeVos's exemplar for choice. DeVos recounted that, as a child, Denisha had failed the third grade twice and moved from school to school. Then, her godmother enrolled Denisha in a Florida school choice program, and her life turned from "struggle" and "difficulty" to "triumph."[57] Indeed, Denisha, herself an advocate of market-based reform as a young adult, accepted a job working for DeVos at the Department of Education.

Expressing passion for her cause, DeVos rallied her supporters to create and sustain market publics that would fight for school choice. In a speech to the American Federation for Children, which she previously led, DeVos mobilized her troops: "Our cause is both right and just. You and I know the fight will not be easy. The opponents of modernizing our education system will pull out all the stops. They will not go quietly into the night. But we should take heart, because our reasons for fighting are noble." DeVos committed herself and her supporters to an unwavering movement for change. She promised that "we will never, ever back down in our effort to give [children] the great education they deserve."[58] DeVos's representation of school choice as a shared struggle—"our cause," "our reasons for fighting," "we will never, ever back down"—evidenced the constitutive force of her advocacy to stress shared interests and build unity and resolve among dispersed actors. As the top education official in the United States, DeVos had the opportunity to articulate a prominent vision of education and human relationships. Foregrounding individual action, this vision required cooperation—ostensibly voluntary and mutually beneficial, in Friedmanian terms—to come into fuller view. Achieving market-based education reform demanded the engagement of a market public.

Yet DeVos's efforts to bolster public commitments to market reforms were often met with protests from people who opposed her vision for education. On her first attempt to visit a school as education secretary, she retreated when met outside the school by protestors.[59] After DeVos accepted her first graduation speaking engagement at Bethune-Cookman University, students and alumni of the historically Black institution circulated a petition urging the school to rescind its invitation. The president held firm, but the petition drew more than fifty thousand signatures. During the speech itself, some graduates silently conveyed their opposition to DeVos by standing and turning their backs to her.[60] Not surprisingly, some commentators joined the students and alumni in objecting to the school administration's decision to invite DeVos. Citing the secretary's ignorance of the history and significance of HBCUs, Mary Curtis, of ESPN's The Undefeated website, wrote that "DeVos came to the university hoping, perhaps, that some of the stature of its pioneering founder, Mary McLeod Bethune, might rub off." However, Curtis pointed out an important difference between the school's founder and the secretary: "Bethune earned her honored status with a lifetime of civil rights activism."[61]

A few months later, in another prominent episode, Secretary DeVos traveled to Cambridge, Massachusetts, to deliver a high-profile speech on school choice at Harvard University. Outside the event venue, hundreds of protestors rallied to denounce her ideas and to support public schools. Loudly voicing their views, the protestors' chants occasionally could be heard inside the forum where DeVos spoke. There, additional protestors silently expressed dissent—some by standing with unfurled banners, others by standing with raised fists. They did so despite a warning that protestors would be removed by some of the more than two dozen police officers present, who quickly acted on this warning. In the upper level of the venue, police let protest banners, which students had attached to railings, remain.[62] In her speech, DeVos appeared defiant, declaring "I've been called the 'school choice Secretary' by some. I think it's meant as an insult, but I wear it as a badge of honor!"[63] Nevertheless, frequent protests at speeches and other events dampened the reception of her market advocacy.

Innovating Education Delivery Systems

Across her public advocacy, Betsy DeVos argued for innovating the means of delivering education to students. In her 2015 South by Southwest Education Conference address, she insisted that "we must revolutionize our education delivery system." During her confirmation hearing, DeVos promised that "I will be a crusader for parents and students and the quality of their education, not for specific systems and not for specific arrangements of how school is delivered." As education secretary, she sought to redirect attention from existing "delivery system[s]" to outcomes. At a conference on education and technology, for example, she urged educators, administrators, and policymakers to "build a system centered on knowledge, skills and achievement—not centered on delivery methods." DeVos maintained that "our education delivery methods should then be as diverse as the kids they serve."[64] But what are the implications of distinguishing education from its "delivery"? Highlighting delivery systems implies a discrete product that consumers may obtain in different ways. Purchasing a new smartphone, for example, may occur in a brick-and-mortar retail store or via a website. The method that a consumer employs to purchase this product does not alter its character. Does this hold for education?

John Dewey did not think so—at least not for a democratic education. He held that the radical character of democracy, its fundamental principle, arises in the alignment of means and ends: "Democratic means and the attainment of democratic ends are one and inseparable."[65] So, too, with a democratic education. As with democracy, Dewey emphasized processes, not outcomes, in his vision of education. As I explained in chapter 1, Dewey believed that training proceeds directly, but education could unfold only "indirectly by means of the environment." To train is to dictate: to seek a specific outcome through efficient means. Education entails a relationship between teacher and student that cultivates agency and aspirations in the learner, making experience meaningful and enabling the student "to direct the course of subsequent experience."[66] Democratic education foregrounds process; learning is the means and the end. In contrast, a focus on delivery systems sacrifices means to predetermined, static ends. In multiple speeches, DeVos explicitly urged a focus on ends, not means, which would support the opportunity for every family, every student, to choose their proper education.[67]

Delivery systems needed innovation because the delivery system embodied in the traditional public school system reflected the designs of an earlier era and an eclipsed economy. The nation needed "a transformation that will open up America's closed and antiquated education system."[68] The existing public school system represented the needs and interests of an industrial economy, but continued competitiveness demanded success in a new economy. At the American Enterprise Institute, DeVos painted a picture of stultification: "Think of your own experience: sit down; don't talk; eyes front; wait for the bell; walk to the next class; and repeat. Students were trained for the assembly line then, and they still are today."[69] The economy had changed, but education remained the same. An industrial economy required routine, repetition, conformity. Workers needed to know their place—in the assembly line and society—and act as a human extension of the machine. But a new economy demanded transformation, disruption. In her speech, DeVos displayed images of change in other areas of society, for example, showing an image of an operating room from the 1930s, and then displaying an image of its contemporary equivalent. Yet her images of classrooms from the past and present revealed striking similarities: desks, chairs, and more. These images underscored the verbal message—change constituted a prima facie good. The nature of a particular change warranted no further investigation. The disruptive innovations of a technoliberal economy necessitated newness.[70]

Innovation required bold thinking from individuals who questioned established practices and institutions and discarded perceived limitations. In a speech to the National Lieutenant Governors Association, DeVos challenged her audience to "compete—with each other, and with every other country in the world—to find the best ways to deliver an excellent education." She reminded them that "putting a man on the moon and a computer in every home were [once] unthinkable ideas." Yet innovators found a way. Elsewhere, she celebrated the achievements of Henry Ford, who "didn't stop creating after his revolutionary Model T car," and Steve Jobs, who "didn't stop improving after the first iPhone," and other corporate titans. "Leaders. Inventors. Innovators. They never stop. Educators shouldn't either."[71] In statements like these, DeVos compared what she saw as the closed, defensive, antiquated system of public education and the open, dynamic, forward-looking world that surrounded it. In distinguishing educators from leaders, inventors, and innovators, she also indicated that change within the education system would arise from outside the education system in the markets that thrived on competition and choice. DeVos called for an army of entrepreneurs to battle an outmoded status quo. She pledged to get Washington "out of your way," which would unleash "new and creative thinking." In return, DeVos promised to highlight "out-of-the-box approaches."[72] These contrasts—a government-backed industrial system demanding conformity and obedience against a market-based technological system inspiring creativity and invention—recalled the Friedmans' contrast of government conformity and market diversity. Like the Friedmans, DeVos represented "Washington" as inimical to ingenuity, while she embraced "innovative disruptors."[73]

In DeVos's discourse, innovation ostensibly rendered obsolete all that preceded it, but the implications of this process remained uncertain. For instance, elucidating the "tremendous breakthroughs in nearly every sector of our society," DeVos recounted how she could "video chat with my six darling grandchildren from anywhere in the world." The capacity of new communication technologies to connect families physically separated by hundreds of miles invited praise, and DeVos lauded their virtues: "With a few swipes and taps on the same device, I can access more—and more current—information than what's contained in any brick and mortar library."[74] Yet the supposed benefits of this feature appear more ambiguous. As consumer goods, iPads and similar devices cost money—both in the initial purchase and in maintaining the hardware's compatibility with evolving technology. Even cords and adapters may change from year to year, requiring new purchases. In comparison, libraries often share their information with patrons at no cost. Further, tablets typically are personal devices, while libraries often engage their local communities by hosting special events, community meetings, and other activities. In these ways, libraries offer people information and experiences inaccessible through even the most up-to-date tablet.

By dissociating means and ends, DeVos articulated parallel trajectories that facilitated a comparative history of innovation across a range of industries—automotive, computer, medical, and education. Disconnecting means and ends suggests that different means can serve a particular end, and a particular means can serve different ends. This asserted relationship enabled DeVos to argue for the diversification and innovation of delivery systems for education, just as a market actor may support different systems for the delivery of telephone service and products. In this way, her dissociation facilitated the transferability of market models. For instance, although Amazon began as a bookseller, it has developed a delivery system that appears capable of selling just about everything—books, electronics, clothes, food, data storage, and perhaps education.[75] Separating means and ends makes interchangeable the items delivered through a particular system, allowing entrepreneurs to apply innovations across industries.

Thinking Outside the District Against the Education Establishment

Acknowledging her public struggles, DeVos professed not to care, since she regarded herself as an outsider to the "education establishment," even though her cabinet post made her a high-ranking national education official. Indeed, she did not wish to ingratiate herself with the so-called education establishment, telling the Conservative Political Action Conference that "my job isn't to win a popularity contest with the media or the education establishment here in Washington." Innovators always faced doubters and haters who ridiculed their ideas. Their ridicule arose from self-doubt and fear. Reframing the meaning of the protests against her, DeVos urged an audience of policymakers at the American Legislative Exchange Council (ALEC), which advanced school-choice legislation at the state level, to join her in regarding "the 'excitement' [as] a badge of honor. . . . Our opponents, defenders of the status quo, only protest those capable of implementing real change."[76] Both ALEC and DeVos had received their share of protests. Both ALEC and DeVos challenged the education establishment.

As an outsider working inside the Department of Education, DeVos believed that she could offer a distinctive contribution to help spur market-based reforms. She noted that most of her public life had been spent on the outside: "Outside Washington. Outside the LBJ Building. Outside 'the system.'" Standing outside for over thirty years had spared DeVos the debilitating effects of long-term government service. Just as government stifled innovation and demanded conformity, governmental officials, whether by natural inclination or training, operated as conformists. Existing programs and policies marked the limits of their vision. DeVos countered that "maybe what students need is someone who doesn't yet know all the things you can't do." Even as secretary of education, she continued to share her preference for events with "thinkers" and "doers" rather than affairs in the "stuffier, acronym-laced halls" of DC.[77]

References to an education establishment appeared across DeVos's public statements. Most often, she named this establishment itself as a nefarious actor. Sometimes, she identified specific actors, particularly teachers' unions and experts, as constituting segments of this establishment. Teachers' unions cared only about maintaining the resources they controlled and the privileges they accumulated. For instance, DeVos told her Harvard audience that "the union bosses made it clear: they care more about a system—one that was created in the 1800s—than they do about students. Their focus is on school buildings instead of school kids." As she criticized unions, DeVos distinguished these organizations from individual teachers, whom DeVos said she trusted to work for their students. Experts operated with arrogance, insisting that they knew more than teachers and parents. On this score, DeVos rebuked the reforms of both Democratic and Republican predecessors, since both exhibited the same flawed approach: "Both approaches had the same Washington 'experts' telling educators how to behave."[78] Their arrogance arose in the insistence that a single, top-down formula could be applied successfully in diverse classrooms across the nation.

The education establishment issued orders and expected compliance. Structured hierarchically, the establishment generated plans from a central command in Washington and then disseminated these plans across states and local districts. In this structure, information flowed in one direction; the establishment neither solicited nor tolerated feedback. Central control "sidelined" teachers, who were "not allowed to be part of the solution." Instead, the "'system' tells them when to teach, how to teach, and what to teach." Insisting on a rigid chain of command, the system punished teachers for insubordination. DeVos had collected what she regarded as egregious cases of administrators denying teachers any autonomy: "There was Matt, who was berated for not being on page 72 of the lesson plan on a certain day of the calendar. And there was Jed, who was repeatedly told to 'keep it down' because his class was 'having too much fun' learning."[79] Offered without any specifics or context, the disciplining of Matt and Jed reinforced an image of bureaucratic overreach led by Washington. Surely, any reasonable person would grant teachers the leeway to instruct their students according to a suitable, tailored pace. And only a robotic disciplinarian would take the fun out of the classroom. But the education establishment and its functionaries were neither reasonable nor humane. They had long since lost sight of appropriate educational ends, caring only for power.

Seeking a monopoly on decision-making consistent with its desire for monopoly control of the education industry, the establishment treated any show of initiative and innovation, however minor, as an existential threat. DeVos rebuked what she characterized as "a zero-sum myth" regarding school structures and learning "perpetuated by the education establishment." She responded that "education is not a zero-sum game. . . . There is no one right way to help kids learn, and just because a school educates children differently than you might propose to does not make them the enemy." She maintained that no one held a "monopoly" on innovation and creativity.[80] Yet, monopoly thinking appeared to shape education so long as Washington placed itself in a controlling position. In *Capitalism and Freedom*, the Friedmans contrasted market and government flows of power. They held that "economic power can be widely dispersed. There is no law of conservation which forces the growth of new centers of economic strength to be at the expense of existing centers." To the contrary, they contended, markets encourage decentralized decision-making. However, the Friedmans believed that "there seems to be something like a fixed total of political power to be distributed."[81] DeVos's criticisms of an education establishment followed this stipulated distinction. She characterized this establishment as constantly on guard against the rise of rival power centers and quick to eliminate any potential challengers. DeVos advocated a market-based alternative that would facilitate the simultaneous flourishing of diverse educational approaches.

Perhaps most alarming, the education establishment threatened to usurp the primary role of parents in teaching their children. In multiple speeches, DeVos warned of this potential outcome. For example, to the Alfred E. Smith Foundation, she reported on "many in Washington who seem to think that because of their power there, they are in a position to make decisions on behalf of parents everywhere." This disclosure suggested that government power continued to grow, unless checked by a countervailing force. Nor did government power respect institutional boundaries. Presumably, even enthusiastic supporters of traditional public schools would not want government decision-making to replace their own judgment. Yet, with Washington making decisions for parents, "in that troubling scenario, the school building replaces the home, the child becomes a constituent, and the state replaces the family."[82] Perhaps DeVos did not sketch this dystopic vision as a literal forecast, but it resonates with the fear of tyranny that has driven neoliberal rejections of government. If the education establishment could dictate the schools that children attend, would it dictate the values that children uphold? Would it dictate that children accept government institutions—and not parents—as the ultimate authorities in their lives? For their part, the Friedmans believed that diminished public faith in "big government" could "restore a belief in individual responsibility by strengthening the family and reestablishing its traditional role in instilling values in the young."[83] When she focused on the wonders of innovation, DeVos delivered a more positive message about the future of education. When she addressed the power of the education establishment, DeVos warned of the baneful consequences of failing to adopt reforms.

Choosing the Right Fit

Since the passage of the original ESEA, across administrations and ideologies, reformers have targeted various objects and people for amelioration: funding systems, curricula, standards, testing, dress codes, students, teachers, principals, parents, and more. DeVos's campaign for choice focused on a putatively more basic consideration: fit. DeVos diagnosed the problem with education as compelling students to attend schools that potentially did not "fit" them; choice appeared as the solution by enabling students to select the right educational option. At times, DeVos framed this problem and solution as an issue of equity, arguing that a poor student's zip code, which serves as a geographical marker of deprivation, should not limit their future.[84] On this point, she kept bipartisan company, as President Barack Obama, too, had decried the disparities of zip codes for children from poor and wealthy families.[85] Intimating this equity frame, DeVos observed that "the affluent and the powerful" have always had, and will continue to have, choices regarding their children's education. This observation broached a fundamental problem with the traditional, neighborhood-based system of public schooling: property tax funding and residential segregation have combined to produce and sustain significant inequalities across districts and locales.[86] However, DeVos did not acknowledge the structural problems suggested in her claim, nor did she favor structural solutions, which she cast as tyrannical. Perhaps more telling that DeVos saw fit—and not inequality—as the basic problem with public education was her insistence that fit constituted a concern for all students. She repeatedly contended that "even the most expensive, state-of-the-art, high-performing school will not be the perfect fit for every single child."[87] As this quote exemplifies, DeVos did not pursue the logic of an equity argument to make comparative claims about the different options and resources available to poor and rich children. Instead, she focused on individuals—every individual, as an individual, without regard to their family's socioeconomic status.

Fit focused education reform on the uniqueness of each and every student as an individual. Recalling the Friedmans, DeVos's pairing of fit and choice articulated the individual as distinct in interest, ability, and value but universal in motivation. The education "experts" in Washington disregarded human distinctiveness, preferring one-size-fits-all solutions that sustained their power by treating students as indistinguishable and interchangeable. Presumably, by succumbing to the routine of the assembly line, even contemporary students would not question their place in a hierarchy. The establishment, DeVos warned, "cares more about a system—one that was created in the 1800s—than about individual students." Alternatively, DeVos imagined "education approaches . . . as varied as the students they serve."[88] Contemporary students needed customized approaches tailored to their interests and aspirations, just as they customized their social-media personae and other extensions of their selves. A "19th century assembly-line approach" had long outlived its usefulness. Students required "learning environments that are agile, relevant, and exciting" to keep pace with a dynamic, technology-driven economy. DeVos exhorted, "Students need to be prepared for professions not yet imagined. The pace of technological change and the increasing interconnectivity of the global economy demands individuals who are continually learning and adapting."[89] In this statement, the technological inflection with which DeVos voiced market themes appeared clearly. The quickening pace of technological change powered a global economy. In this environment, individuals had no choice but to change themselves. Standing still in a technological economy would lead an individual to fall behind, fall into disrepair, and, eventually, fall apart. Disruptive innovations did not announce their presence in advance. Agile individuals could react and adapt, perhaps finding a way to make disruption economically advantageous.

Across DeVos's speeches and statements, as the means for finding the right fit, choice served a variety of functions. The secretary represented choice as an enactment of individual agency in market publics. In the model of a market public, if not necessarily in its practice, choice frees families (or the individuals who act for families) to compare and evaluate potential relationships with education providers, to initiate and terminate these relationships as they see fit. Choice would structure a market public for education with regard to the qualities that DeVos extolled in a technologically attuned pedagogy—agility, flexibility, relevance, change. In this spirit, DeVos maintained that parents required only "relevant and important information" to make judgments about the comparative quality of the educational options available to them: "When parents choose and they are unhappy with whatever the school setting is they will choose something different. And that's the beauty of having choices."[90] Through their choices, parents expressed their judgments and acted on these judgments. In this way, when parents acted, their choices served as a measure of accountability. For instance, during a May 2017 House committee hearing, Representative Nita Lowey asked whether DeVos believed that "private schools that enroll voucher students should be accredited and have to provide evidence of the quality of their programs." The secretary replied that parents have used this funding for "a private school of their choice. Those parents are very happy with and satisfied with that decision. They have made that choice to do that."[91] Her response indicated that choice answered questions about quality; choice signaled customer satisfaction with the product, unless a subsequent choice revealed a change in preference. A chosen program constituted a successful program.

Relatedly, choice offered protection against economic exploitation and discrimination. If parents sent their children to for-profit schools run by companies with highly paid executives, then parents consented to these salaries. If parents signed documents with private schools curtailing the legal rights of their children, then parents willfully relinquished these rights. For example, when pressed by senators about safeguarding the legal rights of children with disabilities who might use federal funds to attend private schools, DeVos retorted that "states have implemented programs that—for disabled students that parents willfully elect into and opt into. Parents are making those decisions. There is no requirement."[92] In these ways, choice operated as self-confirming. The act of choosing provided all of the evidence one needed to accept a choice as appropriate, sound, and fair. Moreover, choice resisted external evaluation by a non-chooser. Individuals could only evaluate their own choices. Efforts by policymakers to identify evidence of quality or safeguards from exploitation and discrimination represented the hubris of the establishment.

As she campaigned for choice, DeVos presented an equivalency of choice. Choice operated independently of its object, offering the same benefits to the chooser across different markets. For example, in her speech at the Brookings Institution, DeVos asked, "How many of you got here today in an Uber, or Lyft, or another ridesharing service? Did you choose that because it was more convenient than hoping a taxi would drive by?" Her questions recognized the disruptive innovation of ridesharing services, which she implied would empower individuals. No longer would someone have to wait uncertainly, or brave inclement weather. She continued: "The truth is that in practice, people like having more options. They like being able to choose between [ridesharing services]. Or when it comes to taking a family trip, many like options such as Airbnb." Why, then, limit choice in an area as essential as education? She proclaimed, "We celebrate the benefits of choices in transportation and lodging. But doesn't that pale in comparison to the importance of educating the future of our country?"[93] As these statements suggest, DeVos saw no differences in the value of choice across industries, including the education industry. Her focus on fit enabled this equivalency by bracketing contextual factors that may have revealed the unevenness of choice for differently situated individuals.

As the solution to the problem of fit, choice respected individual decision-making while promoting the basic value of freedom. DeVos urged audiences to "be clear on what 'school choice' really means." Various methods of tying public funding to individual students, such as vouchers and tax credits, were "just mechanisms" that enabled something more important: "Choice in education is bigger than that." Choice realizes "freedom. Freedom to learn. Freedom to learn differently. Freedom to explore."[94] Freedom appeared as the ultimate value against which other aspirations remained secondary. Even as DeVos decried the limits of zip codes, she would not countenance remedies that abrogated freedom. Equality could inform education reform only through the universal application of choice.

Parents Know Best

DeVos's advocacy for school choice sustained a neoliberal view of knowledge as arising from direct experience. She asserted that "parents know what is best for their children. . . . Parents know better than any politician or administrator the unique needs of each of their children." Parents knew their children better than any other adult, witnessing their development from infancy through adulthood. Parents experienced their children's highs and lows, successes and failures, joys and frustrations. Parents nurtured their children, encouraging them to try new activities and expand their interests. Parents knew their children's abilities. Parents knew the educational environments in which their children would flourish or flounder. Of course, not all parents are biological, guardian parents. Some parents adopt their children; others may lose contact with their children. DeVos did not address these and other diverse families. Instead, her professed support for the family, with a few exceptions, espoused a traditional ideal. On this basis, parental knowledge contrasted with the secondary knowledge of the Washington expert. The expert knew not from experience but by abstraction and generalization. The expert drew from one particular case, experiment, or demonstration and sought to apply its lessons elsewhere. However, DeVos observed that "no two schools are identical" and "no two students are alike."[95] The problems with top-down Washington thinking arose because experts discounted individual distinctiveness in favor of uniform, conformity-driven solutions. Assembly-line approaches came naturally to governments, especially national governments.

Parental knowledge exhibited a humility that contrasted with the arrogance of the education establishment—it knew its limits. Parents did not seek to apply their knowledge widely. They may have shared this knowledge in a neighborly way, but any application rested on an experiential foundation. No one person knew everything, but "people do know how to help their neighbors. . . . Because they know the students. They know their home lives. They know their communities. They know their parents. They know each other." In contrast, the Washington expert, resident of the education establishment, believed that they had all the answers. DeVos bemoaned that "too often, the Department of Education has gone outside of its established authority and created roadblocks" for parents and teachers. She chided this habit: "No parent should feel like the Department of Education thinks it knows better than they what is best for their child."[96] In this way, DeVos sought to align federal education policy with the value of freedom. As the Friedmans wrote, "Humility is the distinguishing virtue of the believer in freedom; arrogance, of the paternalist."[97] In education policy, the paternalist had usurped the rightful role of the parent.

Parental knowledge functioned as a type of proximate knowledge—the knowledge of individuals acting in specific markets. DeVos explained that "when it comes to education—and any other issue in public life—those closest to the problem are always better able to solve it. Washington bureaucrats and self-styled education 'experts' are about as far removed from students as you can get." The education establishment has strained and damaged market relationships—in this case, "a trusting relationship between teacher, parent, and student."[98] In such an exchange, each party should know their role. The interference of the establishment has prevented these parties from fulfilling their agreed-upon obligations.

The Problems of Race and Racism

Across the first two years of her term, DeVos struggled to overcome her ignorant framing of HBCUs as "pioneers of choice," as interlocutors periodically
returned to this remark during subsequent testimony and interviews. At a
House hearing on the Department of Education's fiscal year 2018 budget
request, Representative Rosa DeLauro asserted unequivocally in her opening
statement that "HBCUs were not the product of school choice. They were a
product of our nation's racist segregation." Later in the same hearing, Representative Barbara Lee rebuked DeVos for "completely ignor[ing] the fact
that for many black students, HBCUs were their only choice." The secretary replied simply, "I know that."[99] In a subsequent interview, as a reporter
pressed the point, DeVos responded more assertively, "When I talked about
it being a pioneer in choice it was because I acknowledge that racism was
rampant and there were no choices." She conceded that "I should have
decried much more forcefully the ravages of racism in this country," but
she emphasized that "my last three decades have been working on behalf
of primarily minority families and students to allow them to make choices
for their kids."[100] DeVos invoked her record to underscore a commitment to
equal opportunity across zip codes.

Yet, even if DeVos had decried racism more forcefully, she would have
undermined an equity approach, because her discussions of race and racism,
as with her statements on fit generally, resolutely focused on individuals at the
expense of wider structures that conditioned individual action. For instance,
on two occasions—during remarks at an HBCU congressional luncheon and
in her commencement address at Bethune-Cookman University—DeVos
celebrated the life and achievements of Mary McLeod Bethune. In both settings, DeVos recounted how Bethune began with only $1.50 in her pocket but
worked hard and overcame many challenges in founding a school that would
educate African American youth. At the luncheon, DeVos remarked that Bethune recognized how "the traditional school systematically failed to provide
African Americans access to a quality education—or, sadly, more often to any
education at all." Working to realize her vision, "Mary refused to accept the
status quo." At Bethune-Cookman, DeVos noted that "this inspired daugh-
ter of slaves refused to accept repulsive and systemic racism." She quoted
Bethune on developing "the courage to change old ideas and practices."[101]
Certainly, Bethune's achievements merit praise, and DeVos's admiration
appeared genuine. The problem lies with the individual model of change
suggested by DeVos's biographical account. She represented Bethune as a

woman against the establishment, a visionary who did not accept "no" for an answer. Apart from a passing reference to "systemic racism," DeVos did not contextualize Bethune's story within the wider injustices and inequalities that she confronted and that continue to confront HBCUs and their students. In DeVos's account, Bethune succeeded because she had great ideas and an indefatigable spirit.

When advocates of market-based education reforms appropriate the discourse of civil rights, they transform a collectivist struggle for racial justice into a history of individual advancement. Focusing on the plight of individuals, whose stories they circulate widely, these advocates largely ignore "persistent structural inequalities" that continue to marginalize African Americans and other minority groups. Janelle Scott explains that the use of civil rights language by advocates of market-based reforms "distills the most individualistic aspects of civil rights aspirations while neglecting broader communitarian components."[102] Although she may have regretted her framing of HBCUs, DeVos continued to align HBCUs, K–12 education, and school choice as part of a larger civil rights struggle. Praising HBCUs in a *USA Today* op-ed, DeVos exhorted that "we must follow their lead and apply that same thinking to our K–12 system because the same reality exists: Too many students live without access to quality schools. These children and teenagers are assigned to failing schools based solely on the zip code in which they live."[103] But her framing of this problem in terms of the individual forestalled a fuller understanding of the circumstances of the students she wished to help, including whether the dynamics of race, racism, and markets have produced educational inequalities in the first place.[104]

Seeking the Public in a Technoliberal Public Sphere

Betsy DeVos may have worn the label "school choice secretary" as a badge of honor, but her detractors worried about what her emphasis on choice portended for public education. As one critic wrote, her decades-long advocacy had demonstrated nothing but "contempt for public schools."[105] DeVos countered these criticisms, arguing that her adversaries had falsely approached education reform as an either-or proposition that distorted the dynamics of choice. In her Harvard speech, she warned against definitions of public education that "have become tools that divide us." She identified the "public" as consisting of "students and parents" and the "public money" that funds education as "really their money—the taxpayers' money." Attributing cynicism to the defenders of the establishment, she asked, "Doesn't every school aim to serve the public good? A school that prepares its students to lead successful lives is a benefit to all of us." Recognizing this good, she proposed a unifying definition of public education: "The definition of public education should be to educate the public."[106] In addressing their students' interests, all schools—public and private, nonprofit and for-profit, secular and religious, diverse and homogeneous, offline and online, inclusive and exclusive—meet this definition.

Offering what she regarded as an ecumenical view of education, DeVos sketched a particular vision of the public it serves. She imagined a public of individuals who, throughout their educational experiences, remain individuals. As market actors, these individuals establish relationships with others strictly on voluntary terms. Based on direct knowledge and volition, these relationships limit individuals' responsibilities to others in accordance with their choices. Further, these market relationships do not exert a transformative force on individuals. In this market public, students and their parents enter into relationships with education providers to satisfy an independently identified interest. Providers offer services that align with the interests of their customers; they do not seek to shape customer interests. Affirming the value of all schools, DeVos intimated an aggregative public good that arises through the accumulation of individual interest maximization. Individuals do not deliberate or participate in collective decision-making to articulate a public good. To the contrary, individuals do not need to modify their interests at all. Only the education establishment seeks individual change, and it does so in the name of conformity. According to DeVos's definition, public education expresses its publicity in the terms of a publicly traded corporation. In the abstract, any individual can buy stock in a corporation traded on the New York Stock Exchange, but this market does not guarantee everyone the resources and relationships necessary for participation.

To this market-based vision of a public, DeVos added an optimistic view of the innovative power of technology. Damien Pfister and Misti Yang explain that technoliberals regard politics as a time-consuming and unproductive activity. Instead, technoliberals purport to separate politics and technology, asserting that only the latter respects individual choice. Toward this end, they seek technical solutions that "can bypass the messiness of democracy." While software engineers "build new systems that can replace existing ways of doing things," such as Bitcoin and Uber, "deliberation [is] doomed to failure because [it is] grounded in the mistakenness of human perception."[107] As the Friedmans maintained, deliberation proceeds from a flawed theory of knowledge. Pfister and Yang report on technology entrepreneurs seeking algorithmic solutions to public problems like online hate speech. They quote one technology executive who urges that "we should build tools to help de-escalate tensions on social media—sort of like spell-checkers, but for hate and harassment."[108] The pursuit of technological solutions to public problems like these implies that there is no need for individuals to learn from one another and work together to address shared concerns. In this spirit, DeVos sought to de-escalate debates over the means and ends of public education. Why battle over potentially shared values and aspirations when the market can satisfy the interests of every individual? By detaching means and ends and innovating delivery systems, technology can bring innovations to education that Americans enjoy in the other aspects of their lives.

As education secretary, Betsy DeVos employed her bully pulpit with mixed success. Yet, as with her predecessors, she drew on the energy of state legislators, advocates, and officials in opening up markets in education. In Wisconsin, prior to the November 2018 election, the governor and legislators had made great strides in this effort over the past eight years. They battled teachers' unions to give local school boards and administrators increased "flexibility" over education spending. They expanded vouchers statewide to bring choice to residents in different regions of the state. These efforts illuminate how visions of market-based relationships have transformed education policy.

4

GROWING MARKETS, DIMINISHING DEMOCRACY: THE STATEWIDE EXPANSION OF VOUCHERS IN WISCONSIN

Promoting vouchers, the Friedmans aspired to replace what they saw as the monopolistic structure and coercive authority of public education with a marketplace that would realize individual freedom through choice. Their proposal promised a departure from the status quo that would free individuals from entanglements with others. Frustrating individual agency, the status quo operated with a flawed theory of persuasion and decision-making presuming that people could interact in groups to generate knowledge and render judgment beyond their direct experiences. On education and other issues, these group decisions affected everyone—even the enlightened individual who recognized the proper application and limits of their knowledge could not escape the coercion of the collective. Only a clean break from existing structures would unleash the productive power of the market for all. On this basis, individuals could choose their relationships with others, brokering educational agreements to serve their interests while refusing relationships that would not advance their interests. An education market would manifest the virtues of a market public, offering all participants opportunities to satisfy their interests. In this public, choice ostensibly abates the influence of inequality and control.

In contrast to this normative vision, policy debates over school vouchers have situated individual choice among wider social forces of power, money, and race. Both supporters and opponents of vouchers have identified these forces as crucial dynamics of education reform. On power, supporters have discerned in vouchers a means of empowerment for marginalized, minority, and underserved communities. In Milwaukee in the early 1990s, Representative Polly Williams, a Black community activist and Democratic member of the Wisconsin State Assembly, worked with Republican governor Tommy Thompson to bring vouchers to her city to enable her constituents to work around the racial inequalities of the Milwaukee Public Schools and direct the education of their children in autonomous, community-based schools.[1] Opponents of vouchers have portrayed their relationship to power as vehicles for ideologically driven and profit-seeking individuals and lobbying groups who have pressed for vouchers to satisfy established interests despite a lack of evidence of their educational efficacy and tepid public support.[2] Both supporters and opponents have tied vouchers to the unequal system of public education financing in the United States, which primarily funds schools through property taxes and thus reinforces wealth disparities across communities.[3] Some supporters and opponents also have construed vouchers as a means for making money function as speech and agency. Like the Friedmans, neoliberal advocates have regarded this transformation as an exemplary mode of engagement in a market-based public.[4] Opponents have highlighted its wider inequities, especially as state funding of private vouchers may reduce resources for children in public schools.[5]

Both conceptualizations and implementations of vouchers have long intersected the forces of power and money with race. The Friedmans themselves stumbled over the issue of racism, professing a nondiscriminatory stance while seemingly unable to distinguish the differing magnitude of sartorial choice and choosing to discriminate.[6] The Friedmans may have equivocated on the issue of race, but some policymakers have adopted vouchers to negotiate and perpetuate clear racial divisions. In 1956, utilizing a model that resonated with Milton Friedman's discussion in his original 1955 essay on vouchers, Virginia lawmakers adopted a system of tuition grants that enabled white families to send their children to private schools while the state resisted the Supreme Court's mandate for desegregation.[7] Prince Edward County closed its public schools for five years from 1959 to 1964—until a court intervened—as white families used the tuition grants to continue their children's education while Black families suffered.[8] As Candace Epps-Robertson explains, Virginia senator Harry Byrd, a segregationist and political power broker, praised the school closings as acts of civic engagement. Epps-Robertson argues that this framing "establish[ed] a brand of citizenship based in hierarchies and difference as a means of civic control."[9] This constituted a practice that contrasted with the Friedmans' imagined market public in which power and inequality play no role.[10]

By the early 1990s, in Milwaukee and other urban areas, relationships between vouchers and race had changed. Polly Williams had come to regard the promises of integration as hollow and its mechanisms, such as busing, as placing unfair burdens on Black children. Williams remarked that "we have

desegregation, integration, and transportation. We still don't have education."
She urged her legislative colleagues to "give us a chance to educate our own."[11]
Finished with integration, Williams believed that Black children would do better in schools run by adults from similar backgrounds who were connected to
the children and their community. However, her support of vouchers did not
last long. By 1995, Williams charged that powerful interests in Wisconsin had
coopted vouchers for purposes other than community empowerment.

Wisconsin has experienced a range of policy proposals and arguments for
vouchers. If, as Dewey suggested, democracy represents a particular alignment of means and ends, then Wisconsin vouchers have supported more
and less democratic visions. Kelly Jensen argues that Williams's advocacy
associated vouchers with values of community, empowerment, autonomy,
and equality.[12] Challenging a history of discrimination and broken promises,
Williams discerned a means to promote the ends of fostering democratic relationships in local communities. Yet, even as she sought passage of voucher
legislation, known as the Milwaukee Parental Choice Program (MPCP), her
collaborator, Governor Thompson, pursued vouchers for the market ends of
deregulation and reducing the scope of public institutions.[13] As the MPCP
specifically and school choice policies more generally have expanded in Wisconsin, a vision of democratic relationships has receded and market relations
and publics have become the dominant framework. After his 2010 election,
Republican governor Scott Walker pushed for vouchers in the Racine Uni-
fied School District, one of Wisconsin's largest districts, and subsequently
statewide. A 2015 Department of Public Instruction analysis indicated that
roughly 75 percent of the students participating in the statewide program
had attended a private school in the prior academic year, suggesting that the
vouchers disproportionately benefited students whose families possessed
the financial means to send their children to private schools or students
who had received private scholarships.[14] Addressing this programmatic shift,
Democratic senator Lena Taylor, a Black legislator representing portions of
Milwaukee, argued in a 2015 hearing that vouchers "used to be the program
that Polly Williams created. This program is not that at all."[15]

In this chapter, I analyze policy debates over the statewide expansion of
vouchers through the Wisconsin Parental Choice Program (WPCP). These
debates focused on the passage of the 2013–15 and the 2015–17 biennial state
budgets. The 2013–15 budget created the WPCP, and the 2015–17 budget
increased the income levels for families eligible to participate and instituted
a gradual elimination of enrollment caps for the program. While supporters
of expanded vouchers discussed the need to serve particular populations,

they nevertheless framed their advocacy in terms of a business model for providing education that obscured the ongoing influences of race, power, and money. Further, policymakers supporting voucher expansion achieved their ends through decidedly undemocratic means. The materials for my analysis consist of speeches by Governor Scott Walker, legislative hearings, and remarks by attendees at listening sessions on the state budget. This chapter focuses mainly on the debates of the Joint Finance Committee, composed of state representatives and senators, that receives the governor's budget and directs a bill—often with changes—through the legislature.[16]

I begin this chapter by providing a brief history of the growth of vouchers in Wisconsin and discussing the polarized state political climate of the 2010s. Next, I explain how Scott Walker framed the voucher debate as a historical battle for freedom. Turning to legislative debates, I analyze how the Republican members of the Joint Finance Committee envisioned a new market for education including both public and private schools, and I consider funding concerns voiced by state and local education officials. I then foreground the ways that power, money, and race shaped visions and dynamics of ostensibly neutral markets, including the antidemocratic processes of expanding vouchers statewide.

Means and Ends for Vouchers

In her advocacy of vouchers, Polly Williams balanced individual and community concerns. As a policy tool, vouchers permitted individual Milwaukee parents to choose a private school for their children instead of their assigned public school. Yet Williams supported vouchers to advance her community. She did not hide her interest in helping Black children, and she asserted that she would work with anyone—regardless of party affiliation—to achieve this end.[17] Williams's position reflected a shift among Black education activists in Milwaukee from favoring integration to asserting community autonomy. Confronting the resistance of the city school board and superintendents, Black Milwaukeeans engaged in a years-long, multifaceted campaign for school desegregation that combined protest, legal challenges, and political action.[18] While these struggles produced some successes, like a 1976 federal court finding that the Milwaukee school district "intentionally created and maintained" a segregated system, the larger process underscored for Black families their limited power in city government and in the Milwaukee school district.[19] As Jim Carl explains, these experiences "helped to generate a reform movement within Milwaukee's Black community that embraced local control of public schools as a means to raise minority achievement."[20] Local control found a home in community schools that primarily had been educating minority students in the city.

Starting with seven schools and three hundred students, the MPCP steadily expanded in the number and types of schools involved, participating students, the total cost to the Milwaukee Public Schools, and the income eligibility for families participating. After the 1994 midterm elections, Republicans gained majorities in the Wisconsin State Assembly and Senate, and an expansion of the MPCP appeared imminent. A business-led coalition, encouraged by the neoliberal Bradley Foundation, pushed to include parochial schools in the MPCP. In response, Williams and other Black legislators who had voted for the original program withdrew their support. When policymakers debated statewide expansion in 2013, the MPCP had grown to include more than one hundred schools and nearly twenty-five thousand students.[21] Since the funding of the MPCP reduced state aid to the Milwaukee Public Schools by a specified amount for each student enrolled in a choice school, the growing program meant decreased aid for the city's public schools. In its first year, the program cost the Milwaukee Public Schools roughly $700,000 in state aid. By 2013, this figure had increased to more than $50 million.[22] Subsequent changes to the MPCP also increased the income eligibility for families participating in the program. By 2015, a family of four earning up to $73,401 ($80,401 for a family of four with married parents) could obtain a private school voucher.[23]

Expansion proceeded despite signs of problems with some choice schools. One of the inaugural schools, Juanita Virgil Academy, closed in the middle of the school year during the first year of the program, leaving seventy-one MPCP students to return to public schools after the semester had already begun. In his analysis of the school, John Witte identified a host of concerns: a principal who joined the school after fall classes had begun and was quickly fired, transportation issues, overcrowding, a lack of books and classroom materials, and more.[24] During the first six years of the MPCP, three choice schools failed midyear and another failed during the summer. Some other early choice schools operated on the verge of closure, but the infusion of MPCP funds enabled them to survive.[25] School closings have been a persistent problem for the MPCP. Forty-one percent of schools that participated in the MPCP at some point between 1991 and 2015 had closed. The Department of Public Instruction mandated some of these closures for schools that failed to meet statutory requirements, while other closures were initiated by the schools themselves. The closure rate for start-up schools, which did not exist prior to their participation in the MPCP, was a shockingly high 67.8 percent, and start-ups constituted the large majority of school closures overall.[26] While business failures may be acceptable for traditional markets, for education they cause serious disruptions for students, families, and communities.

In 2013, Governor Scott Walker worked with the Republican majority of the Joint Finance Committee to bring vouchers to the entire state. Initially, policymakers limited the Wisconsin Parental Choice Program to five hundred students and twenty-five schools in its first year and one thousand students and fifty schools in its second year. However, in 2015 the legislature passed and the governor signed a bill that removed these caps on students and schools. In their place, the bill placed no constraints on the number of schools that could participate and gradually eliminated limits on student enrollment (as a percentage of a district's total student population) by 2026.[27] The 2015 legislation also changed the funding source for the WPCP: while previous funding had been provided through general purpose revenue, the legislation prescribed that new students enrolling in the WPCP would be funded by a reduction in their districts' state aid. For the 2016–17 school year, nearly $23 million that would have gone to school districts in state aid was redirected to private schools.[28] The 2015 legislation also established a "marriage bonus" that effectively enabled married parents to earn an additional $7,000 in household income without losing their eligibility. A married couple with two children could earn up to $52,263 and remain eligible for the WPCP, a figure that compared favorably with the 2015 statewide median household income of $55,638.[29] A highly publicized 2015 memo by the Legislative Fiscal Bureau estimated that total state costs for the WPCP could range from $600 to $800 million between 2015–16 and 2024–25.[30]

The enactment of the WPCP occurred amid what some analysts have referred to as a period of "unprecedented growth" for vouchers in the United States.[31] Florida created the first statewide voucher program in 1999, and Ohio expanded its voucher program from the city of Cleveland to the entire state in 2006. More recently, Indiana and Louisiana adopted statewide programs. These developments have been guided by the advocacy of governors and legislative leaders. However, at the ballot box, voucher referenda have failed consistently. Since 2000, voters have rejected vouchers in such politically diverse states as Arizona, California, Michigan, and Utah by wide margins.[32] In the wake of a 2008 referendum defeat in Utah, voucher advocate and attorney Clint Bolick lamented that the opponents of voucher referenda need only "raise the specter that public schools may be harmed, and the electorate is likely to vote no."[33] Along these lines, polling support for vouchers drops considerably when respondents consider the potential of reduced funding for public schools.[34]

As vouchers have expanded, advocates and analysts have advanced mixed purposes for these programs. Advocating for vouchers in 2013 and 2015, Republicans on the Joint Finance Committee called for a new business model for public education. Nevertheless, committee co-chair Representative John Nygren rebutted arguments against vouchers from committee Democrats by highlighting the plight of disadvantaged children: "This is a program focused on those kids in poverty to give them an opportunity to actually be successful in life, rather than being on our welfare programs, rather than being in our corrections systems."[35] Nygren's references to the alternatives of impoverishment and imprisonment suggested that even as he mentioned helping children, he also accounted for cost savings. Moreover, neither Nygren nor any of his Republican colleagues advocated for structural reforms to distribute resources more equitably among wealthier and poorer communities. In this way, their advocacy resonated with the dynamics of a market public by emphasizing considerations of economic value and the primacy of individual agency. Expressing concerns over the "'social justice' rhetoric" that had circulated in some public campaigns for vouchers, in 2010 prominent school-choice advocate Frederick Hess urged a shift to a primarily economic campaign. Appreciating the "politically marketable" circumstances of poor urban Black families, Hess retorted that focusing on vouchers as a "moral crusade" led to unrealistic promises about success and did not connect with suburban parents whose children attended generally well-functioning public schools.[36]

Act 10, Polarization, and Public Education

Running for governor amid a severe economic downturn, Scott Walker highlighted the themes of economic recovery and job creation. He did not campaign on what would become the signature issue of his entire governorship. Nor did he inform his Republican colleagues in the state legislature until after his inauguration. Even Republican legislative leaders expressed shock as they learned of his plan: advancing a "budget repair bill," the newly elected governor would eliminate collective bargaining rights for the state's public employee unions and mandate organizational changes that would destabilize their finances and dramatically reduce their ability to recruit and retain members.[37] As tens of thousands of public school teachers across the state digested this news, Governor Walker introduced his first biennial budget, which cut state support for K–12 public education by more than $800 million, the largest reduction in state history.[38] The governor articulated a clear connection between these two developments: Act 10, as the Wisconsin Budget Repair Bill would come to be known, provided local school districts the necessary tools to absorb unavoidable budget reductions. In a March 2011 guest column published in the *Wall Street Journal* shortly after he released his budget, Walker insisted that "our reform plan gives state and local governments the tools to balance the budget through reasonable benefit contributions."[39] Walker argued that unions had contributed significantly to the state's budget woes and that union members should contribute their fair share to help the state regain solvency.

Facing a climate of fiscal austerity, and engaging weakened teachers' unions, many school districts across the state deployed the financial tools from Act 10 to cut employee benefits and reduce staff. In the years after the passage of Act 10, the salaries of public school teachers declined by an average of $2,000, and their out-of-pocket contributions to health insurance increased dramatically. In the 2010–11 school year, teacher contributions to their health insurance premiums averaged 5 percent. Seven years later, this figure more than doubled to 12 percent—and the contributions by district varied widely, from no employee contributions in a few districts to more than 25 percent in others.[40] Further, 73 percent of districts across the state reduced their instructional staff in the school year after Act 10 was passed. The largest cuts occurred for librarians, whose numbers declined by almost one-tenth. Reading specialists faced a nearly 5 percent decline from the 2010–11 school year. Overall, districts across Wisconsin employed 1,446 fewer public school teachers in the 2011–12 school year than the previous year.[41] One study of Act 10's impact on teaching in diverse districts across the state reported increased class sizes, more course assignments for teachers, less one-to-one time between teachers and students, unilateral policy changes, and higher teacher turnover.[42] Unsurprisingly, districts—especially smaller, rural ones—struggled to hire new teachers.[43]

As successive state budget cuts followed, the tools from Act 10 appeared to many local public school officials and community members as an unsustainable measure. In a 2015 listening session with the Joint Finance Committee, Laura Myrah, superintendent of the Whitefish Bay School District, recounted that "since the 2011 reductions to education and Act 10 legislation," the district had made significant budget reductions. However, these reductions "have come off the backs of employees through salary freezes, changes to health insurance benefits, and drastic reductions to post-employment benefits. But those tools have been exhausted."[44] The district faced ongoing budget challenges, and teachers were leaving its schools for alternative types of employment. Similarly, Dominic Madison, superintendent of the Brillion Public Schools, explained to the Joint Finance Committee that his district had "wrung all that we can out of staff salary and benefits with the tools that have been given to us."[45] As these comments illustrate, the inadequacy of Act 10 appeared as a common refrain throughout the listening sessions. Moreover, local officials reported that teachers "have handled it very professionally and continue to work extremely hard" under difficult conditions.[46] But continuing cuts placed districts in an untenable position. Wauwatosa community resident Karen Suarez Flint regarded the ongoing actions of state policymakers as a betrayal: "With the passage of Act 10, you demanded school districts operate more like businesses with cuts to salaries and benefits, layoffs to dedicated staff, and even outsourcing. The school districts complied, and now you change the game again."[47] In his 2011 *Wall Street Journal* guest column, Governor Walker asserted that the tools provided in Act 10 would generate more than enough savings to compensate for "the reductions in state aid."[48] Yet, even if local officials initially accepted this claim, their experiences illuminated the clear shortcomings of Act 10.

Act 10 did not introduce polarization to Wisconsin, but the legislation severely exacerbated developing trends. Fearing budget cuts to public education, the Teaching Assistants' Association (TAA), the labor union representing graduate student workers at the University of Wisconsin–Madison, had organized a protest for Valentine's Day, February 14, 2011. Three days before the protest, which the organizers had not anticipated, Governor Walker introduced his Budget Repair Bill. In what became the first mass protest against Act 10, the TAA led a thousand protestors to the State Capitol to deliver "I heart UW" valentines to the governor's office in support of public education.[49] In the days and weeks that followed, successive protests swelled to a hundred thousand participants. Public employees from across the state traveled to Madison to join the demonstrations. The Madison Metropolitan School District cancelled classes for days because of a shortage of teachers. National unions, too, traveled to Madison to show their solidarity.

Mass marches and other protests drew national media attention to Madison.[50] The day after the Valentine's Day march, the Joint Finance Committee held a public hearing on Act 10, and hundreds of people signed up to testify. At 3:00 a.m. on February 16, the Republican co-chairs called an end to the hearing, even as people continued to wait their turn to testify. Democratic committee members began an impromptu, all-night informal hearing, and protestors camped out in the State Capitol, beginning a weeks-long continuous occupation of the building, in which protestors chanted, sang, and fed and cared for one another.[51] On February 17, 2011, to deny Republicans a quorum, Senate Democrats left the state to an "undisclosed location" in Illinois. As recall efforts of some Democrats and Republicans began, the Assembly debated the Budget Repair Bill the following week. After a series of unsuccessful clandestine meetings with departed Democrats, Senate Republicans ordered a conference committee to approve the bill without the presence of Democrats. On March 11, 2011, Scott Walker signed Act 10 into law. The next day, Senate Democrats returned to Wisconsin to the cheers of protestors gathered at the Capitol.[52]

The passage of Act 10, protests, and cuts to public education represented a shift from a more bipartisan approach that had characterized state relationships with public employees and education in past decades. In 1959, Wisconsin became the first state to enact legislation that recognized public employees' rights to organize and bargain collectively.[53] During his years in office from 1987 to 2001, Governor Thompson worked productively with public-sector unions, earning the endorsement of the Wisconsin chapter of the American Federation of State, County, and Municipal Employees for his 1994 and 1998 reelection campaigns. In a 1997 speech, Governor Thompson boasted that "Wisconsin has collectively bargained with state employees for twenty-five years. By working together, we've created a positive atmosphere for state employees and enhanced services to our citizens."[54] From this perspective, Act 10 represented a fundamental change in relationships among the state, local school districts, and teachers' unions. Further, as the departure of the Senate Democrats illustrated, Act 10 exacerbated already worsening relationships among the political parties and citizens. Throughout the 2010s, news accounts and analyses identified Wisconsin as one of the most polarized states in the nation.[55]

Because Republicans controlled the state Assembly and Senate in 2013 and 2015, they appointed twelve of the sixteen members of the Joint Finance Committee, which was cochaired by one Republican member of both the Assembly and Senate. During this time, Tony Evers served as the state superintendent of public instruction, which is a nonpartisan, elected constitutional office. Even so, legislators viewed Evers as a liberal, and his interactions with the committee generally exhibited support from Democrats and varying degrees of opposition (and rare support) from Republicans. During the two hearings examined for this chapter in which Evers testified—one in 2013 and one in 2015—both Democrats and Republicans actively participated. During the executive sessions, Democrats used their full allotted time to speak while only a few Republicans took part. This is likely because the Republicans knew they had the votes to pass their budget and defeat any unfriendly amendments, so they did not perceive a need to engage their Democratic colleagues in debate. The committee passed the Republican education budgets and defeated all of the proposed Democratic amendments by a straight-party, twelve-to-four margin.

A Governor and a President

Scott Walker deeply admired Ronald Reagan, and he associated his policy aspirations with the president's accomplishments. When the governor informed his cabinet about the Budget Repair Bill, he invoked his hero: "You know, this may sound a little melodramatic, but thirty years ago Ronald Reagan . . . had one of the most defining moments of his political career, not just his presidency, when he fired the air traffic controllers." Ostensibly a labor action, in Walker's view, Reagan's decision changed the course of global history. The firing "was the first crack in the Berlin Wall and the fall of communism because from that point forward the Soviets and the communists knew that Ronald Reagan wasn't a pushover." The governor contended that Wisconsin faced an analogous situation. Strong action would engender monumental change: "This is our moment. This is our time to change the course of history."[56] Separated by three decades, in Washington, DC, and Madison, Wisconsin, a president and a governor heard the call of history. Against forces that would shackle individuals to the coercive will of the collective—communism, unionism—they defended freedom and freely chosen relationships between individuals.

In their first inaugural addresses, both Reagan and Walker addressed economic downturns that helped carry them into office. They both blamed an overreaching government that trampled on individual freedom and the prosperity it delivered. Promising a new era, as I noted in chapter 3, President Reagan declared that "in the present crisis, government is not the solution to our problem; government is the problem."[57] Governor Walker also promised change, asserting that "what is failing us is the expanse of government. But we can do something about that starting today." Although unsuccessful, Reagan pledged to abolish the US Department of Education during his campaign. Walker did not mention his Budget Repair Bill during his campaign or inaugural address, but he succeeded in weakening what he regarded as baneful public institutions. In his inaugural address, Walker promised that he would focus on "creatively improving our education system so that our children can be competitive in a global marketplace."[58] The world had changed, and public education needed to change with it.

In his major speeches from 2013 to 2015, Governor Walker repeatedly promised to give every child in the state access to a great education. In his 2013 budget address, he held that "since wealthy families have a choice because they can pay to send their children to a private school, we give low-income and middle-class families an opportunity to also choose a viable alternative for their sons and daughters."[59] Referencing class, Walker implicitly acknowledged the inequalities that attended an educational system funded by residential (racial, financial) segregation. However, like his Republican colleagues in the legislature, his policy prescriptions did not veer from an individualistic, nonstructural orientation. Further, in mentioning the middle class, Walker signaled a normative shift in his vision of choice. As vouchers, private school tax credits, and other measures grew, policymakers would no longer target poor families exclusively; rather, they would align choice with the individual as such, regardless of class standing, and they would work within the context of state politics to realize individual freedom where it had been previously denied. In these ways, insisting that "every child should have access to a great education" repositioned the child referenced in this declaration.[60] "Every child" did not invite a comparative accounting of resources available to different children. Rather, "every child" positioned each child (through their families) as the universal "Friedmanian" subject pursuing their self-interest and expressing their agency through choice.

As choice appeared to be the proper exercise of each individual, only a child's parents could answer the question of fit between a student and a school. In his signing statement on the 2013 budget, Walker explained that "every school doesn't fit every student—which is why this budget includes a statewide expansion of school choice."[61] A focus on fit recast the purpose of vouchers from the early-1990s program that Polly Williams and others had supported. Fit individualized education, connecting it to self-interest rather than social redress—wider social structures of race and class did not warrant consideration for a market public. Further, judgments about fit demanded direct knowledge. In his 2015 State of the State address, as he geared up for a presidential run, Governor Walker placed even greater emphasis on themes of choice, fit, and freedom. He pledged that his administration would "continue to empower families to make the choice that is right for their sons and daughters." He would stand against the institutions and actors that sought to deny market agency: "No need for bureaucrats or politicians to make that choice—I trust parents. Give them access to objective information and they will make the choice that is best for their children."[62] Far from the families who sent their children to school, bureaucrats and politicians lacked the necessary knowledge to choose for others. Moreover, in choosing for others, they transfigured individual students and their families into groups composed of interchangeable members. From the perspective of a market public, these larger groupings disrespected individual diversity. Traditional public schools treated individuals as uniform neighborhood residents.

Engendered by his policies, Walker contended, an education marketplace had arisen in Wisconsin. In a 2015 guest column in the *Des Moines Register*, making his case to prospective Iowa presidential caucus-goers, he held that "in 2011, we changed that broken system in Wisconsin. Today, the requirements for seniority and tenure are gone. Schools can hire based on merit and pay based on performance."[63] Previously, union rules concerned more with power and privilege than performance had constrained the personnel decisions of local districts. Walker's policies had replaced regimentation with competition. Now, districts could align their workforce to respond flexibly to consumer demand. For their part, parents could behave as market actors in choosing among schools that would compete for their children. An insistence on accountability had provided parents with the information they needed to make individual decisions.

Envisioning a New Market for Education

Against democratic visions, market-based publics offer alternative alignments of means and ends, foregrounding individual choice as the means for realizing the end of freedom. Nevertheless, as they supported the statewide expansion of vouchers, the Republican-majority members of the Joint Finance Committee associated various ends with vouchers—improved educational outcomes for all students, cost savings, new incentives for public schools, accountability—that, when amplified, ultimately appeared as corollary benefits of choice. By definition, a traditional system that assigned children to school by residence failed the test of choice and freedom. Yet majority committee members employed these other ends, particularly educational outcomes and cost savings, to rebuke public education. Further, these varied ends underscored the need for a new business model for education in which consumers could choose among public and private options.

Although their judgments of success differed, majority committee members urged Superintendent Evers and their Democratic colleagues to focus on educational outcomes, rather than what they regarded as an undue focus on money. At the conclusion of Superintendent Evers's March 2013 appearance before the committee, co-chair Senator Alberta Darling returned to an *Education Week* state report card that she had referenced at the beginning of the hearing. The report card ranked Wisconsin eighteenth among states in education performance. Moreover, she noted that the Legislative Fiscal Bureau informed her that some higher-ranked states spent less per pupil than did Wisconsin. Evers called attention to "biases" in the rankings, but in her concluding remarks Senator Darling remained undeterred: "We have to be able to compete. And our taxpayers have to know what their investment is. And our kids cannot wait. . . . We cannot wait to be competitive with the rest of the country. . . . We want outcomes."[64] As Darling's impatience (she repeated the phrase "we cannot wait" several times) and call for competition suggested, the majority committee members associated presumption with change, viewing a necessary restructuring of public education as beyond debate. This presumption implicated public school advocates like Superintendent Evers, who acknowledged directly in his testimony and his interactions with Republican and Democratic committee members that the state's public schools needed to improve in different areas.

With change as the motivating force, and freedom as the underlying principle, majority committee members discounted troubling evidence of the performance of private schools participating in the MPCP. During the committee's May 2015 executive session, Senator Lena Taylor noted that a recent report had concluded that of the ten lowest-performing schools in Milwaukee, seven were voucher schools. More broadly, she explained that "we know from studies that the schools that are failing and the schools that are succeeding are all types." These varied outcomes across school types challenged the presumption in favor of privatization. By itself, creating more voucher schools would not improve outcomes—and the high failure rate of "start-ups" suggested that expansion would harm many students. By increasing funding for private schools, the committee was "only putting public schools at a larger and larger disadvantage," preventing these schools from educating their students.[65] On a similar note, in the same meeting, Senator Jon Erpenbach observed that if the committee had treated all the voucher schools in Milwaukee as constituting their own independent district, this district would receive a failing grade by the committee's own measures. Yet these arguments did not persuade the majority committee members to vote against expansion, because the actual outcomes of the MPCP schools did not undermine their standing as options in an education market.

Since a growing education marketplace would affect all K–12 schools in the state, public schools would need to generate cost savings to compete. In the March 2013 hearing, Representative John Klenke asked Superintendent Evers, "What are you going to do to bend your cost curve?" Representative Klenke pointed to teacher benefits as a key component of this curve. He speculated that since teachers did not engage in physically taxing labor, they would live for many years in retirement at taxpayers' expense. Further, specifically citing Milwaukee, Klenke held that education properly occurred in the classroom, yet the number of administrators and other nonteaching personnel in the city and other districts had driven up the cost of education. The numbers indicated an unsustainable trajectory: "You have a very high-cost model to deliver education." Klenke exhorted that Evers must "change the cost curve so that we can deliver education in a new way." When Evers responded that the Department of Public Instruction had worked hard to improve efficiencies, Klenke affirmed this work but insisted on the need for "transformation."[66] Continuing to push on teachers' benefits, Representative Klenke implied that Act 10 had successfully enabled local districts to absorb recent state budget cuts, but that its tools would be insufficient going forward. On this point, Klenke stated a view that local administrators articulated in listening sessions. Yet Klenke approached this position from a contrary perspective—rather than demonstrating the need for more state funding, the limits of Act 10 demonstrated the need to maintain pressure on public schools to transform their delivery model. As an economic good, education could be delivered variously, and public schools needed to explore these options. Focused on delivery, local districts might reshape their workforce to eliminate benefits, for example, so they could get their product to the market more cheaply. Klenke intimated that Evers's attention to efficiency represented a futile effort to maintain a failing model. Transformation—market innovation—would force public schools to find genuine, long-term cost savings or risk going out of business. While these possibilities might worry teachers, they ultimately would benefit the education consumer.

High-cost pensions and administrator-laden districts suggested to the majority committee members that public schools continued to support and respond to the wrong incentives. They did not behave as market actors, and they did not demand this behavior from their employees. Indeed, public schools and districts continued to act as bureaucratic entities that sought to preserve their power and protect themselves from the threats of private schools. Yet this action betrayed a sluggishness and lack of motivation that explained poor outcomes. Markets demanded dynamism and energy. Lauding the school performance grants proposed by the governor, Representative Pat Strachota maintained that these grants represented an effort to fund public education in "a different way." Tying funding to outcomes, these performance grants would enable policymakers and administrators to "incentivize people." Advancing a market model, Strachota explained that "if you own a business, that's how you treat your employees."[67] She asserted that in the private sector, when a company does well, its employees do well. When a company does poorly, its employees suffer the consequences. Superintendent Evers responded that incentive grants operating in other states had not produced positive outcomes—bringing this policy to Wisconsin would only reward wealthy districts that already met prescribed standards. Seen through the lens of a new business model, Evers's response reflected a desire to avoid competition.

For some committee members, past policies had wrongly retained the anticompetitive incentives of the bureaucratic public school system. In both the 2013 and 2015 hearings in which Evers appeared, Representative Dale Kooyenga called attention to what he regarded as the perverse incentives of existing choice programs among the public schools. For the open enrollment program, which permitted a student from one local district to enroll in a public school in a different district, the original district retained the monetary difference between their per-pupil budgetary authority and the lower, state-provided per-pupil allocation allotted to the new district. Kooyenga expressed puzzlement at this arrangement: "That's a remarkable business model. . . . You lose a customer but you get to keep a portion of the sales."[68] In 2015, with regard to Milwaukee, Kooyenga charged that the open enrollment program incentivized the city's school district to fail: "In a business context, you can maximize your revenue by decreasing your customers. If Milwaukee Public Schools decreases their number of students, they can maximize their revenue because they don't have the cost associated with teaching a child." The legislature did not demand positive outcomes from the Milwaukee Public Schools, so the district did not produce positive outcomes. Left unsaid in this conclusion was the restriction of motivation to a profit-loss calculation. Why would someone want to teach a child except for profit? Kooyenga saw the possibility of maximizing revenue through fewer customers as an "inherent motivation."[69] He did not credit teachers' and administrators' commitments to their students and their communities as possible reasons why they might wish to keep and educate students in the Milwaukee Public Schools. For Kooyenga, no sound market reason could explain this interest, and nonmarket reasons did not register.

While interests balancing individual and community appeared murky to Representative Kooyenga, majority committee members purported to see the interest of parents clearly—to seek advantages for their children. And this self-interest outweighed all others. For Senator Leah Vukmir, the best evidence for the success of vouchers arose in high "parental satisfaction" and growing "demand for the program." This market did not evaluate individual interest; it provided opportunities to satisfy individual interest. Like the governor, Senator Vukmir "trust[ed] [parents] to make the best decision for their kids." Against charges that statewide vouchers would undercut the authority of democratically elected local school boards, Representative Nygren retorted that "more information for parents is the ultimate local control."[70] By developing school report cards and other measures, legislators would enable parents to act as informed consumers. Rather than controlling education markets, school boards could only offer parents one option in a diverse marketplace.

Stifling the Competition

If vouchers served as the means to the end of expanding an education market that encompassed public and private schools, opponents of expanding vouchers regarded the shift of state resources for developing markets as undermining the capacity of public schools to perform. Noting that the 2011–13 budget, which followed Act 10, enacted the largest education cuts in state history, Superintendent Evers maintained that voucher expansion and property tax reductions in the 2013–15 state budget consumed its increased funds for education; indeed, public schools would receive a funding cut for the first year of the budget. He urged the Joint Finance Committee to "stop the continual defunding of public education and approve a state budget that truly invests in public education." He explained that overall the budget flatlined funding for public schools while increasing voucher spending by 32 percent. Rather than serving students across the state, the budget "pits public school kids against voucher and independent charter school kids."[71] While majority committee members envisioned a market spurred by competition and innovation, Evers foresaw a harmful, zero-sum battle for finite resources.

During the 2013 and 2015 listening sessions, dozens of local administrators, teachers, parents, and students offered firsthand accounts of the consequences of insufficient state support for public education. Jill Underly, an elementary school principal and the incoming superintendent for the rural Pecatonica Area School District, explained that her school could not afford a full-time nurse. Instead, they could only pay a nurse to visit the school once weekly. She recounted an interaction with a young boy who came into her office crying: "Asking him what was wrong, he said his tooth hurt." Underly looked into his mouth with a flashlight and discovered that "he had lost a filling in the back of his mouth. He couldn't eat; he couldn't drink. He couldn't concentrate in school. Talking to his mother, I finally figured out that they couldn't afford to get it fixed."[72] In sharing this story, Underly conveyed two messages. First, despite the polarizing discourses that cast rural and urban areas of the state as holding disparate educational interests, need existed across the state. Second, Underly underscored the varied roles that public schools played in their communities, including arranging dental care for some students.

Other speakers addressed the effects on classroom instruction. Challenging the assumptions of legislators like Kooyenga, Amanda VanRemortel, an elementary school music teacher from Green Bay, explained how she drew from her personal finances to provide her students with necessary learning materials: "In my classroom, I buy supplies that I believe my students need. I spend upwards of $500 personally for my classroom and students every year." These expenditures presented a confounding case study of profit maximization, since VanRemortel did not receive a higher salary in return. Perhaps the youngest person to address the Joint Finance Committee directly was Lucy Herman, an eighth grader at St. Croix Falls Middle School. In addition to her classroom instruction, Herman had learned lessons about the difficulties of school funding: "My school is only scraping by on the money we make on fundraisers." Even so, she reported that her math class "ran out of graph paper. . . . We ended up having to print sheets out on the computer and use the back of old assignments."[73] Like her teachers, Herman learned to survive with less.

In interactions with Evers, majority committee members retorted that local communities could recover reductions in state funding for public education through referenda. In particular, in both 2013 and 2015, Representative Dean Knudson pressed this point during his interactions with Superintendent Evers. He noted that Evers had discounted the increased funding for public education in the budget because this funding largely went to property tax reductions. While Knudson agreed with this analysis insofar as Evers had correctly identified the effect of the state funding, he responded that Evers had overlooked a benefit of this funding change: "What it has also led to is that local voters are approving referenda questions at a rate, just remarkably different than before Act 10 and before those property tax cuts." With regard to the increasing frequency and approval rates of referenda, Evers and Knudson agreed. Indeed, earlier in the hearing, Evers remarked that "people are going to referenda in droves." But they disagreed about the implications of this trend. Evers maintained that funding through referenda did not provide districts with financial stability from year to year, which impeded planning. Moreover, referenda did not increase funds for public schools; rather, they shifted the source of funding from the state to local communities. Considered in light of the differences in wealth in communities across the state, an increased reliance on local funding would exacerbate educational inequalities. Some communities could afford referenda while others could not—and some communities passed referenda and still cut their district budgets. As Christine Weymouth, superintendent of the Mauston school district, explained, even if her community passed an upcoming referendum, "we will still need to make cuts in staffing."[74] Either Knudson did not consider these possibilities, or he saw them as acceptable consequences of market competition.

Power and Money

As legislators and the governor represented their cause as a struggle for individual freedom against the coercion of bureaucratic institutions, voucher lobbying groups in Wisconsin developed a more comfortable relationship with state power. By the end of January 2013, as the push for voucher expansion began, pro-voucher groups had hired some serious legislative firepower—three former Republican Assembly speakers. Jeff Fitzgerald, who had just retired from state politics after serving for two years as Assembly speaker, joined former speakers John Gard and Scott Jensen as registered lobbyists for school choice organizations. The Associated Press observed that "the proliferation of former Assembly speakers on the school choice issue shows how advocates for expanding vouchers plan to focus on this year's legislative session to push for changes."[75] Fitzgerald and Gard worked for the influential lobbying group School Choice Wisconsin, whose president, Jim Bender, had worked previously as a staffer for Fitzgerald. Jensen worked for the Wisconsin chapter of the American Federation for Children, which Betsy DeVos had chaired prior to her nomination as education secretary.

Pro-voucher groups also dedicated significant financial resources to the campaign for statewide expansion. In a 2012 "election impact" report, the American Federation for Children boasted about its investments in the state: "With expenditures of $2,392,000, the American Federation for Children and the AFC Action Fund engaged in hard-fought, successful battles to ensure educational choice majorities in both chambers of the legislature."[76] Of these funds, the American Federation for Children spent over $300,000 in a single state Senate race. One report estimated that pro-voucher groups had outspent voucher opponents by an almost ten-to-one margin from 2003 to 2013.[77] The combination of money and past legislative experience made voucher lobbyists a familiar face to the people in the State Capitol. During one listening session outside of Milwaukee, as private school teachers and students organized by School Choice Wisconsin stepped up to the podium to speak, co-chair Senator Alberta Darling introduced them as "Jim Bender and his group, please."[78] Darling offered this introduction not to discount the speakers—Jim Bender did not address the committee—but as a statement of recognition. Her introduction also exemplified the combined force of the disproportionate symbolic and material resources available to more privileged and powerful publics. In voicing her recognition, Darling implicitly acknowledged the relationships that Bender had built with the committee, as well as the material resources employed by his group to further the interests of School Choice Wisconsin and the majority members of the committee.

Democratic committee members and participants in the public hearings charged that the influence of the voucher lobby—not freedom, nor enhanced educational outcomes, nor cost savings, nor accountability—determined the expansion of vouchers in Wisconsin. During a listening session in Green Bay, Brenda Warren, president of the Green Bay school board, referenced a recent Legislative Fiscal Bureau analysis that found no educational gains for voucher students in comparison to public school students in Milwaukee. Indicating that vouchers would not "suddenly . . . work in Green Bay and elsewhere," Warren asserted that "I am frustrated that my local control is being usurped by out-of-state money and outside lobbyists pushing unsuccessful voucher programs on our community."[79] Representative Chris Taylor pointed to the lack of accountability for voucher schools. Unlike public schools, which needed to account for their use of state funding, private schools faced no such requirement: "We're just essentially [giving a] taxpayer subsidy no longer available for public school [to] private school." Although past performance and current safeguards raised concerns, Taylor identified the rationale for expanding vouchers: "The elephant in the room is this, I mean, this is the biggest player in Wisconsin state politics." While choice may have outweighed poor results for some committee members, Taylor saw money outweighing both. Likewise, Senator Erpenbach held that the committee majority supported voucher expansion because of "the amount of money that's been spent." Erpenbach challenged his colleagues that so long as they continued on this path, they should "acknowledge the fact that, yeah, we are being run by the highest bidder."[80] These criticisms of the voucher lobby's business practices resonated with Milton Friedman's portrayal of the capitalist wanting protection for oneself and "freedom" for others.

If voucher lobbyists held such great power that they could shape the legislative agenda, then the children served by public education lacked comparative political power. During one listening session, Doug Perry, a school board member from South Milwaukee, made this comparison starkly: "My constituents are a little bit different than yours, though. My constituents, most of them, are children. And they don't really have a voice here today. They don't have a voice. They don't vote and they don't, they don't donate to . . . political campaigns." Similarly, Kim Schroeder, vice president of the Milwaukee Teachers Education Association, insisted that legislators explain why "our students [are] less in worth to you than ALEC [American Legislative Exchange Council] and your big money."[81] By 2015, as Governor Walker's presidential aspirations had become clear to citizens across the state, speakers referenced his desire for power in comparing the constituencies who could and could not influence state education policy. Appleton resident Richard Gussey accused the governor of crafting his policies to appeal "to the right wing of the Republican party in the hopes that he receives the party's presidential nomination."[82] Together, these comments outlined a cynical political calculation: Wisconsin schoolchildren did not vote, but party stalwarts did. In calling out improper influence, voucher opponents flipped the monetary motivations asserted by voucher supporters. While supporters ascribed monetary incentives to actors in an education market, opponents identified monetary incentives at the base of political decision-making.

Vouchers and Race Revisited

From the early uses of vouchers in the South as a means of avoiding integration, to the Friedmans' dubious prediction that their continued use in Virginia would produce integration despite policymakers' intentions, to their adoption in Milwaukee as Black community members voiced frustration with the failures of integration, vouchers and race have always been linked and their relationship has been in flux. With the election of Scott Walker as governor, the relationship of vouchers and race changed once more. The WPCP did not target Polly Williams's former constituents, and the MPCP had long since dashed the hopes of its early advocates. Vouchers had been a fixture of Milwaukee education for more than twenty years, and Black children still did not receive an adequate education. Thandeka Chapman and René Antrop-González maintain that market theories of education fail to account for the convergence of financial and social capital that sustain "whiteness as property" and perpetuate uneven choices for white and Black families. In wealthy white communities, "the high regard for the schools is supported by the lack of people of color, the limited number of poor students, and the property value of the homes."[83] Illuminating how market reforms constrain the agency of their putative beneficiaries, Chapman and Antrop-González explain that the individualist orientations of these reforms obfuscate the structural forces of poverty and racism that influence interactions in market publics. Choosing among generally inferior options in Milwaukee, Black children suffer grossly unequal education experiences in comparison to white suburban children.

The poor performance of vouchers did not dampen debates about racial legacies and ongoing struggles for racial justice. Both supporters and opponents of privatization referred to education as "the civil rights battle of the twenty-first century," as Representative Kooyenga asserted during a 2015 executive session of the Joint Finance Committee.[84] Explaining that he recently read one of Frederick Douglass's autobiographies, Kooyenga shared his awe-struck reaction to Douglass's description of learning to read as a enslaved person: "The man changed our world, and he said that part of the change he was able to make in our world was that his freedom was rooted in his ability to read." Kooyenga expressed frustration with the status quo, with talk: "We need to do something. Just execute." But he was not the only member of the Joint Finance Committee to reference Frederick Douglass. Later in the same meeting, Senator Lena Taylor offered Kooyenga a different Douglass quote. She retorted, "Why don't [you] use the quote that says, 'Where justice is denied, where poverty is enforced, where ignorance prevails, and where any one class'—look around—'any one class is made to feel that society is an organized conspiracy to oppress, rob, and degrade them, neither persons nor property will be safe.'"[85] Taylor suggested that the majority committee members did not need to discover a suppressed market to locate the source of Milwaukee's struggles; rather, they needed to recognize the larger structures that have kept Black Milwaukeeans disproportionately poor, uneducated, and imprisoned.

Senator Taylor exhorted her colleagues to examine the larger contexts that have shaped the (lack of) education for Black children—contexts that the state legislature helped to create and sustain. Referencing the majority committee members' call to focus on outcomes, she asserted that "our outcomes are horrific." She enumerated a substantial range of challenges that confronted Black children in Wisconsin and, especially, Milwaukee. The state sustained the worst achievement disparities in the nation among Black and white students. The nation's highest poverty rates resided in Milwaukee. Only 4 percent of students in Milwaukee Public Schools met standards for college readiness. In fifty low-income schools primarily serving students of color in Milwaukee—public, charter, and voucher schools—only 8 percent of students demonstrated reading proficiency. And yet Taylor's colleagues supported "a budget that is so void on dealing with the crisis disparity that we have. It's almost morally corrupt, because you have to begin to wonder, 'Do we care, or is it by design?'" Rather than educating Black children, Milwaukee schools suspended Black children at the highest rates in the nation, which, Taylor explained, decreased their likelihood of receiving a diploma and increased their likelihood of being imprisoned. In this dire situation, Senator Taylor grieved: "I'm suffocating; I can't breathe."[86] Her lament recalled the dying words of Eric Garner ten months earlier, who repeated the phrase "I can't breathe" as NYPD officers choked him to death. In the months since, the phrase had entered public culture as a symbol of police harassment and violence toward Black people and, more generally, structural racism. In the committee room, Taylor struggled to convey the magnitude of the situation facing her constituents; she could not breathe. As the only Black legislator on the Joint Finance Committee, she struggled to engage her colleagues' understanding of the contexts and implications of their policymaking; she could not breathe.[87]

Representative Kooyenga and Senator Taylor both cited Frederick Douglass, but they drew different lessons from his words. Kooyenga read in Douglass's autobiography the story of a man who bettered himself under the most extreme conditions imaginable. Drawing inspiration from these efforts, Kooyenga wanted to facilitate the agency of contemporary Black children who suffered. In this way, as Lisa Flores explains about pro-voucher discourse generally, Kooyenga advanced a representation of Black children as "'trapped' or 'stuck'" in underperforming schools, denied "the choice that, to many, is fundamental to ideals of American mobility and freedom."[88] Recognizing that Douglass confronted structural obstacles during his life,

Taylor argued that change would not happen for Wisconsin's Black children until legislators directly addressed the structural conditions they faced. Until then, all types of schools would fail Black children. Structural inequalities also affected the ability of poor children and their parents to address the Joint Finance Committee. Senator Taylor saw herself as "the voice for them, for their parents. Stories matter. I just don't know whose stories matter. I'm hoping their stories matter."[89] To rewrite stories of suffering, legislators needed to address wider contexts of inequality and oppression. Senator Taylor called for "wraparound services" that would combine education with health care and other services needed by the poor families she represented.

Kooyenga's call to help children circulated a changed representation of Black people and yet proposed familiar solutions. Flores observes that unlike the threatening racial figures that haunt debates over typical social policies, school choice advocacy often offers a sympathetic portrayal of a "racialized figure . . . as the impoverished and disadvantaged victim of greedy teachers and politicians who consistently put their own interests above those of marginalized student populations."[90] On this score, Kooyenga demanded action—he no longer would abide the profit-seeking behavior of the educators in the Milwaukee Public Schools. Black children in the city deserved the opportunity for training as capable market actors just like their white peers.[91] Yet this sense of urgency reconfigured social change as individual change. Like Douglass, Milwaukee children could improve themselves under trying conditions. Even so, this positive identification of contemporary children with Douglass maintained historical categories of deservingness that have sorted poor people into populations warranting and not warranting assistance.[92] Good Black children, through the choices of their parents, went to schools that fit them. Bad Black children went to prison. The school-to-prison pipeline that Senator Taylor decried reappeared as a consequence of bad choices.[93] Indeed, the commitment to granting choice to poor Black families intensified the ascription of personal responsibility for educational outcomes. Granted their freedom, individuals needed to choose wisely and accept responsibility for the consequences of their decisions. Before the availability of choice, its absence explained the poor educational outcomes of disadvantaged students. With the availability of choice, bad decision-making would explain ongoing poor outcomes. And ongoing poor outcomes, in turn, likely would reassert representations of poor Black families as undeserving.

As poor Black children confronted an array of structural forces that inhibited their agency, they also encountered the biases of the Joint Finance Committee itself, whose members assumed that they could discern the needs, interests, and motivations of these children and the adults in their lives. This assumption appeared most clearly in the debate over an item in the 2015 majority budget titled the Opportunity Schools and Partnership Program (OSPP), which effectively authorized a private takeover of low-performing public schools in Milwaukee.[94] The provision created an autonomous commissioner who would act separately from the Milwaukee school board. Choosing each year from a list of the city's underperforming public schools, the commissioner could transfer the management and property of these schools to private operators of voucher and charter schools. Senator Darling and Representative Kooyenga developed the OSPP without consulting any of the legislators representing Milwaukee.

Defending both the program and its exclusive development, Senator Darling stressed the importance of the appointed commissioner acting independently of the elected school board. Darling maintained that "the commissioner will also be boots on [the] ground to keep the pressure on the school board. They will both be free from the school board's authority and they will be free to perform." As this description suggests, the commissioner would act as an entrepreneurial agent freed from the constraints of bureaucracy. A market innovator, the commissioner would act boldly and decisively without having to wait for an official stamp of approval. This entrepreneur would be focused on outcomes, not established lines of authority and accumulated power. Darling underscored the pressure that this competition would place on the Milwaukee school board: "If we take this pressure off today, what will happen in a couple of weeks, the school board will say, 'We don't have to do it anymore.'"[95] Without this market pressure, the board would revert back to its old ways, accepting failure as a regular education outcome in Milwaukee. And if it took two white suburban legislators in Darling and Kooyenga to demand change, then so be it—the children in Milwaukee deserved better.

Making plain the racial dynamics of the OSPP, Senator Taylor chastised her colleagues for presenting themselves as "the great white hope." She expressed incredulity that they did not seek input from the city's representatives: "I just can't imagine why you couldn't talk to any Milwaukee legislators." Moreover, the bill's authors behaved duplicitously. When word of the proposal's inclusion in the budget circulated in the Capitol, their staff rebuffed Taylor's inquiries: "When my office asked, and we were told there was nothing, and then something came out." Darling and Kooyenga professed concern for the plight of Taylor's constituents, but they expressed no interest in hearing from them. Instead, they imposed another market option in the city unilaterally. Senator Taylor distilled their process: "You guys are not really good at listening to the people."[96] Neither Darling nor Kooyenga replied to this comment, but their market logic spoke for itself: insufficiently incentivized, the Milwaukee school board betrayed suspect motives. It did not care to deliver a great product at a great price. And Milwaukee legislators did not appear as suitable business partners, for they lacked sufficient competitive drives.

Market Ends Justify Antidemocratic Means

Advocates of expanding markets confronted a potential paradox in pursuing this end. If markets stood as the surest guarantor of individual freedom, then their campaign for further marketization could have invited the polling of individual preferences, in deference to choice. Yet, as this chapter demonstrates, the results of a poll of Wisconsin residents would not have produced a unanimous decision. Indeed, a March 2013 Marquette University Law School poll found that only 37 percent of respondents favored expanding vouchers to the entire state. The poll also found that 84 percent of respondents with children in their household expressed satisfaction with their local public schools, while only 13 percent of such households expressed dissatisfaction.[97] Pro-voucher legislators, then, faced the very same problem of coercive decision-making that the Friedmans rebuked—they would have to compel individuals to participate in education markets against their stated preferences. Perhaps the resolution of this paradox lay in a distinction of market development from market operation: markets safeguard freedom, but sometimes individuals need to be forced to practice their freedom.

In a literal sense, majority committee members avoided the sunlight of publicity when they expanded vouchers statewide. When the Joint Finance Committee held listening sessions around the state, the proposed budget called for expanding vouchers to nine additional districts out of the more than four hundred public school districts in the state. However, shortly after 1:00 a.m. on June 5, 2013, after ten hours of closed-door meetings, confirming rumors that had circulated just days before, Republican legislative leaders announced to the press a revised budget that included the expansion of vouchers to every public school district in the state. At 1:25 a.m., the Joint Finance Committee reconvened and distributed copies of an omnibus education bill to its members. As copies of the education budget circulated, Representative John Richards reminded the committee chairs that at the start of the current legislative session, Assembly speaker Robin Vos had pledged that "we weren't going to be conducting our business in the middle of the night."

Richards proposed that the committee recess until 9:00 a.m. so that members could consider the budget they had just been given. A recess also would permit "the public" to "see what we're doing in the light of day." Speaking next, Senator Jennifer Schilling pointed out that no public hearings had been held on the provision to expand vouchers statewide. She observed that even as members disagreed, the committee had typically maintained "a healthy respect for process." The late-night introduction of a new policy violated this respect: "This is not the way to develop good public policy."[98] Schilling also asked for a short recess, but the committee co-chairs denied these requests.

Even when the budget proposed expanding vouchers to nine additional districts, multiple speakers at each of the four 2013 listening sessions urged the committee to remove this provision from the budget to consider it as separate legislation. For example, John McMullen, president of the Tomah school board, stated, "We would respectfully request that you remove the private school voucher expansion proposal from the budget. This is a fundamental change in education policy that should be introduced and debated away from the budget to allow more public discussion and scrutiny."[99] Others argued that as a policy change, voucher expansion did not constitute a budgetary issue. The budgeting process did not serve as a proper vehicle for public participation, since much of the Joint Finance Committee's work consisted of communication with agency heads and negotiations with the governor's office. While citizens could speak briefly at listening sessions, unlike witnesses at committee hearings, they could not engage in dialogue, through question-and-answer time, with policymakers.

Many speakers at the listening sessions also expressed concerns that voucher expansion would usurp the decision-making authority of local officials. Identifying himself as "one who generally views the world from a conservative perspective," John Acomb, vice president of the Beloit school board, derided voucher expansion as unproven and costly. To compensate for money diverted to vouchers, districts would need to raise property taxes. Further, he held that "it has always been a common-sense conservative perspective that the best oversight of any government program is local."[100] A board of "locally elected community residents" governed the Beloit public schools, while no such authority existed for proposed voucher schools. Referencing his political orientation twice, Acomb demonstrated the negative dynamics of polarization in the state. In both conservative and liberal communities, residents agreed on the value of their local public schools, but the members of the Joint Finance Committee—enabled by the Republicans' legislative control—advanced different visions of education.

Many speakers at the listening sessions projected an alternative vision of human relationships than the new business model favored by the majority members of the Joint Finance Committee. In this vision, individuals do not relate to one another only as market actors connected through voluntary contractual agreements. Instead, they share interests and identities in common, and work together in groups. Public schools serve as both means and ends for sustaining communities. As Sue Todey, president of the Sevastopol board of education, explained, "Our small public rural schools are truly the heart of our communities." Other speakers from diverse locales echoed these sentiments. Nancy Jones, who indicated that she had lived and worked in large and small cities in the state, drew the lesson that "public schools are the heart of each community." Public schools are emblematic of collective engagement and decision-making. Green Bay resident Luann Crowder remarked that "members of a society work together to do what individuals cannot. We pool our resources to pay for things we could never afford on our own."[101] Crowder did not quote John Dewey, but her reference to individuals working together invoked the reciprocal relationship of individual and community that Dewey saw as critical to democratic relationships. Individuals contribute to their communities by supporting local public schools, and communities facilitate individual growth in the classroom and beyond.

Negotiating Tensions of Market Publics

The Friedmans' professional standing as economists gave their normative vision of human relationships special force. As members of an ostensibly truth-telling discipline, they cast aside partisan argument to outline the essential motivations, interests, and aspirations of individuals. Articulating a powerful and potentially paradoxical hybrid of realism and normative theory, they identified the true nature of the human condition in promising a future in contrast with the actual world in which people live—reality stands against the "reality" most people know. Their vision of human relationships and market publics has entrusted contemporary disciples with a desirable and challenging legacy.

Wisconsin policymakers needed to reconcile two tensions as they pushed for the statewide expansion of vouchers. First, they pressed for a model of freedom and individualism in education policy in an environment that they acknowledged had been influenced by race, power, and money. As poor Black children suffered in relation to their wealthy white peers, further marketization promised redress. Yet improved outcomes constituted the original promise of the MPCP, which, according to analyses, it had failed to deliver; large divides continued to exist between the city and suburbs. Advancing markets free of discrimination, then, required obscuring the market forces of residential segregation that had helped create the very inequities that further marketization supposedly would counter. Moreover, negotiating this tension necessitated rewriting the history of civil rights as stories of personal transformation, as Kooyenga's admiration of Frederick Douglass illustrated.

The second tension, extending to schoolchildren from different backgrounds across the state, concerned the means and ends of developing education markets. As the Joint Finance Committee held hearings across the state in 2013 and 2015, they discovered that the large majority of speakers—and, polls indicated, a large majority of Wisconsin citizens[102]—expressed contentment with their local public schools. As potential market actors, these consumers appeared satisfied with the suppliers they already used. To create a statewide market, committee members had to discount the voices of the constituents they heard. Perhaps these constituents could not perceive their lack of freedom. Bound by the state, they did not know what freedom looked like. But the speakers pushed back against this vision, asserting reciprocal relationships of individual and community and ascribing a central community role to local public schools. Outside of the listening sessions, local community groups have championed the cause of public education.

5

CONNECTING SCHOOLS AND COMMUNITIES:
LOCAL ADVOCACY FOR PUBLIC EDUCATION

John Dewey recognized that education evolves through relationships created inside and outside of the classroom. Critiquing formalist philosophies of education, he resisted an approach that locates the origin and consummation of education in the transmission of information from teacher to student. This explains his claim in *Democracy and Education* that "we never educate directly, but indirectly by means of the environment."[1] Education requires the active engagement of teacher and student, as well as other students in the classroom, students and staff elsewhere in the school building, and adults in the school's neighborhood. If a school building brings these different people into physical proximity, their interactions hold the potential to build relationships. Some relationships—such as those that encourage participation and reflection, value the perspectives of everyone in a school, and seek connections with neighbors—can support students in discovering a desire to explore their interests, develop their agency, and act purposefully with others. Other relationships—such as those that devalue the insights and abilities of young people while insisting on clear lines of authority—can actively militate against growth, producing disaffection and alienation and casting school as something to suffer and discard at the earliest opportunity.

Through his key term of community, which connects democracy and education, Dewey outlined his ideas about the particular relationships that an educational environment should facilitate. At times, as I explained in chapter 1, Dewey seemed to invoke community and democracy as synonyms. Still, we may distinguish these terms in Dewey's writings by regarding community as the opportunity for the tangible realization of the more abstract values and aspirations of democracy. In "Creative Democracy," he explained that practicing democracy as a way of life carries the recognition that "democracy is a reality only as it is a commonplace of living."[2] Community provides a framework for such living, mapping out the potential for individuals to build multiple and varied connections and networks they can engage regularly. Not surprisingly, Dewey extended these networks to schools. Beyond the curriculum, schools offer irreplaceable lessons in socialization—for good or bad. If schools offer students opportunities for building relationships by physically bringing people together, community provides the pathways for organizing empowering relationships that articulate common interests and concerns while respecting differences and foster individual and collective growth without subsuming one into the other. As Dewey's vision of a Great Community makes clear, he regarded democracy, education, and community as primarily local undertakings.

Inspired by this vision, interested in finding more democracy-friendly views of education than those I explored in chapters 3 and 4, and perhaps more focused than Dewey on the limits of actually existing communities, in the summer of 2019 I worked with Kelly Jensen to interview thirty-seven public education advocates across the state of Wisconsin.[3] When I first considered writing a book chapter based on interviews with local advocates, I anticipated meeting exclusively with community volunteers. I did not expect to meet with school board members, teachers, administrators, or professional advocates. However, as we began the interviews, I quickly realized that "public education advocate" is a slippery category. We did interview volunteers, but we also interviewed people whose advocacy roles shifted from local volunteer to elected official, teachers and other education professionals who viewed their commitments as extending beyond the classroom into public advocacy, and advocates who worked for nonprofits and education associations. These different positions reveal manifold advocacy networks characterized by relationships that cut across institutional boundaries.

To elicit a wide range of perspectives, I purposely sought to create a pool of interviewees more diverse than the demographics of Wisconsin. With regard to race in particular, I did so in recognition of the roles that race and racism have played in debates over vouchers and other market-based reforms in Wisconsin and elsewhere in the United States. As the case studies in this book demonstrate, advocates from diverse backgrounds historically have supported and opposed vouchers and other market-based reforms as a means for addressing racial inequities in primary and secondary education. The interview pool consisted of more than twice the proportion of African Americans living in the state, more than four times the proportion of American Indians, and slightly less than the proportion of Latinx state residents.[4] With the approval of the UW-Madison Institutional Review Board, we obtained interviewees' verbal consent at the beginning of the interviews to make an audio recording, prepare a written transcript, and quote anonymously from the transcript. Lasting between fifty minutes and one hour and thirty-nine minutes, the interviews followed a semi-structured, open-ended format. The interview protocol addressed five main topics: advocates' backgrounds and aims, their assessment of state-level policies and discourse, their ideas for the future of public education in the state, their views on the relationships of local public schools and community, and their perspective on the relationships among education, community, and democracy.

In starting this chapter with Dewey, I hope to demonstrate the resonance across time of democratic perspectives on public education, perspectives that may offer empowering alternatives to the prominent neoliberal approaches that have occupied recent presidential administrations and many state legislatures. I do not seek to place Dewey and contemporary advocates in the positions of theorist (Dewey) and practitioners (advocates). Without diminishing Dewey's scholarly accomplishments, I do not believe that he articulated a singular perspective on democracy and education. Dewey addressed what I regard as a strong desire of many people to create meaningful human connections, to work with others to solve shared problems and achieve mutual goals, to support both individual advancement and group solidarity. Dewey himself responded to his critics by grounding his ideas historically: he did not construct a Platonic ideal and demand that humans live up to it. Rather, he represented his approach as learning from human activity—the values that people express and the actions people take to realize them. And the contemporary advocates we interviewed did not cast themselves as practitioners of a timeless philosophy, nor did they cite Dewey as their inspiration. Instead, they spoke of the value of community in terms of their goals and the relationships and networks in which they located themselves. They amplified the power of community with respect to the people they saw themselves as working with and fighting for. The relationship I imagine between Dewey and contemporary advocates is characterized not by hierarchy but equality. Indeed, as this chapter proceeds, Dewey's voice recedes and the advocates' voices take center stage.

In important respects, the contemporary advocates we interviewed said more than Dewey did, especially on the subjects of community, locale, and race. Their insights illuminate what I described in chapter 1 as the promise and the limits of Dewey's vision for democracy and education. Indeed, consistent with Dewey's views, these insights reveal the limits of any single perspective and the value of engaging multiple perspectives through democratic relationships. While Dewey championed a Great Community, these advocates elucidated the dynamics of the local communities they participated in, the various communities they worked with, the communities in which they felt welcome and from which they experienced exclusion. They appreciated the challenges of community in its theory and practice. Our interviewees described their politics on a range from reformist to radical, yet, across these differences, they offered compelling reasons for building communities. One African American advocate, who elucidated clearly the structural racism that harms Black and Brown children in the Madison public schools, nevertheless maintained that "education is paired best when [it's] rooted in home, in community, in a grounding." In these comments, we may value community, as I suggest with Dewey, as a place for people to stand. A contemporary vision for democracy and education may draw productively from Dewey and advocates like this insightful theorist and practitioner.

I begin this chapter by developing a concept of community as a network of purposeful human relationships that mediates identity and difference. I then explicate five themes from our interviews with local public school advocates: capacious community, community resources, communities divided, challenges to community, and communities and democracy. These themes illuminate the ups and downs, satisfactions and frustrations, successes and failures of community-building. If community is to embody democracy as a way of life, then it requires active engagement. This framework asks more of people than treating democracy and community as stable, independent entities, but the potential benefits may justify the effort.

Conceptualizing Community

Communities constitute particular, purposefully created and sustained sets of human relationships. Against the self-interested individual of the market, communities represent an effort to hold the I and we in productive relationship. As networks of human activity and interaction, communities enable participants to discover, develop, and pursue what they may regard as shared interests, concerns, and goals. In *Keywords*, Raymond Williams writes that the historical usage of the term community connotes "relations" and "common."[5] Some theorists have emphasized the common, but my perspective regards community as the mediation of identity and difference, both for individual members themselves as well as for the collective of a particular community.[6] Wary of consensus, concerned that a primary focus on the common may enforce conformity and construct rigid boundaries, contemporary scholars have considered how communities may productively maintain themselves through disagreement and dissent. For example, Linnell Secomb regards the "repression of difference and disagreement in the name of unity and consensus" as destructive of the "engagement and interrelation of community." While I share this view, I do not subscribe to Secomb's reconceptualization of community as a prior condition of sharing "that allows the human existence to be."[7] This approach attenuates the purposeful action entailed in the creation of communities. Humans may be born and live among others, but we do not actively relate to all others; indeed, sometimes we purposefully dissociate from people we find objectionable. Further, even within and among communities, disagreement and dissent constitute purposeful communicative acts.

If we find inspiration in Dewey's call to live democracy as a way of life, we do not need to view all relationships as democratically oriented, nor do we need to view everyday life entirely through the lens of community. Although I regard market-based approaches to education as structurally flawed, I do not wish to see markets disappear from existence; for example, I happily shop for food each week at the local grocery store. As a type of community, democratic communities arise through networks of democratic relationships. They typically mediate individual and collective with a view toward the public dimensions of living lives together, solving problems, pursuing shared goals, and seeking ameliorative social change in view of the ends of justice, freedom, and equality. Mary Stuckey and Sean O'Rourke illuminate the promise of democratic communities as they envision inclusive political community "rooted in a kind of radical democracy that allows for and even celebrates robust, passionate rhetoric and a corresponding broader array of 'acceptable' discursive forms."[8] Further, like Dewey, we may identify democratic communities by their inward and outward practices, in the ways that individual participants relate to one another and the ways they relate to other communities. For instance, seeking empowerment within a particular community at the expense of other communities violates democratic ends. In this spirit, some of the advocates we interviewed explained that even as they sought to advocate for the children in their local schools, they did not do so to the detriment of children elsewhere and they explicitly opposed education policies that pitted students in different districts against each other. A commitment to respectful and vibrant intercommunity interaction reflects people's shared experience of living within and among many communities.

Because public education can only bolster students and society when tending to justice, freedom, and equality, it requires democratic communities inside and outside the classroom. Along these lines, Silvia Cristina Bettez maintains that learning communities can encourage students to "practice interdependence" and enact "social responsibility towards others."[9] Students, too, participate in multiple communities. They bring the experiences of diverse communities into the classroom, and their classroom experiences may instruct their actions elsewhere. This dynamic presents both a challenge and an opportunity, as public school advocates recognize that we live in a structurally unequal and unjust society and yet seek to enlist the potentially transformative power of education. Toward this end, democratic communities in schools may orient themselves toward curricular and extracurricular activities. Working together, teachers and students may organize classrooms to call attention to and discuss societal inequalities and model egalitarian practices. School clubs may explore shared interests, develop members' agency, and address issues in their communities.[10]

My perspective on community foregrounds the productive power of relationships. If we reduce community to an aggregation of individuals or a group, we arrest its movement and vitality. The dynamism and energy of community arises from the mediation of people and perspectives and the fluidity of the in-between. In this spirit, Gregory Clark characterizes the collectivity of community as "a process rather than a state of being."[11] Community does not represent a fixed achievement, nor does any participant possess membership as a commodity. Participants enact their relations with one another, unsettling stagnant conceptualizations of membership and suggesting potentially textured and varied connections and vibrant ethical practices. For instance, in their analysis of the rhetoric of the Reverend Richard Allen, the first bishop of the African Methodist Episcopal Church, Glen McClish and Jacqueline Bacon consider some of his writings to illuminate how Reverend Allen related the individual and the collective in the African American community in Philadelphia in the late 1700s and early 1800s. In a pamphlet narrating the heroic actions of Black Philadelphians who cared for sick people during a yellow fever outbreak in the city in the 1790s, Allen and his co-author Absalom Jones cast heroic individuals "as members of a collective rather than as unique actors with merely personal claims to honor and integrity." Against white people's tendency to praise individual African Americans as exceptions to a larger group, Allen and Jones "stand with the collective and affirm that they all share the traits that deserve commendation." Noting praise they received from white Philadelphians, they presented themselves "not as elevated individuals but as leaders fundamentally a part of—and authorized by their commitment to—their community."[12] Allen and Jones resisted reductions of individual and group; they expressed a network of relationships, which included enslaved people, that supported and fought for individuals in community.

Lived relationships convey contextualized meanings, layered meanings, historically resonant meanings that add depth to particular networks, gainsaying scholarly models that imagine preferred human relationships in comparatively anonymous terms. In her influential argument against the politics of community, Iris Marion Young offers the model of the city, which presents denizens, especially those with socially marginalized experiences and views, "a welcome anonymity and some measure of freedom." Young characterizes city life as "the 'being-together' of strangers. Strangers encounter one another, either face to face or through media, often remaining strangers and yet acknowledging their contiguity in living and the contributions each makes to the others."[13] Yet even as a city offers residents stranger relations, it facilitates relationships built on different degrees of familiarity, commitment, affection, and solidarity. A person experiencing social marginalization in one locale may desire the relative anonymity and freedom of the city, but they may also look to create urban communities with others. Indeed, these communities may provide social supports that bolster one's sense of self and confidence to act freely. The people we interviewed spoke repeatedly of the power of community as a source of solidarity, a respite from the irritation, anger, and indifference of others, a restorative space for evening out the highs and lows of their advocacy.

Purposefulness motivates community relationships, situating individual and collective agency as a critical resource. In the world in which people practice community, agency appears as an unevenly distributed resource that variously enables and constrains people's abilities to direct their lives individually and in coordination with others. Both material and symbolic constraints, often in a mutually reinforcing manner, frustrate people's ability to act. Addressing these constraints, Karlyn Kohrs Campbell characterizes agency as "the ways in which individuals accept, negotiate, and resist the subject-positions available to them at given moments in a particular culture."[14] My own subject-position as a white male professional has offered me opportunities denied to others. For example, both of my children have attended public schools serving students from a range of socioeconomic backgrounds, including children from Latinx immigrant families. As a parent with a flexible work schedule and a well-paying job, I am better positioned to attend school functions during the day and in the evening and to donate to school fundraising campaigns than a parent who may have a fixed work schedule and who may lack adequate financial resources. Symbolically, as a professor in a city shaped importantly by its major university, I hold a privileged social position when I do attend school functions in comparison to a parent employed in a blue-collar position. Engaging a historical case, Darrel Wanzer-Serrano addresses the dynamic of community and agency in his study of the New York Young Lords, who were active in the city in the late 1960s and 1970s. Throughout the study, Wanzer-Serrano explains how the Young Lords unapologetically asserted their agency. He writes that "the Young Lords' community control rhetoric functioned as an agency that enabled certain kinds of discursive and political opportunities."[15] In this case and others, calls for community control may enact people's abilities to strengthen the relationships of community.

Even as they valued the local as an important site for community-building, our interviewees did not conflate community and local. As my analysis demonstrates, one locale can host multiple local communities. As I discussed in chapter 1, in *The Public and Its Problems*, Dewey tended to equate local with locale in his vision of a Great Community. Although he alluded to other types of connections in *Freedom and Culture*, Dewey did not explicitly consider the potential role of diversity within a particular locale. He wrote that "democracy must begin at home, and its home is the neighborly community,"[16] but Dewey did not discuss how the residents of a neighborhood may perceive community differently. This gap in his theorizing broaches a longer tradition of philosophical thinking about size, scale, community, and communication. From Aristotle onward, philosophers have worried about the prospects for community among many people separated by long distances.[17] Yet these worries have implicitly and explicitly configured the problems of community as logistical, neglecting the exclusions and inequalities that may shape action within a manageable terrain. Only by explicitly refusing a rendering of local as a singular space may we imagine more diverse communities and recognize multiple community affiliations.

As several scholars have observed, community necessarily involves a dynamic of inclusion and exclusion.[18] When we direct our energy to some networks of relationships, we devote less effort to others. When we develop particular interests and concern ourselves with some problems, we neglect others. Constraints on agency also shape community boundaries—prejudice and structural inequality foreclose some perspectives and interactions. Boundaries reflecting wider inequities and relations of power may police community participation. Attending to diversity and multiplicity cannot eliminate community boundaries, but such boundaries may garner greater attention, exhibit greater porousness, avail themselves to transformation, and support affiliations consistent with values of justice. Recognizing these challenges, Bettez promotes "critical community building" that enables participants to "question dominant norms" and "further one another's critical thinking, particularly around issues of power, oppression, and privilege."[19] She offers an approach for engaging and reconfiguring community boundaries productively. Alternatively, if we try to avoid boundaries altogether, we confront at least two disempowering options. One would be to conceive of a universal community, assuming that all humans potentially could affiliate with a single public project. Yet this effort would reproduce universalizing public discourses, such as the preamble to the US Declaration of Independence, that articulate an inclusive subject and countenance particular exclusions. As a second option, we could follow the Friedmans and reject community altogether, insisting that each of us is only and always an individual, and that our individuality alone affords opportunity.

Rather than obscure exclusions or deny human connections, scholars and advocates alike should acknowledge the inevitability of community boundaries in theory while contesting unjust exclusions in practice. In her analysis of homeless advocacy, Melanie Loehwing offers one case of a powerful reconfiguration of community boundaries centered on the meal-sharing efforts of the Orlando, Florida, chapter of Food Not Bombs (FNB), an antihunger activist group. Loehwing explains that FNB used meal-sharing as "a way of intervening in unjust community exclusions." Toward this end, the Orlando chapter hosted and photographed regular public meals in a prominent downtown park, finding themselves the target of an arrest campaign and disparaged by the mayor as "food terrorists." Although the police typically intervened, Loehwing holds that photographs of the peaceful meals and police interference circulated "sights of community anew, countering invisibility with constitutive visions of what the community could look like if different values and norms of civic relationships were enacted."[20] This case suggests that to the extent to which communities draw attention to commonalities—and they do—the common need not appear as a preexisting condition. Of course, some communities may take for granted a sense of shared interests and concerns, which excludes new perspectives and participants. But FNB's practices of meal-sharing illustrate that people can construct common concerns, even amid wider societal structures that represent some people as other and suspect.

Capacious Community

The local advocates we interviewed spoke differently about their public schools than did the national and state-level officials I discussed in chapters

3 and 4. Holding together its means and ends, these local advocates held an expansive view of education. Expressing different degrees of openness to charters and the potential for public and private schools to work together, these local advocates did not treat education as a discrete, fungible, stable product that can be delivered through variable new technologies. Settings matter, people matter, environments matter—these contextual factors place schools and communities in capacious relationships. Education represents more than technical training and job preparation; schools relate to communities in numerous ways. A Latina teacher working in one of the larger districts in the state remarked that schools "build a sense of community. It's a place where everyone goes, and they're a part of something. It connects kids. It connects families." In these comments, connection appears as crucial to education. Separating means and ends blocks the process of education, which ineluctably proceeds among people. Interviewees identified a variety of connections built through local school activities, including play groups, theatrical performances, sporting events, voting sites, meeting spaces, recreation spaces, and more. Some interviewees explained that they wore T-shirts from the local public schools to express their affiliations. One white male advocate working with rural districts quipped that in some small districts, "if they go to [the] state tournament, you might as well just lock up the doors and turn off all the lights because people are leaving town." In these various ways, interviewees represented public schools as hubs of activity, resources for collective identity formation, nodes in multiple networks, generators of conversation and critical thinking, and more—for children and adults alike.

Reflecting the distinct circumstances of their students and the communities they engaged, some schools served these communities to stabilize lives threatened by inequality and poverty. That some students' basic needs were not met—in both urban and rural areas—illuminates different degrees of precariousness across local communities, revealing levels of urgency in the need for community-building and broaching the emotional character of communities motivated by positive and negative valences like hope and fear. One interviewee, an African American retired teacher and current advocate from Milwaukee, addressed the challenge of homelessness for some of her students. She discussed the profound educational impact on students who lacked basic resources that many students and families never considered, such as the ability to shower in the morning or change clothes. Even providing clothes to students presented challenges, since "they're moving around. They can't carry all this stuff with them." This advocate identified "local control, structure, and consistency" as crucial for creating communities in which children could succeed. For students whose lives lacked stability generally, school presented a critical opportunity—perhaps a unique opportunity—to establish it, which this advocate regarded as essential. Yet this advocate's insights should not reinforce a reductive, stereotypical understanding of poverty as an urban phenomenon, as rural advocates also addressed the need for schools to serve students suffering through poverty. One white male advocate explained that he worked with rural schools that had set up food pantries, clothing drives, and health clinics. While separating ends and means of education treats student needs as uniform, these advocates and others pointed to critical disparities among individuals and groups.

Articulating the theme of coming together, particularly in comparing public schools to private schools, a number of interviewees expressed some variation of "the public schools serve all students." From one perspective, this is a statement about inclusion that describes the fact that public schools cannot turn away eligible students in their districts, unlike private schools that select among applicants. As such, this statement carries the tensions of community boundaries, invoking exclusion as a counterpoint to its affirmative embrace of inclusion. The "everyone" of a local public school lives amid widespread residential segregation by race and class, already excluding someone from its facilities and communities. Even within a district or attendance area, perceptions of belonging may limit formal practices of inclusion, such that some students may feel engaged as community members, while others may feel isolated or alienated, and such feelings may comport with unequal structures of race, class, and gender. The universal everyone betrays the particular experiences of someone and someone else. From another perspective, the statement functions as an ethical commitment, an imperative to treat children equally and fairly and to promote engagement across difference. Our interviewees' advocacy strongly suggests that they did not offer this statement as an empty claim. Further, their advocacy indicates that schools can only fulfill this commitment through practice, via the active engagement of children and adults in their communities.

By engaging local residents, public schools can create and participate in local communities, and, in turn, these local communities can support the activities occurring inside school buildings and classrooms. By bringing neighbors into school buildings and by venturing out to noneducational settings, advocates can practice engagement. Neighbors who feel welcome in public schools—who regard these schools as part of their relationship networks—may see themselves as stakeholders of public education. Against the individualism so prominent in contemporary political culture, one white educator-advocate spoke of the potential for developing programs that bring neighbors to school to "learn about our obligations to one another . . . and find ways to creatively forge ways to be in those obligations." In this spirit, this interviewee directed community-based arts programs. Another interviewee, a white woman who had served as a school board member, recalled efforts to establish informal education dialogues in her city. Noting the proliferation of myths about public education, she retorted that "the only way to debunk those myths would be to engage with citizens, with parents, with taxpayers, with businesses so that we could form a more collaborative approach." Across multiple dialogues consisting of diverse interlocutors, a judgment emerged that countered the prevailing state policy trend of valuing education as narrowly instrumental: participants "agreed that the most important thing we could do is develop students holistically." In these dialogues, means and ends aligned. Participants did not begin by extrapolating from technical data like test scores but asked broad-based questions regarding the role of public education in people's lives. In turn, they looked beyond standard measures like test scores to imagine education capaciously.

The clearest vision of wide-ranging school-community relationships may have been expressed through interviewees' references to the Milwaukee Community Schools Partnership, a collaboration of the Milwaukee Public Schools and the United Way of Greater Milwaukee and Waukesha County. As the program title suggests, community schools seek greater connections among educators, students, parents, and neighbors.[21] When we conducted our interviews, only a small number of Milwaukee schools participated in the program, but advocates inside and outside the city saw its promise. The collaboration addresses themes of leadership, equity, and culture, eliciting different visions of vibrant relationships from advocates. One Milwaukee advocate, a white male retired teacher, envisioned maximal connections that relate schools and communities "in multiple ways," including "honor[ing] the community," "build[ing] on the knowledge and strengths of the community," and involving "significant parent leadership." In these ways, a community school constitutes a democratic community. Various stakeholders can offer ideas and perspectives, and no single person can exercise absolute decision-making. Valuing collective judgment, a community school does not absorb individuals and their distinctiveness; to the contrary, its energy arises from the interaction of perspectives. One African American educator whose school had recently joined the partnership explained that education needs to "get away from big box curriculums." Across a network, particular communities express their individual attributes.

Beyond formal partnerships, some advocates praised the actions of schools to affirm specific cultures even as students participated in varied communities. One African American teacher explained the value of centering Black lives in history and society for her students. She characterized this curricular focus as "getting our scholars to embrace their greatness despite their circumstance." In other aspects of their lives, these young African American scholars saw Black cultures denigrated, Black children attacked by white authority figures both in and out of school, Black adults denied stable employment and imprisoned. Through many messages, a larger society instructed these children to discount their ideas and contributions. Although they could not unilaterally change this wider world, teachers and staff at this elementary school could build a supportive community to generate understanding of larger structures while cultivating individual and collective agency. A Latina interviewee addressed the theme of cultural affirmation in terms of her own development as an advocate and, subsequently, an elected official. Working with others to secure adequate resources for a primarily Latinx school, she recounted that when "we started meeting and providing training for folks and having those conversations . . . we actually found our voice collectively to be like, 'Our stories are very similar.'" Conversations facilitated through education advocacy enabled recognition of shared experiences and concerns, fostering a desire to build a supportive and assertive community.

Community Resources

Across the interviews, discussions of community resonated polyphonically with the perspective I develop in this chapter—some advocates explicitly identified relationships as foundational for community-building, while others noted the roles of shared experiences, identities, and interests (themselves recognized in relationships). Identifying various materials for constructing communities, interviewees collectively appreciated the active efforts entailed in these processes. An American Indian educator differentiated between community as proximity and community as an intentional project. The former treats community as a spatial marker delineating an already existing entity, which manifests the conflation of community and locale that scholars should resist if we wish to envision community as the mediation of identity and difference. The latter recognizes that commonality, whether a shared zip code or some other attribute, does not in itself create community. Community as an intentional project references active engagement, valuing the perspectives of others, "efforts to learn with and from each other." This educator facilitated summer workshops for K–12 public school teachers seeking to incorporate American Indian studies curricula in their classrooms. He explained that successful workshops depended on building relationships among participants. Considering their distinct work in the classroom and their interactions at the workshop, relationship-building meant that participants "really invested in building each other's capacity," creating communities that outlasted the workshops. A distinction between communities of proximity and purpose crystalizes the critical work of the advocates we interviewed, who have sought to create and expand networks of relationships to strengthen local support for public education and to create ties across the state. Their very advocacy gainsays any claim that community arises automatically. The example of American Indian studies workshops also intimates varied resources available for community-building, from time and structure to curiosity and respect. Other interviewees also identified a range of potential resources.

A key resource for community-building entails critically engaging prevailing local assumptions and practices of community. To the extent that these ideas go unquestioned, communities may become static, reducing openness to new individuals, perspectives, and groups. An unexamined community may operate as a community of proximity—proximal in location, outlook, identity, power, privilege, prejudice, and more. In the classroom, the American Indian educator quoted above recognized that for some non-native students he might have served initially as a stereotype of otherness. He explained that "sometimes I'm playing against that stereotype." In this way and others, he sought to "teach from multiple perspectives" and "make the strange familiar and the familiar strange." In doing so, he believed that he could break down potential boundaries rooted in bias and suspicion and encourage students to reimagine relationships with others and to build new relationships on diverse grounds. A Latina advocate discussed her practice of critically engaging community as she worked with Latinx families for adequate education resources. She asked questions regarding "what is community?" and "who gets to practice community?" to assess local power structures that disregarded the perspectives of Latinx families. In this context, forming new and supportive communities for marginalized families meant challenging reigning ideas of community that oriented the local school district and city politics. She explained that some white city residents had staked their claims for voice and resources on long-standing ties to the city. From this approach, generations of residence supposedly constituted an unassailable, foundational community. Yet this strategic act of history-making ignored the histories of others: "We've been experiencing this for generations, too. . . . You haven't acknowledged us." Further, this historical claim denied new city residents the opportunities to create and affiliate with multiple communities. By calling out the power dynamics of such claims, this advocate sought to generate community resources for residents with varying histories from diverse backgrounds.

To critically engage established community practices is to assert one's own agency, which can serve as an empowering act especially for individuals and groups who see themselves as ignored and/or discounted by others. An African American advocate in Madison highlighted the importance of "community control" to the work of their organization. In determining their priorities and evaluating existing city and school district policies, this advocate asked, "What does it mean for Black people to really have power?" Part of the answer involved localizing decision-making to the students and families at specific schools, rather than relying on centralized organizational structures. Asserting their own agency in interacting with district officials, this advocate also sought to facilitate the agency of their communities. Revealing another dimension of this issue, Milwaukee advocates recounted the well-established history of white suburban legislators making decisions for the majority Black students and families in the city's public schools. From the original voucher program onward, the state legislature had developed a series of policies aimed at the city that treated its schoolchildren, in the words of one African American advocate, as "guinea pigs." Yet Milwaukeeans did not dictate policy to the suburbs, especially the wealthy white suburbs from which legislators cast themselves as the city's saviors. Working with others, this advocate sought to resist usurpations of agency.

Agency serves a crucial role for securing necessary investments in local public schools and the communities they engage. Even so, individual and collective agency may not ensure sufficient investments in education, nor may agency overcome inequalities across communities in Wisconsin. A white rural advocate referenced the "75 to 80 percent" statewide passage rate of local referenda as evidence of community investments in public education. Yet the need for referenda underscored inadequate investments at the state level. Further, successful referenda did not eliminate needs, such as increased teacher pay. This rural advocate cited dire circumstances in some small districts where teachers' families qualified for free and reduced-price meals. A white advocate from Milwaukee addressed how inadequate and unequal investments complicated the task of hiring qualified teachers. This advocate recalled hearing about online teacher certification programs, which lacked the training of university-based programs, that offered "Black Friday" and "Cyber Monday" sales discounts. Having attacked public education for ten years, the state legislature responded to resulting teacher shortages not by increasing investments but by lowering qualifications, which only exacerbated district-to-district disparities. In this spirit, the Milwaukee advocate imagined two classrooms, the first in a poor district like Milwaukee and the second in a well-funded, wealthy suburban district. He observed that the need to hire a Cyber Monday–certified teacher likely would arise in only one of these scenarios.

As interviewees' own practices suggest, advocacy constitutes an important resource for community-building. The people we interviewed understood their important roles even as they sometimes expressed concerns over the difficulties of sustaining local advocacy networks. A highly networked white advocate addressed the challenge of trying to work with local people to develop organizing skills without burning them out. She observed that a key component to these efforts entailed "old-school relationship-building" within and across communities, institutions, and roles. Still, "activism fatigue and the feeling of voicelessness are probably the two biggest barriers" to sustaining local engagement. Our interviewees discussed various strategies for maintaining and restoring their energy amid victories and defeats, including adding elements of fun and joy to their work and drawing strength from supportive networks. Individually, advocacy as a resource could be depleted over time, but collectively individuals discovered means of generating new energy. One suburban Milwaukee advocacy organization developed a postcard campaign for their state representatives. As one white advocate explained, knowing the voting records of their representatives, group members did not see this campaign primarily as a means of changing legislators' minds. However, she explained that her group launched the campaign to raise public awareness and engage others in their communities, potentially generating more resources for advocacy. Some of the teachers we interviewed talked about their advocacy as consistent with their vision of education as bolstering young people's lives. In a poignant moment, a Latina elementary school teacher recalled how she explained her current advocacy to former students: "I wanted to look out for you. . . . Because that's what is important to me, that you're okay, and that you get a good education." This teacher resisted a view of education as confined to the classroom, acting instead as an educator in varied relationships.

If advocacy serves as a resource for community-building, then perhaps one of its key contributions involves inviting people to imagine their worlds differently. Toward this end, some advocates mentioned storytelling—specifically, success stories of public schools—as an important strategy. One white interviewee in particular highlighted the power of stories for her advocacy: "It's a story that's going to save us, if anything does." Others expressed hope in the potential for education success stories to shift negative perceptions of public schools, especially when community members and policymakers could experience storytelling firsthand. A white Madison advocate reported that she had witnessed people's perceptions shift when they visited public schools: "When you get people in the schools and they see some of the things that are happening in the classrooms and what kids are doing, it's a real eye-opener." Critics of public education do not lack stories; to the contrary, public figures like Betsy DeVos have shared many stories that supposedly reveal the limits of public schools. Local advocates supporting public schools have needed to fight for resources at material and symbolic levels—to argue for better-paid teachers and well-maintained buildings, for example, they have needed to counter negative images and circulate vibrant visions of community that invite widespread affiliation.

Envisioning a Great Community, Dewey imagined networked local communities that could learn from each other and enliven each other. In their advocacy, our interviewees have built numerous and varied connections locally and across the state to sustain expansive networked communities that demand support for public education. Several advocates mentioned connections with individuals and groups elsewhere in the state. These connections have emboldened advocates, as one white advocate from a small town explained: "There was no morale if we felt like we were the only ones in the state. We needed to know we were in it with other people." In a prominent case, as we began our interviews in the summer of 2019, hundreds of public education advocates participated in a sixty-mile march to Madison to urge greater state funding for public education.[22] The march began in the small town of Palmyra, which faced the closure of its local school district because of insufficient funding. Some interviewees referenced their experiences in Palmyra and during the three-day march, including one African American advocate from Milwaukee. She noted that both rural and urban districts suffered from the state's failure to support public education adequately. Recalling parent comments at the start of the march in Palmyra, she noted that "it was very similar to what parents are saying in Milwaukee. . . . If you can get those people together, that really is going to change the narrative." Multiple interviewees addressed shared interests and concerns across rural and urban school districts.

Communities Divided

Dewey typically discussed community in positive terms as a forward-looking concept and practice for reinvigorating democratic human relationships that combines local attachments with global cosmopolitanism. He understood that local community practices historically have not been uniformly positive, but he did not dwell on these shortcomings. He acknowledged this side of community in references to past local life as sometimes "stagnant" and "isolated." He acknowledged, too, that political boundaries, which implicate community as a vehicle for democracy, could foster "jealousy, fear, suspicion and hostility." But he insisted on the necessity of reviving vibrant local communities: "Unless local communal life can be restored, the public cannot adequately resolve its most urgent problem: to find and identify itself."[23] Similarly, as I discussed in chapter 1, Dewey recognized the prevalence of racism in the United States, but he did not analyze how racism shapes human relationships and efforts at community-building.[24] In contrast, our interviewees considered these issues, including racism and other obstacles for community-building, extensively and thoughtfully. Neither naïve nor cavalier, they valued community in the face of structural inequality, prejudice, and intolerance, sometimes calling for communities connected through shared experiences of marginalization and oppression and other times seeking to build relationships across such differences. Their insights mark the outlines of Dewey's perspective in terms of its potential and limits. This evidences my contention that Dewey holds contemporary value for scholarship and practice when placed in dialogue with others. In chapter 1, I placed Dewey in dialogue with scholars like Eric Watts and Eddie Glaude, Jr.; in this chapter, I foreground our interviewees as dialogue partners.

A nationwide problem, racism's destructive force has been felt acutely in Wisconsin. During the years addressed in this book, a steady stream of academic and media reports have documented that Wisconsin and its two largest metropolitan areas of Madison and Milwaukee exhibit some of the worst racial disparities in the nation on a range of measures such as education, employment, health, and public safety.[25] Interviewees of different backgrounds discussed the dynamics of racism on a local, everyday level, including how race has divided communities and forestalled community-building. An African American advocate from Madison explained that the Black youth she worked with often have "internalized anti-Blackness." Rather than seeing themselves as targeted by racism, they blamed themselves for others' prejudice. For example, they believed that "we need the police in our schools because we're bad people." To encourage the agency of these young people, this advocate taught them about the history of Black people in the United States and contemporary struggles for racial justice. She worked actively to reshape self-understandings that internalized external prejudice. Indeed, this advocate expressed deep skepticism about the capacity for mainstream educational institutions to treat Black children fairly and meet their needs adequately: "I have very little faith in public education and its ability to support and love our children." Rejecting market-based approaches as only exacerbating inequality, she discerned a need for Black communities to create new institutions to educate Black children.

Other interviewees from diverse backgrounds saw the potential for community-building through existing educational institutions, even as they considered the challenges of racism and racial division. Yet building communities that may address these issues honestly requires some difficult conversations, which may challenge potential interlocutors across racial identities. An African American educator in Milwaukee saw her relative newness to the teaching profession as an advantage in facilitating these conversations, but she did not underestimate the work. She anticipated some reluctance and defensiveness from her colleagues: "When you have to say white supremacy. When you have to say racism. When you have to say white privilege. . . . It's difficult for people, because people sometimes take that as an attack, especially people who have been educators for twenty-plus years." Advocates could not sidestep these issues if they wished to develop diverse communities that supported their members. Advocates also had to confront policies that exacerbated division. Contextualizing his comments with regard to gross educational disparities and disproportionate incarceration rates in the metro area and state, a white suburban Milwaukee advocate exhorted that "you make a whole community by enriching everybody." Yet policies facilitating student movement between the city and suburbs, such as open enrollment programs, sometimes have worsened district inequalities even as they have benefited specific participants by removing engaged and vocal families of color from public schools in Milwaukee while neglecting the families that remain.

While the issue of race tended to arise in interviews with advocates from larger cities and school districts (and not just Madison and Milwaukee), some advocates from smaller towns and districts identified religion as a potentially divisive force. These advocates lived in small towns with well-established private religious schools that benefited financially from the statewide expansion of vouchers. Some of our interviewees noted new buildings by religious organizations in their towns and wondered if public voucher dollars had indirectly supported the construction. Others observed that religious institutions in their towns had explicitly—and, in some cases, aggressively—positioned their schools as superior alternatives to public schools. One white advocate relayed the conflicts she experienced as a public school teacher and member of a church in her town. Explaining that school funding had become a divisive issue, she recalled instances where children attending private schools reported that school staff had told them to urge their parents to vote "no" on an upcoming district referendum, in an effort to deny additional funding to their competitors. Further, she recounted listening to conversations in church in which fellow congregants discussed a desire to increase religious-school enrollments while avoiding the "riffraff" from the public schools. These actions had intimidated candidates for local public office, who hesitated to criticize local private schools because they needed the votes of private school parents to serve as public school board members.

Some advocates cited geography—in particular, different neighborhoods and towns within a single district—as a potential source of division. The case of one financially struggling district stands out. The district itself serves two different towns, each with a distinct idea of the role of their local public schools. One town sees itself as a relatively self-sustaining network that values its public schools as sources of uplift, identity, and pride. The second town sees itself as a bedroom community for a larger neighboring municipality. Many families in this second town have used open enrollment policies to send their children to the public schools in the larger neighboring district. When the local district crafted a referendum to address drastic financial shortfalls that threatened its very operation, support and opposition fell along predictable lines—a majority of residents in the first town wished to save the public schools, while a large majority in the second town expressed skepticism and/or indifference to the district's financial woes. As one out-of-district white interviewee put it, the second town dismissively said to the first, "We don't need you. You need us." A white advocate in the first town recounted the widespread hostility faced by those who campaigned for the referendum. A village leader in the second town erected a "vote no" banner in front of their lauded, five-star public elementary school. When high-school students canvassed in support of the referendum, they were sometimes greeted by adults swearing at them in opposition. In response to one young canvasser, an adult male defiantly pulled down his pants and exposed his naked ass. When the local fire department in town two put up a sign congratulating the public school's girls' dance team for their regional championship, some residents complained. These incidents demonstrate that the local offers no guarantees for community-building. One might retort that each of these towns could build its own communities, but as residents have formed multiple communities within and across these towns, they have done so under the looming threat of school closings.

Challenges to Community

Challenges to community formation and maintenance may arise among potential local participants, as I elucidate in the previous section, as well as from forces outside of a particular locale. Community divisions reflect both local and global developments, such as the convergence of religious affiliation and political ideology that may inform both public policy and human relationships. In this section, I focus on challenges that emerge primarily from outside of local relationship networks at the level of state policy and powerful lobbying interests. These factors generate additional layers of difficulty to community-building, suggesting that even when people commit themselves to working within and across differences, other actors and conditions may create obstacles. Referencing this dynamic, I do not offer a pessimistic diagnosis. To the contrary, communities always exist in fields of constraint.[26] Sometimes, constraints hamper individual and collective effort. Other times, people may leverage constraints in working hard to build thriving communities that support their members. Interviewees identified three sets of challenges—well-financed lobbying, state funding policies, and legislative behaviors—that they have engaged in their efforts to build communities that value public education.

Interviewees understood that big money and insider lobbying facilitated the statewide expansion of private vouchers. They recognized that a handful of individuals and organizations led efforts to create and expand education markets in the state of Wisconsin—literally, when asked whose voices were heard loudest in the State Capitol on education policy, most interviewees who named a specific person or group cited one of only a few names. Explaining that she knew of the desire of some corporate interests to profit from public education, one white advocate observed that she had not realized the degree to which "corporate money had infiltrated our political system and our parties, and how they had pointed to Wisconsin and said, 'This is where we go next.'" Under these circumstances, ideas for K–12 education policy arose not from local individuals and groups working most closely with public schools, but from corporate patrons and their lobbyists. Interviewees rebuked competition and vouchers as means for improving children's educational experiences. Referencing thirty years of vouchers in Milwaukee, one white advocate flatly rejected the notion that competition "raise[s] all boats." Rather, competition "creates winners and losers." As the city's public schools struggled with basic issues like hiring teachers and controlling class size, private voucher schools advertised their amenities to prospective customers. She cited the example of one lavish voucher school, featuring a saltwater pool in its natatorium, that had recently opened in the city. A wealthy financier from the suburbs built the school and named it after himself. Although the project cost millions to complete, the revenues from vouchers would enable this individual to recoup his investment in just three years.

Some advocates explained that the state funding formula and state-imposed revenue limits on local districts created additional obstacles for their efforts to build strong school-community connections. One white interviewee from northern Wisconsin pointed to the complicated state funding structure for public schools, charter schools, and voucher schools that made it difficult for ordinary folks to understand the relationships between their tax dollars and their local public schools. She explained that public schools stood third in line for funding behind independent charters and voucher schools. Further, the state legislature restructured voucher funding to effectively flow through local districts, giving local residents the false impression that a greater share of their property taxes went to local public schools than the actual amounts these schools received. This advocate and others fought for transparency, writing resolutions calling for clarity from the state government and encouraging local school boards across the state to vote for these resolutions. Some advocates also worked with their mayors and other local officials to develop inserts for their local property tax mailings explaining how much of each public tax dollar was redirected to fund private voucher schools.

A related financial issue that interviewees addressed concerned district-by-district revenue limits that the state put in place in the 1990s to limit property tax increases and shift the proportion of education funding between the state and local districts.[27] Specific to each district, these revenue limits reflected past spending levels and local wealth. The governor and legislature instituted these limits with a promise of increased state funding—two-thirds of the total cost—that never arrived. Moreover, as the state reduced its funding for public education in recent years, the revenue limits have remained. One white advocate from Milwaukee decried the unequal revenue limits as constituting "a state policy that discriminates against students depending on where you live." According to this advocate, the passage of Act 10, which I described in chapter 4, worsened inequalities. He explained that if the state government valued children in the Milwaukee Public Schools at the same level as some of the city's more prosperous suburban neighbors, the district would have between 90 million and 130 million additional dollars in annual revenue. These differences directly affected children's education experiences, since "revenue limit differences equate to buying power" that hindered the district's relative ability to hire well-trained teachers in comparison to its neighbors. Noting the state's worst-in-the-nation achievement disparities, he maintained that "we have a system perfectly designed to get us there." In these ways, revenue limits have functioned as a material constraint on community formation that informs advocates' agendas within local districts and across wider networks.

As a third major challenge, interviewees referenced legislators' behavior, which ranged from disregard to outright hostility toward constituents who disagreed with them on state education policy. A recurring theme across the interviews concerned the difficulties of getting legislators to meet with advocacy groups in their districts and to attend public forums that groups created for community discussions of education policy. Gerrymandering had worsened this problem, as some legislators understood their constituents in electoral terms that divided citizens in their districts by political party. Some interviewees recounted interactions in which legislators explicitly told advocates that "I don't have to meet with you," since the legislators held seats that did not depend on the electoral support of strong pro-public education groups. Interviewees shared other instances of legislative non-responsiveness to constituents: empty chairs for incumbents at candidate forums, hearings that invite public input but direct legislation toward predetermined outcomes, lame-duck legislation and cynical procedural maneuvers. Legislators acting in these ways betrayed visions of relationships and community that reset the inward and outward orientations of democratic communities as stark choices, rendering democratic commitments suspect. A reluctance or refusal to meet with potential non-supporters among one's constituents may serve a legislator tactically, but this orientation also may forestall the formation of communities across ideology that can mediate alienation and hostility. Indeed, this legislative stance suggests an all-or-nothing approach to community that demands unconditional assent from potential participants.

In some cases, interviewees reported, legislators engaged advocates in openly hostile ways. One white advocate whose financially struggling district faced potential closure recounted a message from one of their state representatives indicating that local residents "deserved" their fate. Another white advocate from central Wisconsin recalled a stern lecture about respecting district boundaries from her ostensibly pro-public education representative when her advocacy group signed a joint letter in support of public education that was sent to the entire legislature. The most striking case concerned the public shaming of a constituent by their representative on social media after a misunderstanding or disagreement (the constituent characterized their inter-action as the former; the legislator represented it as the latter) regarding a visit by public schoolchildren to the State Capitol. A staffer for the representative called this advocate to help arrange a photograph with the representative and perceived this advocate to be unenthusiastic about the possibility. When word of the call reached the legislator, he reacted by denouncing this advocate as an ideologue on his Facebook page and on local talk radio. Other right-wing groups joined the charge and posted this person's home address on their social media channels. Web pages hosted discussion threads in which some area residents denounced this advocate as unreasonable and hypocritical. For their part, this advocate felt outrage at the public shaming and puzzlement that their representative never tried to contact them. Rather than attacking a constituent, this advocate explained, their representative could have called to understand their respective views on education. Sadly, this representative's behavior appeared consistent with—if not a more intense manifestation of—a troubling dynamic in which privatization has made public education, which historically had been a subject for bipartisan support and pride in Wis-consin, a partisan issue.

Communities and Democracy

Negotiating challenges to community formation and addressing potential community divisions, our interviewees nevertheless discerned meaningful connections among community, democracy, and education. In the intro-duction to this chapter, I reference historical resonances between Dewey's writing on democracy and education and the insights our interviewees offer. When asked about their ideas of democracy, our interviewees discussed a range of qualities that resonate variously with Dewey's work: concerning oneself with common interests and goods, expressing one's voice on pub-lic affairs, living life according to one's interests and potential, facilitating inclusive public practices that enable different people to contribute equally, participating in collaborative decision-making, and building productive, vibrant, and mutually valued relationships with others. Demonstrating an appreciation of the role of power in ostensibly fair processes, some interviewees articulated concerns that existing democratic institutions and procedures reflect and reproduce societal inequalities, such that certain processes taken in isolation, like majority rule, could perpetuate unjust social relations.[28] But most of these advocates saw more nuanced visions and practices of democracy, which do not isolate narrow means over wider ends, as addressing their concerns.[29] These different perspectives underscore the importance of democratic relationships to vibrant public life in diverse societies.

Some interviewees emphasized the importance of relationships for engendering democratic practice, rather than assuming, as Dewey cautioned against, that democracy proceeds by its own momentum. One white Milwaukee advocate located the work of democracy at the grassroots level to ensure that ordinary folks could act purposefully to direct the course of their lives. She held that "you can't take it for granted that democracy in and of itself is going to be the thing that fixes stuff. . . . It's never done. We're never done." Because democracy operates as an ongoing process, individuals need to work together to address shared concerns and to prevent democracy from circulating as a free-floating signifier, which powerful interests can co-opt for nondemocratic ends. Centering institutions and procedures at the expense of human action also threatens to abstract democracy by locating its primary operation with external figures and forces that act on and sometimes against community interests and aspirations. One white Madison-area advocate discerned the foundation of democracy in "how we connect to each other, how we build community where we live." At this level, democracy appears as accessible and meaningful, a process that individuals instantiate through their own activity and in cooperation with others. Far from narrowly circumscribing possibilities for action, this local vision sustains a global outlook—in this context, attention to state education policy—while identifying efforts for change in local and translocal networks.

Against the individualism embodied in education markets, our interviewees identified a mediation of the individual and collective through recognizing mutual obligations and supporting collaborative decision-making. Several interviewees decried what they regarded as a diminished sense of a public good in contemporary political culture. As one white advocate remarked, supporting public schools constitutes a practice of mutual responsibility: "This is the common good. This is what we're supposed to be funding with our money." In contrast, vouchers convert public money into private property, potentially eclipsing "what makes democracy work." While the recipients of vouchers might see the program through the lens of self-interest, the education of the state's youth affects everyone—even those who opt out of public school classrooms. Through their actions, our interviewees have reenergized the prospect of a public good and encouraged its proliferation by building relationship networks to support schooling that will address disparities and affirm diversity inside and outside the classroom.

While the Friedmans expressed skepticism toward group decision-making, many of our interviewees valued collaborative decision-making as bolstering processes and outcomes. One white Milwaukee advocate addressed these potential benefits with regard to her volunteer work with teenagers. She explained that "we talk a lot about [how] in democracy we're not always going to get what we want but we're going to try to understand where the other side is coming from." In a polarized climate in which people, including some legislators, dismiss alternative perspectives, this serves as an important lesson. This advocate maintained that "we only get to those spaces where we make collective decisions if we're in the room together making the decision." In this way, collaborative decision-making potentially mediates individual-group conflict by avoiding all-or-nothing standards of judgment: a group of diverse interlocutors can disagree about the merits of a proposal and yet individuals can see themselves respected through the process of reaching a decision.[30] As one white interviewee noted, collaborative decision-making also promotes fair decisions by involving "the people who those decisions affect." In contrast to the Friedmans and other neoliberals, this advocate and others saw the knowledge base for group decision-making as generative and solicitous of individual perspectives.

Practicing democracy in the ways our interviewees envisioned invokes the power of voice, both as an aspect of individual agency and as a collectively shared commitment to meaningful participation.[31] Our interviewees recognized that their own actions could not guarantee reciprocal actions from others, even as they emphasized the importance of speaking and being heard. One African American advocate explained that democracy "means having a say. It doesn't mean I'm always going to get my way, but it means that I feel like I've been heard, and not just heard, heard and taken seriously." As this observation suggests, voice connotes a relational dynamic among interlocutors through which participants in a discussion listen actively to one another. Elsewhere, I refer to this dynamic as "heedfulness," which entails a mutual practice of signaling to dialogue partners that present interactions will inform relevant future activities.[32] Heedfulness need not entail agreement, but it does suggest that the interaction will influence one's perspective on an issue. Advocates cannot assume that this dynamic will inform their encounters. For example, during the Joint Finance Committee listening sessions I discussed in chapter 4, speakers who addressed the committee sometimes wondered aloud whether the legislators were actually paying attention. Our interviewees could not control others' actions, but they could develop arguments addressing different perspectives and modeling reciprocal engagement. On these points, some advocates saw schools as important sites of praxis.

Articulating concerns about structural inequalities and societal prejudices, some advocates indicated the need to critically engage democracy itself. A polysemous term, democracy seemingly supports a potentially wide range of rules and procedures; some of these may orient themselves toward values of justice and equality, but others may perpetuate unjust and unequal social relationships.[33] An African American Madison advocate urged caution in thinking about "how we create popular mechanisms where everybody can give input, but still protect the most vulnerable." This concern appears especially acute when considered together with the city's significant racial disparities on measures of individual and community well-being.[34] As this advocate explained, "I want to say to you, 'Yes, democracy, and democracy is what we need in schools.' I'm also cautious of saying that to you in a majority white city." For this advocate, as well as most of the other advocates of color we interviewed, a response to racial barriers to participation should arise in more purposeful instantiations of democratic practices grounded in principles of justice and equality. Indeed, this advocate explained that "I am favorable to the idea of real people on the ground being able to impact and influence." But this involves asking hard questions, such as "What does democracy look like when you're not a majority?" On a similar note, a Latina advocate observed that diverse communities in her city experienced democracy differently, which included their access to symbolic and material resources. In her view, the challenge consists of "bring[ing] what we want democracy to be to the people" such that all residents can "feel a sense of belonging" in the city. If, from a Deweyan perspective, community presents an opportunity to make tangible democratic aspirations, then these advocates make clear the need to engage critically ideals and practices as part of an ongoing process of democracy.

In this process, public schools play crucial roles in fostering democratic communities. The African American advocate quoted above saw the promise of education in its publicness. This advocate insisted that only public schools can support Black children to realize their potential: "Schools need to be public. They need to be . . . what public can mean in the best case, which is truly of and for the community, and private is not that." Building vibrant and diverse relationships, mediating the I and we, developing individual and collective voice, supporting collaborative decision-making—these constitute public activities. The American Indian advocate I quoted above identified a critical purpose of public education as "recognizing and redefining a broader sense of 'we the people.'" Acknowledging "some pretty problematic contexts" of the phrase, this advocate nevertheless saw the "true power of that statement" in encouraging reflection about ways to build inclusive and diverse relationship networks that affirm different perspectives. Further, for this advocate, "we the people" suggests local action, encouraging individuals to ask, "How can we be good neighbors to each other?" Education can serve this end by bringing together reflection and action for students and neighbors inside and outside the classroom. In both settings, people may reflect on their own assumptions, biases, values, and beliefs. Together they may act to shape their world productively for individuals and their communities.

Practicing Community

In this chapter, I have sought to accomplish three major tasks: present a democracy-based perspective of public education as an alternative to the market visions I have explicated at the national and state levels; facilitate a transhistorical dialogue between Dewey and contemporary Wisconsin advocates for public education; and illuminate the varying dynamics, opportunities, and challenges for practicing community. Developing a democratic alternative, I began with Dewey's association of democracy and community to identify a vehicle for making tangible his exhortation to live democracy as a way of life and to concretize my commitment to democratic relationships as a basis for human action. Dewey championed community, but he did not explicate this concept like other key terms, such as public and education. I have developed a fluid and dynamic conception of community as a network of relationships.

In facilitating a dialogue between Dewey and contemporary advocates, I have sought to exemplify the value of democratic relationships by showing how their collective insights offer resources for imagining vibrant practices of democracy and education. The partners in this dialogue bring distinct perspectives that offer new insights through their interaction. In his writings, Dewey underscored the value of everyday action as a mode of critical praxis that can turn coordinated individual action into a powerful collective force. Our interviewees explicated the texture and diversity of everyday action through their practices of community-building, unpacking connections among community, local, identity, and difference.

If community maps out networks of democratic human relationships, then contemporary public school advocates add crucial details to this project. Dewey denounced racism, but our interviewees explicated the dynamics of race and racism (and other potential sources of unity and division) in the actual processes of community-building. They shared Dewey's commitment to community but recognized tensions, struggles, and frustrations that accompany community engagement. These insights do not devalue the project but bring it greater clarity. Community-building constitutes a potentially powerful response to market frameworks that severely restrict human motivation and aspiration. Our interviewees illuminated a path forward.

CONCLUSION: MEANS, ENDS, AND PUBLIC EDUCATION

A range of relationships involving people, perspectives, institutions, and practices have oriented my arguments in this book. The various people I have engaged—John Dewey, the Friedmans, Betsy DeVos, members of Congress, Polly Williams, Scott Walker, the Joint Finance Committee, local Wisconsin residents, local public school advocates—all have acted within and across different relationship networks, articulating visions of preferred human relationships, the role of education in facilitating these relationships, and the resources necessary for schools to serve their educational purposes. I have organized these visions, as my cases of Dewey and the Friedmans suggest, in terms of their commitments to democracy and markets. These commitments have produced profound policy shifts in K–12 education, as market mechanisms like vouchers have moved from iconoclastic intellectual exercises and segregationist tactics to national policy goals and statewide systems. At the level of everyday life, rising market visions have induced people to rethink their perceptions of self and human agency as well as their interactions with foundational social processes and institutions like schooling. Comparatively neglected in policy, democratic visions have resonated with the efforts of people building dynamic local networks that ascribe critical roles to local public schools. My cases illuminate how these competing visions have pulled schools in different directions, even as the conduct of schooling need not require mutually exclusive actions in specific contexts. However, as I observe in the introduction, we need to align our means and ends with what we want to accomplish.

Through my own relationship networks, including new networks established through the writing of this book, I have oriented myself strongly toward democratic relationships, democratic education, and engagement directed toward building egalitarian, inclusive, and just communities and publics—an end that has long oriented my scholarship. My confidence in the realization of this vision has waxed and waned as I have considered various challenges to building democratic practices and institutions shaped by these values. I am acutely aware of the influence of market visions even as I believe firmly that the local discourses I have explicated present strong evidence of the potential for wide-ranging, self-aware, robust democratic communities. I also appreciate that neoliberalism operates among other democratic antagonists, such as rising authoritarian and white nationalist publics in the United States and other Western countries. In a series of interviews and lectures that occurred after the election of Donald Trump as US president, Wendy Brown argued that neoliberalism has engendered "enormous rage from a predominantly white population that has had its economic and social sense of entitlement *dethroned* by neoliberal capitalism."[1] At the same time, its pro-market, antidemocratic discourse has paved the way for self-professed "strongman" leaders who promise to restore (white) privilege to people who see themselves as threatened by social change. Composed through varying mixtures of neoliberalism, white nationalism, and authoritarianism, antidemocratic visions of education will not promote just alternatives to antidemocratic politics and publics.[2]

By highlighting the themes of markets and democracy, I also have sought to underscore the circulation and interconnections of discourses across sites and situations, particularly national, state, and local levels of engagement and academic, governing, and political institutions and settings. In this spirit, if all the various actors referenced in this book could have agreed on one point, they may have accepted the claim that no one person, practice, or institution will shape the future of public and private education in the United States. For the Friedmans, DeVos, and like-minded legislators, agreement about the unlikely emergence of a single, individual influence may stem from two sources: their professed faith in individual freedom and the impropriety of one individual making educational choices for another, as well as their frequent self-representation as "outsiders" combatting an education establishment. For Dewey and many of the local advocates we interviewed, no individual influence can shape the future of education because its shape depends on the participation of many actors through public deliberation and decision-making, and because conducting these processes fairly and inclusively requires engaging diverse perspectives, especially those of people marginalized by established relations of power and privilege in local communities. Recognizing multiple and varied influences invites us to consider the connections across the various cases I have explored in this book.

In this conclusion, I draw from my various cases to consider the dynamics, entailments, and implications of market and democratic alignments of means and ends. Beginning with markets, I argue that market relationships as a model for human relationships obscure and disavow the very connections, qualities, and institutions on which they rely. They also obscure and legitimate the harms they bring to different individuals and groups in diverse and unequal societies. Extending these relationships to schooling reproduces existing relations of power and privilege that limit some children's agency and personal development. Democratic relationships offer a potentially empowering alternative, but only if we consider honestly the exclusions and limitations of existing democratic institutions and practices as well as existing public schools. Without attending to larger questions of freedom, equality, and justice, we cannot expect the neighborhood public school to serve the needs of all children. Even as we must advocate for justice, we should affirm that public schools need democratic communities, and democratic communities need public schools.

The Limits of Market Means and Ends

In the preceding chapters, I discussed how pro-market advocates dissociate educational means and ends in their critiques of public education. Betsy DeVos wished to modernize educational delivery systems, while Scott Walker and pro-voucher members of the Joint Finance Committee sought to refashion public schools as one option in a wider education marketplace. According to these advocates, diverse students would all receive a sound education, but their families would choose its delivery method. Yet these dissociative strategies do not reflect a basic unwillingness to align means and ends. Rather, these strategies function to displace public schools as preeminent societal institutions and to insinuate other means and ends for education. Dissociation serves to delegitimate public schools' claims to educate a populace, or, in market terms, to break the hold of a public education monopoly. Dissociation disrupts the coherence of educational processes, permitting the transfer of market techniques across "industries" and reconstructing the subjects of education as market actors. By constructing education as a discrete package that individuals may receive separately and variously, dissociation redirects education away from potentially mediating the individual and the collective in the cultivation of democratic publics and toward a role of preparing individuals to pursue their self-interests in market publics.

For pro-market advocates, educational systems run properly when individuals can exercise their personal freedom by choosing among varied options. Organizing educational systems and human relationships generally, individual-freedom-choice constitutes the foundational conceptual clustering of market relations. As a material force, individual-freedom-choice governs neoliberal politics and policy and encourages subjects to comport with market incentives and penalties. As an idealized vision, this clustering imagines individuals as unencumbered by responsibilities and obligations to others (outside of the family), capable of making self-interested and informed choices about how to live, whom to engage, and where to educate their children as, in the Friedmans' terms, "responsible individuals in embryo."[3] The material and ideal converge in private voucher programs that recuperate tax dollars for individual families to direct to the schools of their choosing. In this vision, the comparative availability of choice also provides a measure for judging the historical status, whether healthy or under threat, of freedom and the individual. Advocacy of individual-freedom-choice connects the Friedmans, DeVos, Walker, and pro-market members of the Joint Finance Committee.

Articulating their vision, advocates represent individual-freedom-choice as a perspective that celebrates and protects individual distinctiveness. Observing that every person is different, advocates argue that substantiating individual-freedom-choice in educational systems and practices would enable everyone to pursue their own interests, finding the best educational fit for themselves or their children. A strength of this vision presumably lies in its stand against coercion and conformity. When individuals encounter others who think differently, they should recognize this difference and respect others' autonomy. Relationships develop as individuals seek to satisfy mutual interests through exchange with other individuals. This perspective regards itself as operating with humility—a person cannot know enough about others' interests to judge them or to compel change. Respect for difference and individual agency requires accepting another's statement of self-interest as a transparent presentation of their desire. Shared commitments emerge not in common cause, collective identity, or coordinated agency but in the recognition that everyone benefits by deferring to individual self-interest.

While advocates depict markets as neutral arbiters of human activity, such that competition would drive improvement among all schools in education markets, individual-freedom-choice illuminates the values of market relationships. Most explicitly, individual-freedom-choice themselves are values, and foregrounding these values advances specific visions of human relationships. Valuing the individual, market relationships dismiss the collective or variations of individual and collective. Upholding freedom as their primary value, market relationships do not consider its relationship to other potential values like equality, solidarity, or justice. Isolating choice, market relationships discount the power of identity, care, camaraderie, and other potentially generative qualities of relationships. Moreover, my discussion of individual-freedom-choice has invoked a host of secondary values, such as respect, humility, and autonomy. Without these secondary values, which imply the need for practices, institutions, norms, and shared commitments that neoliberal advocates explicitly deny, the individual cannot exercise their freedom as choice. Further, this primary value cluster represents its means and ends— choice as means, individual freedom as ends—as content-free, thereby facilitating the realization of different ends for different individuals. For example, if one family prefers a religious education for their children, they may direct their tax dollars to private schools, while a family preferring a secular education may enroll their children in public schools. Lost in this scenario are the choices enabled and foreclosed by the pursuit of market relations.

Professing neutrality, individual-freedom-choice dramatically limits the possibilities for human agency through its championing of the autonomous individual and its delegitimization of the social. From this perspective, people's relationships consist entirely of chosen relationships. People owe no debt or gratitude to others; personal successes and failures arise through individual actions. Yet the difficulty of consistently asserting one's independence from collective affiliations and networks remains, as demonstrated by the neoliberal elision of individual and family. Melinda Cooper maintains that the neoliberal turn to the family as a socializing and stabilizing force betrays its unacknowledged reliance on collective action. Referencing the Friedmans and others, Cooper holds that obligations within families "sustain the otherwise inexplicable freedom of the neoliberal individual."[4] Perhaps this is why Betsy DeVos expressed such alarm that an unchecked education establishment would reconfigure the public school as home and the state as family, or why Scott Walker placed parents and "bureaucrats" in an either-or relationship regarding decisions about the right schools for children.[5] Across my case studies, pro-market references to family constitute a partial concession of the limits of atomistic individualism, as people need nurturing, care, and support to develop as capable agents. Still, coordinated activity in human development and everyday life extend beyond the family.

Focusing on the individual ignores the roles of collective identity and agency in shaping individual empowerment and disempowerment. In a positive sense, collective affiliations may inform an individual's identity, motivation for engagement, understanding of the stakes of action, and sense of purpose. In some of her public speeches, as she presented herself as a

DC outsider and praised her audiences' innovative thinking and ability to withstand the force of the education establishment, Betsy DeVos cultivated a collective identity and spirit among pro-market education reformers—she exhorted them to work together as market publics for the cause of freedom. Negatively, an excessive focus on the individual discounts the ways that ascriptions of collective identities and agential capacities to others, often in line with entrenched relations of power, delimit the ability of differently situated people to act as "free" individuals. If individuals exist outside of social relations, then social problems become individual problems. As Wendy Brown explains, "If there is no such thing as society, but only individuals and families oriented by markets and morals, then there is no such thing as social power generating hierarchies, exclusion, and violence."[6] While the Friedmans illustrated this position most boldly in their definition of discrimination as taste, pro-market advocates in my other cases also articulated this orientation. For instance, Wisconsin State Representative Dale Kooyenga gleaned from his reading of a Frederick Douglass autobiography the lesson that Douglass the individual overcame difficult odds. Referencing Douglass's efforts to learn to read, Kooyenga celebrated him as an exemplar of hard work and self-determination. In this spirit, individual successes warrant praise, while individual failures warrant self-recrimination.

As a thoroughly negative attribute, market freedom cannot recognize varying degrees of freedom and unfreedom for differently situated individuals. Freedom from the strictures of unchosen relationships and governing institutions may eliminate constraints for people with the symbolic and material resources to pursue their interests, but this freedom cannot eliminate the constraints of deprivation, marginalization, and subjugation. Freedom without considerations of equality and justice simply reproduces the advantages and disadvantages of the status quo. For example, vouchers may free parents to send their children to ostensibly better-fitting schools outside their residential districts, but the exercise of this freedom cannot control the availability, supplemental cost, and inclusiveness of educational alternatives. These alternatives may select among applicants and require that parents provide their own transportation for children. Inside classrooms, they may reproduce societal hierarchies among connected insiders and isolated outsiders. Moreover, parents choosing vouchers from positions of relative deprivation still lack the freedom to enroll their children in well-resourced neighborhood public schools, which may constitute their foremost desire. As Janelle Scott observes, market reformers dissociate their preferred plans from broader critiques of "social inequality and fail to adequately provide for equal access to high-quality, well-resourced, and diverse schools."[7] Under market relations, coordinated efforts to address wider structural issues appear as "unfreedom" insofar as their redress threatens the unfettered activities of wealthy parents who may have to disavow privileges, which they may defend as rights. As David Harvey explains, market-based notions of freedom draw on its resonance in democratic societies but sharply circumscribe its practice by delinking freedom from complementary democratic values that promote equitable opportunities.[8]

Even as the freedom of individual-freedom-choice purports to stand against coercion, market relations regard coercion as an exclusively political phenomenon, without recognizing the force of economic coercion. The Friedmans asserted that governments concentrate power while markets disperse power. Placing his trust in parents, Scott Walker rebuked "the expanse of government," promising to "empower families to make the choice that is right for their sons and daughters" against "bureaucrats and politicians" who would choose for them.[9] Betsy DeVos claimed to welcome the enmity of the education establishment, because this meant that she was disrupting their control. In these cases, coercion emanated from seats of political power, whether in Washington, DC, or Madison, Wisconsin. But these advocates did not criticize other situations where parents may feel compelled to relinquish their freedom and choice. For instance, parents of disabled children may sign away federally protected rights for their children because they do not value these rights, or they may do so because they desperately want to help their children and see the forsaking of rights as the price of entry to a well-resourced private school. In this latter scenario, coercion through the power of the private school to deny admission may exert a force that produces an outcome detrimental to parents' self-interest. When confronted with this possibility in a congressional hearing, DeVos reiterated the self-confirming character of choice: "Parents are making those decisions. There is no requirement."[10] This response suggests that coercion cannot explain parental decision-making; its application extends only to government action. Similarly, when pro-voucher groups outspent voucher opponents by an almost ten-to-one margin prior to the statewide expansion of vouchers in Wisconsin, the majority members of the Joint Finance Committee did not decry economic coercion; lobbying presumably did not influence their decision-making.[11]

In American culture and other Western societies, the language of choice circulates seductively. Advertisers regularly tell consumers that they should not settle for fewer options—more is always better. Indeed, choice fashions consumer identity, as driving a particular car may construct its operator as a maverick or a good parent. This spirit animated Senator John Kennedy's quip, offered during an exchange with Betsy DeVos at a congressional hearing, that he can find six different types of mayonnaise at his local grocery, but children in his home state of Louisiana have far fewer educational options.[12] This spirit of choice facilitates advocates' characterization of education as an industry, bolstering calls like Representative John Klenke's admonition to State Superintendent Tony Evers that public educators need to "change the cost curve so that we can deliver education in a new way."[13] Presumably, competition engendered through expanded choice would drive down public education costs. This assertion neglects how transferring market choice to education propagates an idea of choice as context-free and limited in consequence to the individual who chooses.

A market affirmation of individual choice obfuscates its wider consequences for the people affected by the reverberating dynamics of public engagement and public policy, challenging market depictions of choice as self-confirming. Educational institutions require collective investment. No individual, save the altruistic or self-interested wealthy patron, can build and staff a school, much less a district of schools. However, every year the aggregate decisions of numerous individuals to use private vouchers cost the Milwaukee Public Schools tens of millions of dollars. In some small and rural districts, vouchers and open enrollment costs, which transfer tax dollars across public school districts through individual choices, threaten the very existence of these districts. For students in public schools across the state of Wisconsin, policies putatively responsive to individual choices carry collective consequences. On public issues like education, parents using public tax dollars do not simply make a choice for their children alone, as Scott Walker and other market advocates would have it. Against their depiction as self-confirming, market choices warrant greater scrutiny. Yet others affected by these choices have no recourse to public deliberation under market relations. As market actors, they can choose to move their children, if private educators accept them and space is available, but they cannot demand public transparency, accountability, and decision-making. These limitations make clear the narrow vision of individual-freedom-choice, which simply cannot imagine—much less engage—complex and diverse interactions across networks of human relationships.

The limited vision of individual-freedom-choice raises questions about the role of education for market relationships. Across my cases, market advocates valued education, devoting much of their energy to the creation and organization of education markets, but they did not detail the content and purpose of a proper education. The Friedmans discerned widespread benefits of education in teaching "a minimum degree of literacy and knowledge" and a "common set of values."[14] Stressing innovation, DeVos argued that students "need a customized, self-paced, and challenging education" to learn skills like critical thinking, collaboration, communication, creativity, and cultural intelligence.[15] Focused on budgets, the members of the Joint Finance Committee did not enumerate educational objectives or competencies, but they did address the efficacy of curricula, such as Senator Alberta Darling when she asked State Superintendent Evers to explain Wisconsin's middling standing on comparative, state-by-state report cards.[16] These examples converge in charging education with the task of teaching common values and skills that can provide stable environments for the practice of market relationships. Yet the dynamics of market relationships frustrate this pedagogy.

Individual-freedom-choice may justify a widespread desire for a shared education as motivated by mutual self-interest. Individuals learn a shared set of values so they may operate with the expectation that others will not advance their self-interest through coercion. However, a basis in self-interest renders this pedagogy tactical—individuals may employ putatively shared values when they discern an advantage in doing so. In other situations, such as marked inequalities among prospective exchange partners, individuals may employ coercion without fear of suffering the same. To serve as ethical guides, shared values require understanding, empathy, and commitment. We may appreciate the diverse contributions of people to a collectively valued public life. We may recognize systems of varying advantage and disadvantage and nevertheless try to practice fair and equitable relationships. Market relationships reward an individual's relative lack of awareness of their embedment in wider relationship networks, for interest in a wider perspective betrays the arrogance of the reformer. In contrast, as Dewey held, democratic relationships depend on an awareness of the interrelatedness of human action to orient ethical and purposeful action.[17] A market education confronts the paradox of teaching the very values and practices its advocates disavow.

The problems of a market education relate to its narrow conception of knowledge and what this entails for persuasion and decision-making. As I explain with regard to the Friedmans, neoliberal thinking construes knowledge as gleaned through direct experience. This view of knowledge underlies the statements of DeVos, Walker, and others that parents know best about their children's education. Yet this framework severely limits an individual's ability to interact with others. A market conception of knowledge provides no role for moral imagination, learning about the histories and aspirations of others, locating one's own views within a wider world. Market knowledge reveals the goals of its pedagogy—self-knowledge untroubled by the transformative power of human relationships. Such direct knowledge may instill a false sense of confidence about what one knows and a reluctance to engage others. It necessarily flattens worldviews, spheres of concern, sympathies and allegiances. This also raises the problem of persuasion: on what basis may an individual persuade another to make a different choice? Certainly, champions of education markets confront this problem for their own efforts, as the large majority of schoolchildren in the United States and Wisconsin attend public schools.[18] Once more, market advocates draw on ideas they claim to reject, as the Friedmans, DeVos, and Wisconsin state policymakers all have asked audiences to support reforms that extend beyond their direct experience.

With one-to-one persuasion as its idealized model, individual-freedom-choice struggles to explain wider efforts for social change. Across my case studies, two possibilities appear that embrace antidemocratic means with rising intensity. The first consists of technological apparatuses—from invoking the price system to urging innovation—that seek to "avoid" politics and public engagement. My use of scare quotes suggests the impossibility of avoiding politics on public issues like education. Still, the Friedmans hoped to constrict the political realm and expand markets, thereby reducing the number of decisions made by individuals in their standing as members of a polity. DeVos affirmed innovation as a force for change, celebrating business figures like Henry Ford and Steve Jobs and intimating that technology could avert public debate. The second consists of authoritarianism, which demands adherence as leaders direct politics toward particular outcomes.[19] In my case studies, authoritarian means appeared most explicitly in the actions of the Joint Finance Committee to expand vouchers statewide. Acting in the middle of the night against the wishes of a large majority of Wisconsin residents, the majority members of the committee compelled Wisconsinites to participate in expanded education markets. These legislators sought a particular end, and they employed the necessary means to obtain it. This outcome reveals the unfreedom and restricted choice of individual-freedom-choice: for individuals, freedom and choice operate only as market means. The creation and organization of markets themselves lay outside the purview of the supposedly sovereign individual.

Aligning Democratic Means and Ends

In Dewey's definition of education as a process of making meaningful and purposefully directing human experience, we may discern democratic ends for public education. As a process actively engaged by students, teachers, and others, education may cultivate capacities and dispositions of agency, purpose, and participation while developing specific skills for their realization. A democratic education may support students in living their lives productively in coordination with others, pursuing individual interests while recognizing how relationships shape these interests and build life-enriching collective affiliations. A democratic education may enable students to mediate productively the I and the we, appreciating people's varied and textured participation in multiple groups that contribute to the complex constitution of personhood. A democratic education may foster recognition of the varied consequences of human action, which Dewey understood as the basis of public formation. Individuals do not choose only for themselves; their choices carry consequences for others who must live with the potentially ameliorative and baneful effects of these choices. Against the market representation of publics as aggregations of individuals, a democratic education may illuminate the transformative power of publics for the people who participate in them. Valuing freedom as well as attendant values of equality, justice, and solidarity, a democratic education may encourage exploration of various practices of community and other relationship networks.

As students, teachers, and others explore various modes of engagement and affiliation, they may understand better the constructed character of democratic relationships and the need to tend to these relationships. While market advocates ascribe uniformity and fixity to relationships as instrumental vehicles of exchange, democratic relationships do not develop without the active involvement of participants. Through this process, participants need to consider the preferred qualities and dynamics of their engagements, cultivating relationship dimensions that facilitate mutual growth and development. In contrast to market relationships, self-interest does not function as a solitary constitutive force. Rather, democratic relationships unfold as a joint project that involves mutual understanding and learning about different perspectives, experiences, and values. The constitutive force of self-interest ostensibly preserves the autonomy of the market individual, but democratic relationships illuminate their transformative power, as participants create meanings and experiences that do not exist independently of these relationships. Participants may revise and reform ongoing democratic relationships to account for varied contexts and new developments. As individuals participate in multiple relationships, their identities, interests, and outlooks may widen, potentially prompting reflection and reformulations of individual identity and collective affiliations. Vibrant relationship networks may facilitate better self-understanding and greater empathy for others.

As they extend outward from particular engagements, contextualizing direct experiences and knowledge, elucidating diverse perspectives, and inviting greater participation, democratic relationships may foster the emergence of democratic cultures supportive of vibrant public education. Emulating relationships, democratic cultures would express fluidity, engage difference, and remain unfinished. Democratic cultures would sustain dynamic practices that could resist, as Dewey warned, quietistic views that ascribe an autonomous energy to democracy. Certainly, the expansion of education markets across the United States gainsays the assumption that democracy will thrive as a self-powered machine. Reinvigorating democracy for our contemporary era involves heeding the lessons of scholarship on multiple public spheres and the public engagement of local advocates. Just as community serves as a democratic map for Dewey, a multiple public sphere illuminates potentially productive engagements within and across democratic communities that attend to relations of power and inequality. Although the advocates we interviewed did not employ the scholarly language of public sphere theory, some of them described their advocacy in a counterpublic spirit as articulating alternative identities, interests, and needs with their communities.[20]

We may follow the lead of local community advocates to engage critically our own democratic practices. Just as these advocates questioned prevailing local assumptions and beliefs about community, identifying exclusionary claims to belonging and assertions of privilege, we may reflect on our own practices to call out exclusions, recognize multiple histories, and affirm diverse relationships. A Latina advocate from Madison underscored the need to regard community itself as a practice. She explained that doing so entails expanding one's circle of concern and seeking understanding. Concern for others requires awareness of others, including their opportunities for developing as capable agents and the obstacles in their paths. This advocate offered the specific example of a parent who walks their child to a nearby neighborhood school becoming aware of and investing in the plight of children in their city who ride buses to school for long periods every day: "That's how we practice community. . . . I'm concerned about your child. You're concerned about my child." Building this sense of mutuality and solidarity requires active learning: "We seek understanding. That's a practice." This insight suggests that critically engaging democracy involves resisting the complacency of settled routines and potentially making oneself uncomfortable by seeking out new experiences and perspectives. Our own discomfort may provide us a vehicle for engaging in continual learning. Further, in the pairing of familiarity and change, we may discern the supportive dimensions of democratic communities as well as their energy and creativity.

By critically engaging democracy, we also may invoke it as a normative framework and check against the unequal, dehumanizing, and destructive operations of markets. In a neoliberal age, it is popular to ask how markets can improve democracy, but what if we ask how democracy can improve markets? A democratic critique of markets would consist importantly of elucidating the force of economic coercion in some markets and exchanges and its effective denial of freedom for many individuals. In this spirit, referencing the issue of increasing income inequality, Danielle Allen discerns the egalitarian potential of a democratic education to develop "the basis for forms of participatory democracy that might contest the labor market rules that deliver insupportable forms of income inequality."[21] On their own terms, markets justify inequality—including degrees of inequality that effectively usurp agency and undermine the very "common set of values" on which, according to the Friedmans, a democratic society relies—as the anonymous outcome of innumerable individual choices. Some people choose high-paying jobs, others do not. However, as Allen suggests, these outcomes represent collective decisions that people reasonably may reconsider. Indeed, recognizing the possibility of both political and economic coercion and holding markets accountable to democratic decision-making better promotes individual freedom. In this way, we may articulate an empowering variation of democratic choice.

Achieving democratic ends in public education involves honest discussions of aligning means and ends. Misalignment appears in current structural inequalities, state disinvestment from public education, the impoverishment of particular schools and districts disproportionately attended by students of color, and the circumscribed imaginations and aspirations that these conditions produce.[22] With regard to education markets, my case studies demonstrate that many policymakers favor antidemocratic means toward antidemocratic ends. As a white Milwaukee advocate observed, addressing the state funding formula and Wisconsin's worst-in-the-nation achievement disparities, "We have a system perfectly designed to get us there." Rather than addressing the effects of racial and economic residential segregation and the ongoing influence of racism and insider lobbying, policymakers have turned to test scores and school and district assessments to characterize some public schools as failing. While test scores and district comparisons offer some useful information, they do not address the larger issues affecting public education. Instead, as I explained in chapter 3, test scores and school assessments circulate independently of context, effectively functioning in market terms as monetary valuations and currency. They do not illuminate how inequality is built into the current system of financing public education in Wisconsin and other states. Instead of bolstering reform, they produce a circumscribed imagination of schooling and the challenges and hopes of public education.

Aligning democratic means and ends requires action from more than public schools. Indeed, progress along these lines necessitates disavowing our collective habit of sending societal issues to school and wishing for a fix. On issues of racism, economic inequality, political polarization, and more, reformers often have devised strategies that call for schools to act alone.[23] Public schools can and should play vital, critical roles in processes of social change, but, as our local advocates have demonstrated, the potential efficacy of this work increases through school and community partnerships. Our interviewees addressed various ways in which public schools serve as sites, vehicles, and agents for community formation. Working toward educational equality entails widening these community connections and focusing collective energy on change. In this context, the Milwaukee Community Schools Partnership serves as a promising effort to use the public school as a coordinating point for addressing wider issues that negatively affect education. The promise of this approach notwithstanding, as long as we employ funding formulas that exacerbate wealth disparities across communities, public schools and communities will continue to struggle. Even successful schools, as judged by such measures as high test scores and graduation rates, will suffer from operating in a culture with a narrow view of education.

Individually and collectively, inside and outside of school buildings, we need to expand our vision of education to foreground the crafting of democratic communities. Important skills that can contribute to this kind of democratic revival are familiar to scholars of rhetoric and communication.[24] To build democratic communities, individuals and groups may develop their capacities for imagination, interpretation, analysis, and expression. Learners of all ages may sharpen their abilities to analyze critically the claims of politicians, lobbyists, and media commentators regarding the supposed failures of public education and promise of education markets.[25] Invoking positive associations and practices of community, they may consider various appeals to inspire and motivate others to work together for a vibrant democratic education. Considering their advocacy, they may practice strategies for developing arguments that engage audience values, invoke relevant and compelling evidence, and organize claims into a coherent case. As these rhetorical practices suggest, efforts to achieve this end may draw on what Danielle Allen regards as "education's most fundamental egalitarian value": "its development of us as language-using creatures."[26] As language-using, rhetorical, communicative creatures, people are more than market actors. A market education activates only a small portion of our complex humanity while neglecting the feelings, ideas, attitudes, and desires that make human relationships compelling, enlivening, rewarding. A market education severely shortchanges human agency and aspiration.

To direct education toward the crafting of democratic communities, we should engage the creative power of communication and people's capacity for communicative invention. In this spirit, Dewey ultimately turned to the power of communication to realize the promises of democracy. He championed "a subtle, delicate, vivid, and responsive art of communication" that would "breathe life" into taken-for-granted communicative systems and practices.[27] In my teaching and scholarship, I have understood his embrace of this art as an exhortation to experiment boldly with varied communicative means for democratic ends. Such experimentation would proceed not in the service of a scientific democracy, but a rhetorical democracy that articulates ameliorative alternatives and advocates for their realization. Lest some readers dismiss this project as overly idealistic, I note that local advocates for public education have undertaken this very experimentation. To achieve their goals, these advocates have held rallies, launched marches, hosted forums, developed postcard campaigns, wrote letters, delivered speeches, fostered dialogue, and more. Since we live in neoliberal times, their successes have been varied, yet fundamental, lasting, ameliorative change will only occur through democratic relationships that reform existing political cultures, institutions, organizations, and interest. Connected across historical eras, Dewey and these local advocates recognized that a democratic education may emerge from the ground up.

NOTES

INTRODUCTION

1. Reilly, "I Work 3 Jobs." For a side-by-side rendering of the three different covers, along with previous *Time* education covers, see Will, "From 'Rotten Apples.'"

2. Wisconsin Department of Public Instruction, "Private School Choice."

3. Endres, "Baraboo Christian."

4. Walker, "Why I'm Fighting." See also Beck, "Conservative Study," and Sommerhauser, "New State Data."

5. For example, the Milwaukee Public Schools include both neighborhood and specialty schools. Throughout this book, when referring to the district and all of its schools, I capitalize Milwaukee Public Schools because this is the name of the city's school district.

6. Dewey, *Democracy and Education*, 26–36.

7. Achieving international fame as a Nobel Prize–winning, unapologetic champion of markets, Milton Friedman published an extensive amount of scholarly and popular writings. In addition, as spouses, Milton Friedman and Rose Friedman co-authored several influential books advocating for market approaches to a range of policy issues, including education. Yet, scholars and media commentators, including myself, sometimes ignore Rose Friedman's authorship. Perhaps the most ambiguous statement of their co-authorship involves the 1962 book *Capitalism and Freedom*. The cover named Milton Friedman as author, while the front matter included the phrase "with the assistance of Rose D. Friedman." However, in their later work, the Friedmans referred to *Capitalism and Freedom* as co-authored, as with this reference from their 1980 book *Free to Choose*, in which they explained their changed views of compulsory education laws: "Our own views on this have changed over time. When we first wrote extensively a quarter of a century ago on this subject, we accepted the need for such laws" (162). Here, they did not qualify their co-authorship as one person assisting another. In *School Choice and the Betrayal of Democracy*, I treat the Friedmans' vision of market relationships and education as a joint project. Indeed, their coordinated efforts to articulate market visions, when considered alongside the uneven credit these co-authors have received, intimates tensions with the market embrace of individualism, which I explore in this book. With regard to specific references, I distinguish quotations drawn from co-authored books by the Friedmans, including *Capitalism and Freedom*, and publications that identify Milton Friedman solely as author.

8. Plagianos, "WeWork."

9. For a defense of market communication against democratic deliberation, see Pennington, "Against Democratic Education." For a critique of market reformers' antipathy to deliberation, see Ravitch, "Why Public Schools."

10. Berkshire, "New Public Education Movement." Considering local grassroots discourse in other settings, Katie Garahan analyzes teacher open letters as protests of market-based education reform; see "Public Work of Identity Performance."

11. Dewey, *Democracy and Education*, 5–6, 9.

12. On DeVos's representation as hostile to public education, see, for example, E. Brown, "Trump Picks Billionaire," and Klein, "DeVos Would Be First." On the market-based education advocacy of the Obama administration, especially education secretary Arne Duncan, see, for example, Martin and Lázaro, "Race to Educational Reform," and Scott, "Market-Driven Education Reform."

13. I planned these local interviews in my conceptualization of this project. In the spring of 2019, after having examined national and state discourses, I recruited UW-Madison PhD student Kelly Jensen to assist with the interviews. See Asen and Jensen, "Interviews with Community Advocates."

14. Asen, "Imagining."

15. On different approaches to conceptualizing the public sphere, see Brouwer and Asen, "Introduction."

16. Arendt, *Human Condition*, 183.

17. Hauser, *Vernacular Voices*, 71. Emphasis in original.

18. Young, *Inclusion and Democracy*, 139.

19. Dewey, *Freedom and Culture*, 187.

20. See, for example, Dewey, *Public and Its Problems*, 147–48.

21. W. Brown, *Undoing the Demos*, 41–43.

22. Dewey, *Public and Its Problems*, 149.

23. Condit, "Crafting Virtue," 82. See also Villadsen, "Progress."

24. Dewey, *Democracy and Education*, 54–77.

25. Cintron, "Democracy and Its Limitations," 98. For an extended case against the idealization of liberal democracy, see Cintron, *Democracy as Fetish*. For a discussion of democratic tensions and their impact on local meetings, see Tracy, *Challenges of Ordinary Democracy*, 53–60.

26. See Turner, "Rebirth of Liberalism." In a 1951 essay in which he explicitly invoked the term "neo-liberalism," Milton Friedman explained that neoliberals did not reject state action outright. Rather, a neoliberal project shared the classical "liberal emphasis on the fundamental importance of the individual, but it would substitute for the nineteenth century goal of laissez-faire as a means to this end, the goal of the competitive order" ("Neo-liberalism and Its Prospects").

27. Friedman and Friedman, *Capitalism and Freedom*, 5–6. William Davies discerns the "neo" of neoliberalism in three areas. First, neoliberalism seeks a strong state to reshape society around its ideals. Second, neoliberalism joins economics and politics in a single vision. Third, neoliberalism treats competition as a critical social principle. See Davies, "What Is 'Neo.'"

28. Dingo, Riedner, and Wingard, "Toward a Cogent Analysis," 522–23. For an analysis of public censure directed toward commentators whose unfavorable economic forecasts threaten to disrupt market confidence, see Colombini, "Speaking Confidence." For an analysis of confidence as a topos employed in public discourse to mitigate perceptions of economic crisis, see Abbott, "Widespread Loss of Confidence.'"

29. See Springer, *Discourse of Neoliberalism*, 23–26.

30. A scholarly challenge attending the term neoliberalism relates to its seemingly ubiquitous circulation. Philip Mirowski notes that the term appeared occasionally in the titles of academic books and articles until the 1990s—then its use exploded (see "Political Movement"). Yet widespread use and potential overuse may signal at least two developments: one, that neoliberalism names prominent and consequential aspects of our current era, which I believe; and two, that neoliberalism as a term sometimes substitutes for careful analysis, which I also believe. In *School Choice and the Betrayal of Democracy*, I have sought to reconcile these two possibilities by using the term judiciously and not in

place of critical analysis or conceptual argument. Market relationships, market publics, and market education all illuminate different aspects of neoliberal governance, but they should not be collapsed into the term.

31. W. Brown, *Undoing the Demos*, 31. Emphasis in original.

32. See Van Horn and Mirowski, "Rise of the Chicago School," and Wapshott, *Keynes Hayek*.

33. See American Federation for Children, *2012 Election*; Kemble, "Wisconsin's Voucher"; and Flanders, "Facts." For a view of pro–market education policy coordination from a pro–public education Wisconsin state representative, see Taylor, "ALEC's Attack."

34. Mirowski, *Never Let a Serious Crisis*, 49.

35. Colombini, "Energeia, Kinesis," 179.

36. Ibid., 187.

37. Dean, "Nothing Personal," 3.

38. For a history of cycles of disinvestment and market reforms in Milwaukee, where the nation's first vouchers were implemented, see Miner, *Lessons*. On the broader effects of educational inequities, see Darling-Hammond, *Flat World and Education*. Describing what she refers to as "segrenomics," Noliwe Rooks details a long history of people profiting from educational inequality; see *Cutting School*.

39. Friedman and Friedman, *Capitalism and Freedom*, 109. See also Friedman and Friedman, *Free to Choose*, 13.

40. Wanzer-Serrano, "Barack Obama," 24.

41. Jones and Mukherjee, "From California to Michigan," 402.

42. Ibid., 407.

43. On the individualization of sexism and the focus on market-based responses, see, for example, W. Brown, *Undoing the Demos*, 104–7; Dingo, *Networking Arguments*; and Fraser, "Feminism, Capitalism."

44. Friedman and Friedman, *Free to Choose*, 13.

45. Chaput, *Market Affect*, 117–18.

46. Duerringer, "Rhetorical Arbitrage," 390. Joshua Hanan, Indradeep Ghosh, and Kaleb Brooks write that economy theory "does not so much represent a marketplace that exists *a priori* as it simulates or 'performs' a world that is imagined in its models" ("Banking on the Present," 141).

47. Friedman and Friedman, *Capitalism and Freedom*, 86.

CHAPTER I

1. Dewey, "Creative Democracy," 225.

2. Ibid., 226.

3. Dewey, *Public and Its Problems*, 31.

4. Sandlin, Burdick, and Norris, "Erosion and Experience," 139.

5. Dewey, *Freedom and Culture*, 151.

6. Dewey, "Creative Democracy," 227.

7. Danisch, *Pragmatism, Democracy*, 53–64; Johnstone, "Dewey, Ethics."

8. Olson, "Concerning Judgment"; Stroud, "John Dewey."

9. Borchers, "John Dewey"; Keith, *Democracy as Discussion*, 93–104.

10. Crick, *Democracy and Rhetoric*, 9.

11. Keith, *Democracy as Discussion*, 100–101.

12. Asen, "Multiple Mr. Dewey." For the classic critique of Habermas's account of the bourgeois public sphere, see Fraser, "Rethinking the Public Sphere."

13. See Hauser, *Vernacular Voices*, 64–72.

14. For a critique of the US Supreme Court's equation of money and speech in its *Citizens United* decision, see W. Brown, *Undoing the Demos*, 151–73. Ronald Greene develops the concept of "money/speech" to indicate how the US Supreme Court has "fused money and speech under the norm of free speech" and how it "understands political rhetoric as a financial process" ("Rhetorical Capital," 329).

15. Dewey, *Individualism*, 45.

16. In Nathan Crick's terms, we need to consider how "Dewey might also benefit from a little more rhetoric" (*Democracy and Rhetoric*, 10).

17. Dewey, *Individualism*, 82.

18. Dewey, *Public and Its Problems*, 147.

19. Ibid.

20. Dewey, *Individualism*, 61, 62.

21. Dewey, *Liberalism and Social Action*, 26.

22. Dewey, *Individualism*, 109.

23. Ibid., 57. Matthew Festenstein explicates Dewey's understanding of freedom as an ethical practice that consists of individual choice and growth, as well as a "collective dimension" of participation in shaping the contexts that facilitate individual development; see "Ties of Communication," 109–11.

24. Dewey, *Individualism*, 121.

25. Dewey, *Liberalism and Social Action*, 28.

26. Ibid., 36.

27. Ibid., 40–41.

28. Dewey, *Public and Its Problems*, 15–16.

29. Ibid., 24.

30. Lary Belman identifies foresight as a key quality of Dewey's theory of communication. Belman writes, "Foresight, as a systematic and deliberate process, is an achievement of language" ("John Dewey's Concept," 31).

31. Dewey, *Public and Its Problems*, 30–31.

32. Ibid., 131.

33. Ibid., 151–52.

34. Dewey, *Freedom and Culture*, 187.

35. Dewey, "Democracy Is Radical," 299.

36. Dewey, "Creative Democracy," 228.

37. Dewey, "Basic Values," 276–77.

38. Dewey, "Creative Democracy," 227. Nine years earlier, in an essay titled "What I Believe," Dewey held that "a philosophic faith, being a tendency to action, can be tried and tested only in action" (278). On the experiential character of Dewey's faith, see Eldridge, "Dewey's Faith."

39. Dewey, *Public and Its Problems*, 148, 149.

40. Ibid., 149.

41. Ibid., 126.

42. Ibid., 128, 129.

43. Ibid., 216.

44. Paul Stob argues that Dewey's attention to the local constitutes his most important contribution to the study of the public sphere; see "Kenneth Burke," 242. William Caspary characterizes Dewey's understanding of local communities "as schools of democracy which prepare citizens for effective participation in the more complex and mediated national political discussion" (*Dewey on Democracy*, 10). Robert Westbrook discerns a "wistful" quality to Dewey's turn to local communities; see *John Dewey*, 315.

45. Honneth, "Democracy as Reflexive Cooperation," 775–76. Lloyd Bitzer, too, sees community as prior to public, which leads him to a tautological rendering of their

relationship: "The public which Dewey saw as created by public transactions apparently already existed as a community—indeed as a public" ("Rhetoric and Public Knowledge," 81). Yet a preexisting public would contravene Dewey's view of publics as active, participatory creations.

46. On this point, particularly Dewey's invocation of Thomas Jefferson, see Engels, "Dewey on Jefferson."

47. Dewey, *Public and Its Problems*, 113. Belman identifies "early America [as] the historical source and inspiration for Dewey's ideas about community" ("John Dewey's Concept," 34).

48. Dewey, *Public and Its Problems*, 216.

49. Dewey, *Freedom and Culture*, 177. In *Individualism, Old and New*, Dewey contrasted medieval society with the present. In the former, "communities were local; they did not merge, overlap and interact in all kinds of subtle and hidden ways" (*Individualism*, 113). In contrast, movement and interaction represented a key feature of the Great Society and would need to be utilized in the formation of a Great Community.

50. Dewey, *Public and Its Problems*, 216–17.

51. Ibid., 213.

52. Ibid., 142.

53. Ibid., 208.

54. Ibid., 149, 183.

55. For an extended discussion of the democratic potential of Dewey's aesthetic understanding of communication, see Crick, *Democracy and Rhetoric*, 130–86.

56. Gert Biesta argues that *Democracy and Education* marked a decisive moment in Dewey's writings in which his philosophy made a "communicative turn." Biesta notes the significance of Dewey making this turn with regard to education: "Dewey seemed to have presented his philosophy of communication for the first time in the context of a discussion about education." Reciprocally, "he developed his theory of education as a theory of communication." See Biesta, "Of All Affairs," 26.

57. Dewey, *Democracy and Education*, 2, 3.

58. Ibid., 4.

59. Ibid., 5.

60. Dewey, *Experience and Education*, 5, 8, 24, 55.

61. Dewey, *Democracy and Education*, 15.

62. Dewey, *Experience and Education*, 35.

63. Dewey, *Democracy and Education*, 19.

64. Dewey, *Experience and Education*, 36.

65. Dewey, *Democracy and Education*, 76.

66. Ibid., 76–77.

67. Ibid., 50, 80.

68. Ibid., 83.

69. Thomas Englund writes that Dewey's "emphasis on the relationship between education and democracy as a life form" supports his view of "education as a forum for communication between people with different experiences" ("Potential of Education," 238). Similarly, R. W. Hildreth observes that Dewey's standards for democratic, educational communities indicate that "conditions for growth are enhanced through encountering difference" ("What Good Is Growth?," 37).

70. Dewey, *Democracy and Education*, 98.

71. Ibid., 136.

72. Ibid., 307.

73. Ibid., 310.

74. Ibid., 315.

75. Ibid., 318, 316. In *The Public and Its Problems*, Dewey decried the "enslavement of men, women and children in factories in which they are animated machines to tend inanimate machines" (175).

76. Westbrook, *John Dewey*, 179.

77. Dewey, *Democracy and Education*, 316–17.

78. Westbrook, *John Dewey*, 141.

79. Keith and Danisch, "Dewey on Science," 27, 43.

80. Burks, "John Dewey," 125. Joseph Metz explains that a Deweyan science could serve democracy by testing concepts, principles, and theories; treating policies and proposals as working hypotheses; and allowing continuous observation of the consequences of these policies to facilitate their revision; see "Democracy," 249. See also Morris, "How Shall We Read."

81. Dewey, *Public and Its Problems*, 174.

82. Ibid., 176, 178. Matthew Festenstein argues that Dewey linked democracy and inquiry through the expression of people's interests: "Interests are not incorrigible preferences, but may be clarified and transformed through inquiry," which Dewey saw as occurring "through public processes of debate and discussion" ("Inquiry as Critique," 742).

83. Dewey, *Public and Its Problems*, 208, 209.

84. Dewey, *Freedom and Culture*, 168, 170.

85. Explicating Dewey's claim in "Experience, Knowledge and Value" that "one and the same method is to be used in determination of physical judgment and the value-judgments of morals" (66), William Caspary identifies key similarities between Dewey's conception of applied science and his conception of ethical deliberation; see "One and the Same Method," 448–53.

86. Dewey, *Freedom and Culture*, 166.

87. Ibid., 167.

88. Dewey, *Liberalism and Social Action*, 50.

89. Ibid., 50, 51.

90. Ibid., 51. James Bohman holds that a Deweyan model of democracy fore-grounding inquiry shifts the basis of knowledge in deliberation from individual to social: "The more deliberation is like inquiry the more thoroughly everyone is dependent on everyone else both for their cooperation and for their contribution to the collective organization of knowledge" ("Democracy as Inquiry," 594).

91. Dewey, *Liberalism and Social Action*, 64.

92. Dewey, *Freedom and Culture*, 155.

93. Dewey, *Liberalism and Social Action*, 51.

94. Dewey, *Experience and Nature*, 132.

95. Ibid., 135.

96. Ibid., 141.

97. Dewey, *Public and Its Problems*, 183.

98. See Brouwer, "Communication as Counterpublic."

99. Asen, "Seeking the 'Counter,'" 425–26.

100. Gent, "When Homelessness."

101. Chávez, "Counter-Public Enclaves," 3.

102. Jackson and Foucault Welles, "#Ferguson Is Everywhere," 398.

103. Pezzullo, "Resisting," 349.

104. Hildreth, "Reconstructing Dewey," 783.

105. Arendt, *Human Condition*, 200.

106. Hildreth, "Reconstructing Dewey," 786.

107. Ibid., 790. See also Hewitt, "Democracy and Power."

108. Wolfe, "Does Pragmatism."

109. Ivie, "Rhetorical Deliberation," 278.
110. Ivie, "Enabling Democratic Dissent," 54.
111. Mouffe, *Democratic Paradox*, 102. Elsewhere, Mouffe writes that the adversary is "the opponent with whom one shares a common allegiance to the democratic principles of 'liberty and equality for all,' while disagreeing about their interpretation" (*Agonistics*, 7).
112. McKerrow, "Principles of Rhetorical Democracy," 98–100.
113. See Young, *Inclusion and Democracy*, 44; Hauser, "Rhetorical Democracy."
114. Dewey, "Creative Democracy," 226. In *Democracy and Education*, Dewey held that expanding democratic communities required "the breaking down of those barriers of class, race, and national territory which kept [people] from perceiving the full import of their activity" (87). Referencing Dewey's political activism, Charlene Haddock Seigfried notes his support for numerous women's causes, including "women's suffrage, women's right to higher education and coeducation, unimpeded access to and legalization of birth control, and just wages and worker control of the conditions of work for women as well as men" ("John Dewey's Pragmatist Feminism," 48).
115. See, for example, Davidoff, "Regarding Some 'Old Husbands' Tales.'"
116. Asen, "Imagining." Catherine Palczewski calls attention to restrictive models of public engagement that privilege narrow conceptions of reason and argument; see "Argument," 4.
117. Dewey, *Public and Its Problems*, 211.
118. Watts, "Pragmatist Publicity," 42. Watts notes that Dewey was familiar with Du Bois and other African American intellectuals in New York, making research trips to Harlem and emceeing the 1927 literary award dinner for *Opportunity*, a journal of the National Urban League (57).
119. Ibid., 49.
120. Glaude, *In a Shade of Blue*, 39. While race did not appear as a major theme in Dewey's scholarship, Glaude does see in Dewey's "political choices . . . a desire to end racism . . . [and an] interest in the challenge race and racism posed to his conception of democracy" (17).
121. Ibid., 131, 19.
122. Ibid., 148.
123. R. Slater, "First Black Faculty Members," 102. Slater reports that Columbia could not identify the first Black professor hired at the university.
124. Squires, "Rethinking," 448.
125. Squires, "Black Press."
126. Brouwer, "Communication as Counterpublic," 200. Emphasis in original.
127. Fraser, "Rethinking the Public Sphere," 120.
128. See Sowards and Renegar, "Reconceptualizing Rhetorical Activism"; McCann, "Queering Expertise"; and Larson, "Everything Inside Me."

CHAPTER 2

1. Aune, *Selling the Free Market*, 40. See also Aune, "How to Read." Aune adopts the concept of "realist style" from Robert Hariman. See Hariman, *Political Style*.
2. Friedman and Friedman, *Capitalism and Freedom*, 200.
3. Friedman and Friedman, *Free to Choose*, 193.
4. Friedman and Friedman, "Foundations," 198.
5. Friedman and Friedman, *Tyranny*.
6. Friedman, "Interview," 83. Along these lines, Paul Turpin discerns in *Capitalism and Freedom* an effort to enlist "the reader's identification with moral disapproval of

those who would thwart competition" (*Moral Rhetoric,* 3). See also Colombini, "Energeia, Kinesis," 182.

7. For a distilled discussion of this quality of neoliberal theory, see W. Davies, "What Is 'Neo.'"

8. Friedman and Friedman, *Free to Choose,* 26.

9. Friedman and Friedman, *Capitalism and Freedom,* 13.

10. Ibid., 12. In this example, the Friedmans appeared to stipulate a more isolated existence for Crusoe than the plot of the novel by Daniel Defoe, as they imagined a titular character living entirely "without his Man Friday" and, presumably, other human encounters (12).

11. On the policy influence of the Friedmans, see Peck, *Constructions of Neoliberal Reason,* and Jones, *Masters of the Universe.*

12. See Carl, *Freedom of Choice,* and Hentschke, "Brief and Future History."

13. Friedman and Friedman, *Capitalism and Freedom,* 1–2.

14. Friedman and Friedman, *Free to Choose,* 128, 129, 132.

15. Ibid., 144, 135.

16. Ibid., 297.

17. Friedman, "Interview," 72.

18. Friedman and Friedman, *Capitalism and Freedom,* 4.

19. Friedman and Friedman, *Free to Choose,* 27.

20. Friedman and Friedman, *Capitalism and Freedom,* 33.

21. Ibid.

22. Friedman and Friedman, *Tyranny,* 136.

23. In this sense, the Friedmans' discussion of the individual and the family recalls Hannah Arendt's explication of the classical understanding of the space of the household as a realm of necessity against the freedom of the polis. Only the head of the household achieved freedom, and thus only the head of the household could act in the polis. One may discern a similar dynamic for the head of the family and market relations. See Arendt, *Human Condition,* 28–37.

24. Wendy Brown identifies a similar gendered dynamic in British prime minister Margaret Thatcher's remark from the 1980s that "there is no such thing as society. There are only individual men and women . . . and their families." For this quote and Brown's discussion of its entailments, see *Undoing the Demos,* 100–107.

25. Friedman and Friedman, *Capitalism and Freedom,* 33.

26. As Nancy Fraser and Linda Gordon explain, dependency is an "ideological term" that makes people's struggles appear as "individual problems, as much moral or psychological as economic" ("Genealogy of Dependency," 311).

27. Asen, *Visions of Poverty,* 41–43; L. Gordon, *Pitied but Not Entitled,* 254–56.

28. Katz, *Undeserving Poor,* 68–69, 151–65; Asen, *Visions of Poverty,* 165–223. For an analysis of the racialization of responsibility in terms of a contemporary case, see Foley, "Infantile Citizens."

29. Friedman and Friedman, *Tyranny,* 134.

30. Rebecca Dingo argues that the foregrounding of "personal responsibility" in policy discourses decontextualizes women's poverty by highlighting individual action while obscuring "long-standing ties between poverty and racism" and how "deindustrialization in the United States had caused a drop in middle-class incomes and a corresponding rise in service sector jobs that do not provide benefits for women" (*Networking Arguments,* 4).

31. Friedman and Friedman, *Capitalism and Freedom,* 15.

32. Friedman, *Bright Promises,* 84, 86.

33. Friedman and Friedman, *Capitalism and Freedom,* 12.

34. Ibid., 188.

35. Friedman, "Interview," 70.
36. Ibid., 71.
37. Friedman and Friedman, *Capitalism and Freedom*, 188.
38. Friedman and Friedman, *Free to Choose*, 2.
39. Friedman and Friedman, *Capitalism and Freedom*, 16.
40. Ibid., 15.
41. Ibid., 110.
42. For analyses of race, publics, and counterpublics, see, for example, Bruell, Mokre, and Siim, "Inclusion and Exclusion"; Kuo, "Racial Justice Activist Hashtags"; Jackson and Foucault Welles, "Hijacking #myNYPD"; and Squires, "Rethinking."
43. Friedman and Friedman, *Capitalism and Freedom*, 111.
44. Ibid., 2.
45. Friedman, "Interview," 73, 74.
46. Friedman and Friedman, *Capitalism and Freedom*, 86.
47. Friedman, "Foundations," 203.
48. Friedman and Friedman, *Tyranny*, 55–57, 61, 67, 166–67.
49. Friedman and Friedman, *Capitalism and Freedom*, 14.
50. Ibid., 13. Of the choices presented to the readers of *Capitalism and Freedom*, Paul Turpin writes, "This air of a disjunctive choice that is not really a choice at all indicates the constitutive rhetoric that underlines [the Friedmans'] argument here. No one of good character would be a proponent of collectivism and an enemy of capitalism" (*Moral Rhetoric*, 67).
51. Friedman, "Line We Dare Not Cross," 109.
52. Friedman and Friedman, *Free to Choose*, 66.
53. Friedman and Friedman, *Capitalism and Freedom*, 86.
54. In their discussion of government as umpire who acts in regard to a clearly articulated and consistently enforced set of rules, the Friedmans evoked Friedrich Hayek's discussion of the "Rule of Law" in *The Road to Serfdom*. According to Hayek, in free countries, the Rule of Law prevents arbitrary government action and enables individuals to predict the behavior of others (81, 88–89).
55. Friedman and Friedman, *Capitalism and Freedom*, 26.
56. Friedman, "Free Markets," 183.
57. See, for example, Brouwer, "Communication as Counterpublic," and Fraser, "Rethinking the Public Sphere."
58. Friedman and Friedman, *Free to Choose*, 13.
59. Friedman and Friedman, *Capitalism and Freedom*, 22–23, 34, 117, 188.
60. Ibid., 201, 202.
61. Friedman, "Foundations," 203.
62. Friedman and Friedman, *Capitalism and Freedom*, 23, 24.
63. Peck, *Constructions of Neoliberal Reason*, 121.
64. Burgin, "Age of Certainty," 208–9.
65. Chaput, *Market Affect*, 123–25; Chaput, "Rhetorical Situation," 201–4; Jack, "Milton Friedman's *Free to Choose*," 520, 525–26.
66. Jack, "Milton Friedman's *Free to Choose*."
67. Burgin, "Age of Certainty," 216. See also Peck, *Constructions of Neoliberal Reason*, 117, 123.
68. Chaput, "Rhetorical Situation," 204.
69. On this basis, Habermas formulates a principle of discourse ethics that states, "Only those norms can claim to be valid that meet (or could meet) with the approval of all affected in their capacity as *participants in a practical discourse*" ("Discourse Ethics," 66). Emphasis in original.

70. Friedman and Friedman, *Free to Choose*, 66.

71. Ibid., xvi.

72. Lippmann, *Phantom Public*, 29. Although not a neoliberal theorist himself, Lippmann's defense of the individual against government planning inspired neoliberal intellectuals, who met in Paris (with Lippmann in attendance) in 1938 to discuss his book *The Good Society*. This meeting served as a forerunner of the inaugural 1947 gathering of the Mont Pèlerin Society, which has served as an international network for neoliberal thinkers. For the proceedings of the 1938 Paris meeting, see Reinhoudt and Audier, *Walter Lippmann Colloquium*. On the early history of neoliberal thought, including the Paris meeting and the formation of the Mont Pèlerin Society, see Jackson, "Origins of Neo-liberalism," and Turner, "Rebirth of Liberalism."

73. Lippmann, *Phantom Public*, 41.

74. Ibid., 32.

75. Ben Jackson notes that Lippmann and Hayek exchanged favorable correspondence about each other's work. Hayek lauded *The Good Society* and promoted its wider reception in Europe. In his correspondence to Lippmann, Hayek explained that the book had motivated him to focus more directly on the relationship between intellectual freedom and economic planning. See Jackson, "Freedom, the Common Good."

76. Hayek, *Road to Serfdom*, 66. Milton Friedman wrote the introduction for the book's fiftieth-anniversary edition.

77. Ibid., 64.

78. See, for example, Brockriede, "Where Is Argument?"; Carcasson and Sprain, "Beyond Problem Solving"; Goodnight, "Personal, Technical"; Hicks, "Promise(s) of Deliberative Democracy"; and Kock and Villadsen, *Rhetorical Citizenship*.

79. Friedman and Friedman, *Free to Choose*, 157. Milton Friedman originally proposed the idea of educational vouchers in his 1955 essay "The Role of Government in Education." A revised version of this essay appeared as a chapter in *Capitalism and Freedom*. The Friedmans revisited the proposal for educational vouchers in *Free to Choose* and *Tyranny of the Status Quo*.

80. Friedman, "Prologue," vii.

81. In *Free to Choose*, the Friedmans explained that their policy views had changed such that they no longer supported public financing of education or compulsory attendance laws. They contended that the wealth of the contemporary United States and its "more evenly distributed income" would suffice to enable individual families to pay for the cost of schooling directly. Further, they held that widespread literacy and public recognition of the value of education would motivate most parents to send their children to schools. Nevertheless, they continued to advocate for vouchers as an acknowledgment of the political reality that Americans have supported public financing and compulsory attendance laws. See Friedman and Friedman, *Free to Choose*, 161–63.

82. Friedman and Friedman, *Capitalism and Freedom*, 90.

83. In his argument against democratic education, Mark Pennington defends a minimal set of values that a privatized education system should respect: "toleration, secure possession of property, voluntary contract, and the prevention of violence and fraud" ("Against Democratic Education," 6).

84. Quoted in Hall and Derby, "Gov. Scott Walker." In recent years, other state governors have decried particular college majors as frivolous and unworthy of public financial support. See, for example, Anderson, "Rick Scott," and Seltzer, "Disparaging Interpretive Dance."

85. Friedman and Friedman, *Capitalism and Freedom*, 89.

86. Thernstrom, "Culture of Choice," 35.

87. Coons, "Give Us Liberty," 61.

88. Friedman and Friedman, *Capitalism and Freedom*, 91.

89. Pennington, "Against Democratic Education," 21.

90. Ibid., 30.

91. On rising public concerns about the quality of schooling in the 1970s and 1980s, see Asen, *Democracy, Deliberation, and Education*, 25–26; P. Graham, *Schooling America*; and McIntush, "Defining Education."

92. Friedman and Friedman, *Free to Choose*, 152. On the widespread attention paid to *A Nation at Risk*, see Toch, *In the Name*.

93. Quoted in Friedman and Friedman, *Free to Choose*, 151.

94. Hlavacik, *Assigning Blame*, 34.

95. Friedman and Friedman, *Free to Choose*, 160.

96. Pennington, "Against Democratic Education," 11. Emphasis in original.

97. Friedman and Friedman, *Free to Choose*, 170.

CHAPTER 3

1. Prior to the passage of the 1965 Elementary and Secondary Education Act (ESEA), the federal government had provided only modest support for K–12 education through such programs as the 1917 Smith-Hughes Act, which addressed vocational education, and the 1958 National Defense Education Act, which concentrated on math, science, and foreign-language instruction. See McGuinn, "Education Policy," 191–94, and McGuinn, *No Child Left Behind*, 25–28. The ESEA represented the first significant, wide-ranging federal effort. See H. Graham, *Uncertain Triumph*, and Jeffrey, *Education for Children*.

2. Johnson, *Public Papers*, 1:25–26. Emphasis in original.

3. Ibid., 1:27, 28. Similarly, in testimony before the Senate Subcommittee on Education, Sargent Shriver, director of the Office of Economic Opportunity, linked the potential successes of K–12 education policy and the War on Poverty. US Senate Subcommittee on Education, *Elementary and Secondary Education*, 2614–17.

4. Johnson, *Public Papers*, 1:26.

5. Elizabeth DeBray-Pelot and Patrick McGuinn write that the "ESEA of 1965 enshrined an equity rationale at the heart of federal education policy" ("New Politics of Education," 17).

6. G. W. Bush, *Public Papers*, 1:17. For an overview of accountability approaches across the history of US education, see McDermott, *High-Stakes Reform*.

7. Obama, *Public Papers*, 2:1632.

8. On income, see Krugman, *Age of Diminished Expectations*, 3. For general discussions of the United States in the 1970s, see Carroll, *It Seemed Like Nothing*, and Schulman, *Seventies*. On declining trust, see American National Election Studies, "ANES Guide to Public Opinion"; Davis and Smith, *General Social Surveys*; and Norris, *Democratic Deficits*.

9. Stuart Hall and Alan O'Shea argue that neoliberalism as common sense "offers us frameworks of meaning with which to make sense of the world" ("Common-Sense Neoliberalism," 8). Relatedly, Doreen Massey maintains that a "vocabulary of customer, consumer, choice, markets and self interest moulds both our conception of ourselves and our understanding of and relationship to the world" ("Vocabularies of the Economy," 11).

10. Reagan, *Public Papers*, 1:1.

11. Foucault, *Birth of Biopolitics*, 147.

12. DeVos, "Competition, Creativity and Choice," 5, 9.

13. Pfister, "Terms of Technoliberalism," 37. Pfister extends the work of anthropologist Thomas Malaby, who coined the term "technoliberalism"; see Malaby, *Making Virtual Worlds*.

14. Carter, *Public Papers*, 2:1237.

15. On opposition to busing, see Delmont, *Why Busing Failed*. On growing public concerns with schooling, see Gallup, "12th Annual," 34–35, and Tyack and Cuban, *Tinkering Toward Utopia*.

16. Prior to the launch of the department, federal education policy had been the responsibility of the Department of Health, Education, and Welfare. On the creation and history of the US Department of Education, see Cross, *Political Education*; G. Davies, *See Government Grow*; and Stallings, "Brief History." On Reagan's opposition to the department, and his eventual acquiescence, see Clabaugh, "Educational Legacy," and "Education Dept." For a first-person account from Reagan's first education secretary, see Bell, "Education Policy Development."

17. Thomas Toch explains that *A Nation at Risk* attracted so much attention that "within ten months of its release 150,000 copies had been distributed by the Department of Education, another 70,000 had been purchased through the Government Printing Office, and several million additional copies and extended excerpts were estimated to be in circulation through reprints in the general and professional press" (*In the Name*, 15).

18. Mehta, "How Paradigms Create Politics," 91–93. Patricia Albjerg Graham maintains that *A Nation at Risk* turned "dissatisfaction with the academic performance of most American children [into a] national political issue" (*Schooling America*, 159). See also Goldberg and Renton, "Nation at Risk."

19. McIntush, "Defining Education," 421.

20. National Commission, *Nation at Risk*, 5, 6.

21. McDonnell, "No Child Left Behind," 25; Vinovskis, "Gubernatorial Leadership," 191–93.

22. For an overview of the events leading to the summit, see Vinovskis, *Road to Charlottesville*. On Bush's education discourse, see McIntush, "Political Truancy," and Staton and Peeples, "Education Reform."

23. G. H. W. Bush, *Public Papers*, 2:1279.

24. Clinton, "Foreword," xii.

25. Mehta, *Allure of Order*, 224–32. For an overview of standards-based initiatives in the 1990s, see Jennings, *Why National Standards*.

26. For an overview of NCLB, see Hayes, *No Child Left Behind*.

27. For detailed accounts of the legislative process for NCLB, see ibid., 165–77, and DeBray, *Politics, Ideology and Education*, 81–125.

28. See Apple, "Ideological Success, Educational Failure?"; Burch, *Hidden Markets*; Fusarelli and Fusarelli, "Federal Education Policy"; Henig, "Education Policy"; and Ravitch, *Reign of Error*.

29. See McGuinn, "Stimulating Reform." Emphasizing a connection between charter schools and markets, one critic held that "the privatization of education through charter schools will deliver market-based decision making to the classroom"; see Onosko, "Race to the Top," 2. Noting that both NCLB and Race to the Top promoted "competitive market structures" in education policy, Sarah Galey writes that Race to the Top "maintained the general course set by the [NCLB] law, but focused more on incentives and building state capacity to achieve performance-related goals—using the 'carrot' rather than the 'stick' to motivate reform efforts" ("Education Politics and Policy," S15).

30. On the role of foundations as institutional actors that have promoted market-based reforms, see Reckhow, *Follow the Money*.

31. See McDonnell, "Educational Accountability."

32. See Manna, *Collison Course*; Sunderman and Kim, "Expansion of Federal Power." In this spirit, in its 1973 *San Antonio Independent School District v. Rodriguez* decision, the US Supreme Court rejected the idea that education represented a basic constitutional right. See Ryan, *Five Miles Away*, and Walsh, "Erasing Race."

33. Quoted in Schneider, "'Opt-Out' Movement." On the nationwide resistance to testing, see Kamenetz, "Anti-Test," and Wallace, "Parents."

34. Obama, *Public Papers*, 2:1168.

35. For overviews of the ESSA, see Education Commission, "ESSA," and Meibaum, "Overview."

36. Obama, "Remarks by the President."

37. Paul Peterson, a prominent education scholar and supporter of market-based reforms, has written that the end of the regulatory era represented by NCLB and Race to the Top presents a new opportunity to introduce "competition"—exemplified by charters, tax credits, and vouchers—into American education: "Such competition is the best hope for American schools, because today's public schools show little capacity to improve on their own" ("End," 23).

38. Huetteman and Alcindor, "Betsy DeVos." Fox News television personality and syndicated columnist John Stossel praised the selection. Denouncing "government-run schools," he countered that "my consumer reporting taught me that things only work well when they are subject to market competition. Services improve when people are free to shop around and when competitive pressure inspires suppliers to invent better ways of doing things" ("What's So Wrong").

39. Klein, "DeVos Would Be First"; Mayer, "Betsy DeVos."

40. E. Brown, "Trump Picks Billionaire"; Zernike, "Betsy DeVos."

41. Leadership Conference, "Civil and Human Rights." See also Ujifusa, "Civil Rights Groups."

42. US Senate Subcommittee on Health, Education, Labor, and Pensions, *Nomination of Betsy DeVos*, 4, 42, 21.

43. See Chingos, "Why the Proficiency-Versus-Growth Debate."

44. US Senate Subcommittee on Health, Education, Labor, and Pensions, *Nomination of Betsy DeVos*, 43.

45. Douglas-Gabriel and Jan, "DeVos Called HBCUs 'Pioneers.'"

46. Stahl, "Interview with Betsy DeVos." For news media reactions to the interview, see, for example, Cillizza, "Betsy DeVos' Trainwreck Interview"; Kamenetz, "Rocky Appearance for DeVos"; and Strauss, "Education Secretary Betsy DeVos."

47. See Strauss, "Omarosa Claims Betsy DeVos."

48. US Senate Subcommittee on Labor, Health and Human Services, Education, and Related Agencies, *Appropriations for Fiscal Year 2018*, 27–28, 43–44.

49. US House Subcommittee on Labor, Health and Human Services, Education, and Related Agencies, *Appropriations for Fiscal Year 2018*, 309–10.

50. US House Subcommittee on Labor, Health and Human Services, Education, and Related Agencies, *Appropriations for Fiscal Year 2019*, 271.

51. Lincoln Dahlberg writes that visibility, as a public practice, invites at least two readings, one critical and the other more manipulative. As a critical practice, visibility invokes "insight, illumination, lucidity, recognition, intelligibility and understanding." Less critically, "visibility can also be articulated to describe publicity in the sense of public relations or marketing" ("Visibility," 35).

52. Klein, "Betsy DeVos Finds." On DeVos's "Rethink School" tour, see Klein, "Scenes," and Strauss, "In Front of Kids."

53. On the K–12-related changes in the tax law, see Leamy, "You Can Now Use," and Saunders, "New Tax Law."

54. Scholars in rhetoric and communication, political science, and other fields have conducted extensive research on the presidential bully pulpit. In contrast, to my knowledge, comparatively little scholarship has focused on the public advocacy of cabinet secretaries, especially from scholars in rhetoric and communication. For analyses of the public roles of education secretaries in larger administration campaigns, see Finn, "Education Policy," and Smith, Levin, and Cianci, "Beyond a Legislative Agenda." For reflections from former education secretaries on their public roles (among other aspects of their jobs), see Bell, "Memo to the Secretary," and Riley, "Reflections on Goals 2000." There has been some research on the persuasive opportunities available to state education chiefs. See Hill and Jochim, *Power of Persuasion*, and Rhim and Redding, "Leveraging the Bully Pulpit."

55. Education Commission, "ESSA," 26. See also Weiss and McGuinn, "States as Change Agents."

56. DeVos, "Keynote Address to the Council."

57. See, for example, DeVos, "US Secretary of Education Betsy DeVos' Prepared Remarks at HBCU."

58. DeVos, "Keynote Address to the 2017 National Policy Summit."

59. Klein, "Betsy DeVos Finds."

60. Green, "Bethune-Cookman Graduates."

61. Curtis, "Protests at Bethune-Cookman."

62. Fernandes and Johnson, "Hundreds Protest DeVos"; Natanson, "Hundreds Protest Education Secretary"; Strauss, "When DeVos Spoke."

63. DeVos, "Secretary DeVos Remarks."

64. DeVos, "Competition, Creativity and Choice," 1; US Senate Subcommittee on Health, Education, Labor, and Pensions, *Nomination of Betsy DeVos*, 36; DeVos, "US Secretary of Education Betsy DeVos' Prepared Remarks to the Council"; DeVos, "Prepared Remarks by US Secretary of Education Betsy DeVos to the 2017 ASU."

65. Dewey, "Democracy Is Radical," 299.

66. Dewey, *Democracy and Education*, 19, 76.

67. See, for example, DeVos, "Remarks by US Education Secretary DeVos to the Washington Policy Center," and DeVos, "Secretary DeVos Remarks."

68. DeVos, "Keynote Address to the 2017 National Policy Summit." See also, for example, DeVos, "Prepared Remarks to the National Parent Teacher Association"; DeVos, "Remarks by Secretary DeVos to the Michigan Community College Association"; and DeVos, "Secretary Betsy DeVos Prepared Remarks National Alliance."

69. DeVos, "Bush-Obama School Reform." See also DeVos, "Prepared Remarks to the American Enterprise Institute."

70. Damien Smith Pfister and Misti Yang write that "technoliberalism focuses on contriving technical systems to change culture, at the expense of democratic argument and deliberation" ("Five Theses on Technoliberalism," 253). Argument and deliberation invite inquiry and reflection, potentially questioning the unchallenged optimality of change.

71. DeVos, "Prepared Remarks by Secretary of Education Betsy DeVos to the National Lieutenant Governors Association"; DeVos, "Prepared Remarks by Secretary DeVos to Students."

72. DeVos, "Prepared Remarks by Secretary of Education Betsy DeVos to the National Lieutenant Governors Association."

73. DeVos, "Keynote Remarks at the 2016 Education Choice."

74. DeVos, "Prepared Remarks by US Secretary of Education Betsy DeVos to SXSW."

75. See Easter and Dave, "Remember When Amazon."

76. DeVos, "Betsy DeVos' Entire CPAC Speech"; DeVos, "Education Secretary Betsy DeVos Addresses ALEC."

77. DeVos, "Bush-Obama School Reform"; DeVos, "Prepared Remarks by US Secretary of Education Betsy DeVos to SXSW."

78. DeVos, "Secretary DeVos Remarks"; DeVos, "Bush-Obama School Reform."

79. DeVos, "Prepared Remarks by Secretary DeVos to Students"; DeVos, "Rethink School Tour."

80. DeVos, "Secretary Betsy DeVos Prepared Remarks National Alliance."

81. Friedman and Friedman, *Capitalism and Freedom*, 15–16.

82. DeVos, "Prepared Remarks by Secretary DeVos to the Alfred E. Smith Foundation." See also, DeVos, "Rethink School Tour," and DeVos, "Secretary DeVos Remarks."

83. Friedman and Friedman, *Tyranny*, 136.

84. See, for example, DeVos, "Betsy DeVos' Entire CPAC Speech"; DeVos, "Keynote at National Summit."

85. See Obama, "Remarks by the President."

86. Stephen Macedo writes that "the nexus of home ownership, local funding and control of schools, and the power of local communities to zone to exclude the poor provides enormous positional advantages to those who can afford to live where the best schools are" ("Property-Owning Plutocracy," 33).

87. DeVos, "Keynote Address to the 2017 National Policy Summit."

88. DeVos, "Education Secretary Betsy DeVos Addresses ALEC"; DeVos, "US Secretary of Education Betsy DeVos Addressed the National Association."

89. DeVos, "Prepared Remarks by US Secretary of Education Betsy DeVos to the US Conference."

90. DeVos, "Transcript of Education Secretary."

91. US House Subcommittee on Labor, Health and Human Services, Education, and Related Agencies, *Appropriations for Fiscal Year 2018*, 298.

92. US Senate Subcommittee on Labor, Health and Human Services, Education, and Related Agencies, *Appropriations for Fiscal Year 2018*, 43. In a separate exchange about protections against profiteering by private companies, after DeVos reiterated the protections of choice, Senator Chris Murphy retorted sardonically, "I understand that you have a belief in the market, that that will end up solving the problems that may encounter" (40).

93. DeVos, "Keynote Remarks at the 2016 Education Choice." In support of DeVos, Senator John Kennedy observed during a Senate hearing that "I can go down to my overpriced Capitol Hill grocery this afternoon and choose among six different types of mayonnaise. How come I cannot do that for my kid in school?" Rejecting this equivalence, Senator Murphy subsequently retorted, "The day that we start treating the education of our children like we do the marketing of a condiment is the day that we have given up on our kids." US Senate Subcommittee on Labor, Health and Human Services, Education, and Related Agencies, *Appropriations for Fiscal Year 2018*, 35, 39.

94. DeVos, "Prepared Remarks to the National Parent Teacher Association."

95. DeVos, "US Secretary of Education Betsy DeVos' Prepared Remarks to the Council."

96. DeVos, "Bush-Obama School Reform"; DeVos, "US Secretary of Education Betsy DeVos' Prepared Remarks to the Council."

97. Friedman and Friedman, *Capitalism and Freedom*, 188.

98. DeVos, "Bush-Obama School Reform."

99. US House Subcommittee on Labor, Health and Human Services, Education, and Related Agencies, *Appropriations for Fiscal Year 2018*, 285, 312.

100. DeVos, "Transcript of Education Secretary."

101. DeVos, "Bethune-Cookman 2017 Commencement"; DeVos, "US Secretary of Education Betsy DeVos' Prepared Remarks at HBCU."

102. Scott, "Rosa Parks Moment?," 6, 8.

103. DeVos, "President Trump Delivers."

104. Gooden, Jabbar, and Torres maintain that "proponents of vouchers who use market-based language never consider that the economic hardships faced by students in inner-city schools may be related to markets and race in the first place" ("Race and School Vouchers," 532–33). They argue that proper consideration of race and vouchers requires explicit attention to structural issues.

105. Barkan, "Miseducation of Betsy DeVos," 141. See also Meckler, "Education of Betsy DeVos."

106. DeVos, "Secretary DeVos Remarks."

107. Pfister and Yang, "Five Theses on Technoliberalism," 254.

108. Quoted in ibid., 255.

CHAPTER 4

1. Carl, *Freedom of Choice*, 127–33; Witte, *Market Approach to Education*, 43–46.

2. Kemble, "Wisconsin's Voucher Vultures." Shortly after Betsy DeVos's confirmation as education secretary, the *New York Times* reported that "a new wave of research has emerged suggesting that private school vouchers may harm students who receive them." In short succession, studies of voucher programs in Indiana, Louisiana, and Ohio all indicated negative outcomes for participating students (Carey, "Dismal Results from Vouchers"). Lubienski and Brewer conclude that "although voucher advocates frequently make claims about the effectiveness of vouchers for boosting student achievement . . . the fact is that, in most of these cases, vouchers simply have no discernable or consistent impact on student learning" ("Analysis of Voucher Advocacy," 462). See also Carnoy, "School Vouchers," and Lubienski and Lubienski, "Is There a 'Consensus.'"

3. See Glickstein, "Inequalities in Educational Financing," and Macedo, "Property-Owning Plutocracy."

4. Pennington, "Against Democratic Education." See also Lubienski and Garn, "Evidence and Ideology."

5. Bruecker, *Assessing the Fiscal Impact*; Shuls, "Financing School Choice."

6. Moreover, as I argue in chapter 2, the framing of discrimination as choice obfuscates the structural dynamics of racism.

7. Carl, *Freedom of Choice*, 91–92; Ford, Johnson, and Partelow, "Racist Origins."

8. Casey, "When Privatization Means Segregation"; Gooden, Jabbar, and Torres, "Race and School Vouchers," 524–25.

9. Epps-Robertson, "Race to Erase Brown," 114.

10. The Friedmans addressed the Virginia vouchers in *Capitalism and Freedom*. They explained that school segregation presented a difficult problem for believers in freedom, since its redress presumably required government action. Forced to accept either "enforced segregation or enforced integration," they indicated that they would choose the latter. However, the Friedmans retorted that vouchers presented a solution that resolved this apparent dilemma: "The appropriate solution is to eliminate government operation of the schools and permit parents to choose the kind of school they want their children to attend." Outside of government, individuals could "try by speech and behavior to foster the growth of attitudes and opinions that would lead mixed schools to become the rule and segregated schools the rare exception." Indeed, the Friedmans

offered an optimistic outlook for vouchers in Virginia: "Though adopted for the purpose of avoiding compulsory integration, [we] predict that the results of the law will be very different" (117–18). Given the widely publicized strategy of massive resistance occurring across the South at the time, this prediction appeared to express willful ignorance and/ or bad faith. Further, their call to change attitudes and opinions confronted the tensions of their appeals to persuasion, as I discuss in chapter 2.

11. Quoted in Jensen, "Alternative Ideology."

12. Ibid.

13. F. Brown, "Privatization and Urban Education," 208–9.

14. Wisconsin Department of Public Instruction, "Statewide Voucher Program Enrollment."

15. Wisconsin Joint Finance Committee, "2015–17 Biennial Budget Executive Session (Part 3)."

16. The public portion of the committee's engagement with the state budget consists of three stages. First, after the governor has released a budget proposal, the Joint Finance Committee holds hearings featuring testimony from the heads of state agencies and departments, who endorse and/or raise concerns about the proposed budget and answer questions from committee members. The second stage consists of listening sessions hosted by the committee in different regions of the state in which local officials, including district superintendents and school board members, and nonelected Wisconsin residents may sign up to address the committee. Speakers are typically allocated two minutes, and a single listening session usually lasts an entire day. During these sessions, save for administrative roles like calling up speakers and timekeeping, committee members do not speak. The third stage of engagement consists of a publicly viewable executive session in which the Joint Finance Committee discusses and votes on specific budget allocations and other items for state agencies and departments as well as amendments offered by committee members.

17. Jensen, "Alternative Ideology."

18. Dougherty, More Than One Struggle.

19. The court decision is quoted in Stolee, "Milwaukee Desegregation Case," 246.

20. Carl, Freedom of Choice, 104. In the first few years of the Milwaukee voucher program, prior to the extension of the program to religious schools, large majorities of students attended three nondenominational, independent community schools in the central city. Two of these schools, Harambee Community School and Urban Day School, were successful Black-led institutions serving a predominantly Black student population. The third school, Bruce-Guadalupe Community School, primarily served a Latinx student population. See Carl, Freedom of Choice, 107–8.

21. Pugh, "Private School," 17. In 1996, Williams introduced an unsuccessful bill in the legislature to rescind the 1995 expansion. Carl, Freedom of Choice, 182.

22. Pugh, "Private School Choice Programs," 23. See also Ford, Consequences of Governance Fragmentation, 67–80.

23. Pugh, "Private School Choice Programs," 3. The original legislation limited participation to families with incomes up to 175 percent of the federal poverty level. The family income limit was raised to 300 percent of the federal poverty level in 2011.

24. Witte, Market Approach to Education, 107.

25. Ibid., 85–86.

26. Ford and Andersson, "Determinants of Organizational Failure," 16. Michael Ford reports that roughly 12 percent of total state expenditures for the MPCP between 1991 and 2013 went to schools that closed; see "Funding Impermanence," 899.

27. Pugh, "Private School Choice Programs," 2–3.

28. Bruecker, *Assessing the Fiscal Impact*, 10.

29. Pugh, "Private School Choice Programs," 3; Posey, "Household Income," 3. Families earning up to 185 percent of the poverty level (excluding the "marriage bonus") could participate in the WPCP.

30. Pugh, "Estimated Per Pupil Payments." For examples of the widespread media coverage of this memo, see, for example, Bauer, "Audit"; Beck, "Memo"; and Richards and Hahn, "Vouchers Could Shift."

31. Cierniak, Stewart, and Ruddy, *Mapping the Growth*.

32. Wermund, "Vouchers."

33. Bolick, "Voting Down Vouchers." In 1990, when the Wisconsin superintendent of public instruction imposed additional regulations on the MPCP schools that went beyond the requirements prescribed in the law, participating parents and schools sued. Polly Williams organized the plaintiffs and selected Clint Bolick to represent them. Carl, *Freedom of Choice*, 178.

34. In a 2017 poll conducted by the Associated Press–NORC Center for Public Affairs Research, support for vouchers dropped from 43 percent to 22 percent when respondents favoring vouchers were asked if they would still support vouchers if this meant that public schools would receive less money. Associated Press–NORC Center for Public Affairs Research, "Education."

35. Wisconsin Joint Finance Committee, "2015–17 Biennial Budget Executive Session (Part 3)."

36. Hess, "Does School Choice Work?," 38, 49.

37. Between 2011 and 2017, membership in the Wisconsin Education Association Council declined by 67 percent; see Rochester, "Wisconsin Teachers' Union." For a detailed account of the debates, protests, and drama that accompanied the Wisconsin Budget Repair Bill from two reporters who covered the events, see Stein and Marley, *More Than They Bargained For*.

38. DeFour, "Budget Cuts"; Wisconsin Department of Public Instruction, "Summary."

39. Walker, "Why I'm Fighting."

40. Beck, "Conservative Study"; Sommerhauser, "New State Data."

41. Wisconsin Department of Public Instruction, "Official Report Shows Cuts."

42. Swalwell et al., "In the Aftermath."

43. S. Gordon, "Western Wisconsin Schools"; Milewski, "Blame Attacks"; Richards and Kulling, "School Districts Scramble."

44. Wisconsin Joint Finance Committee, "Public Hearing in Milwaukee (Part 2)."

45. Wisconsin Joint Finance Committee, "Public Hearing in Brillion (Part 1)."

46. Wisconsin Joint Finance Committee, "Public Hearing in Rice Lake (Part 2)."

47. Wisconsin Joint Finance Committee, "Public Hearing in Milwaukee (Part 1)."

48. Walker, "Why I'm Fighting." Governor Walker also made this claim in his 2011 budget address; see "2011 Budget Address."

49. Jaffe, "Fight Against Austerity"; Teaching Assistants' Association, "History."

50. See, for example, Davey and Greenhouse, "Angry Demonstrations in Wisconsin"; Sewell, "Protestors Out in Force."

51. Slosarski, "Jamming Market Rhetoric."

52. Stein and Marley, *More Than They Bargained For*, xvi–xvii.

53. J. Slater, *Public Workers*.

54. Quoted in Bice, "Thompson the Governor."

55. Gilbert, "Dividing Lines"; National Conference of State Legislatures, *State Legislative Policymaking*.

56. Quoted in Stein and Marley, *More Than They Bargained For*, 57. During Walker's short-lived 2015 presidential campaign, news accounts would regularly relay his love of

Reagan. These stories explained that Walker and his wife, Tonette, ate Reagan's favorite foods on the anniversary of the former president's birthday, which coincidentally was the same date as their wedding anniversary. On this point, Governor Walker joked, "Truth be told, Tonette would tell you, I know our wedding anniversary because it's Ronald Reagan's birthday" (quoted in Healy, "How Is Scott Walker"). See also, for example, Prokop, "Scott Walker Loves Ronald Reagan."

57. Reagan, *Public Papers*, 1:1.

58. Walker, "2011 Inaugural Address."

59. Walker, "2013 Budget Address."

60. Walker, "2013 State of the State."

61. Walker, "Excerpt from Governor."

62. Walker, "2015 State of the State." See also Walker, "2015 Budget Address," and Walker, "Walker: We Changed."

63. Walker, "Walker: We Changed."

64. Wisconsin Joint Finance Committee, "2013–15 Budget Briefing."

65. Wisconsin Joint Finance Committee, "2015–17 Biennial Budget Executive Session (Part 3)."

66. Wisconsin Joint Finance Committee, "2013–15 Budget Briefing."

67. Ibid.

68. Ibid.

69. Wisconsin Joint Finance Committee, "2015–17 Budget Briefing."

70. Wisconsin Joint Finance Committee, "2015–17 Biennial Budget Executive Session (Part 3)"; Wisconsin Joint Finance Committee, "2015–17 Budget Briefing."

71. Wisconsin Joint Finance Committee, "2013–15 Budget Briefing."

72. Wisconsin Joint Finance Committee, "Public Hearing in Reedsburg (Part 1)."

73. Wisconsin Joint Finance Committee, "Public Hearing in Brillion (Part 1)"; Wisconsin Joint Finance Committee, "Public Hearing in Rice Lake (Part 1)."

74. Wisconsin Joint Finance Committee, "2015–17 Budget Briefing"; Wisconsin Joint Finance Committee, "Public Hearing in Reedsburg (Part 1)."

75. Associated Press, "Former Speakers Lobbying." In the same story, the Associated Press also reported that two Republican senators—one of whom was Senate president Mike Ellis—stated they would oppose the expansion of vouchers unless the legislation required approval in the affected districts through a local referendum. Given the Republicans' eighteen-to-fifteen majority in the Senate, this would have effectively ensured local community approval of vouchers. However, this provision never appeared in the legislation.

76. American Federation for Children, *2012 Election Impact Report*, 11.

77. Kemble, "Wisconsin's Voucher Vultures."

78. Wisconsin Joint Finance Committee, "Public Hearing in Greendale (Part 1)."

79. Wisconsin Joint Finance Committee, "Public Hearing in Green Bay (Part 1)."

80. Wisconsin Joint Finance Committee, "2015–17 Biennial Budget Executive Session (Part 3)."

81. Wisconsin Joint Finance Committee, "Public Hearing in Milwaukee (Part 3)"; Wisconsin Joint Finance Committee, "Public Hearing in Milwaukee (Part 2)." As Julie Underwood explains, the American Legislative Exchange Council, which has drafted model legislation for state legislatures, supports "privatizing education through vouchers, charters and tax incentives" ("School Boards Beware," 18).

82. Wisconsin Joint Finance Committee, "Public Hearing in Brillion (Part 2)."

83. Chapman and Antrop-González, "Critical Look at Choice," 802. Carrie Sampson and Melanie Bertrand explain that "whiteness as property implies that individuals and groups associated with the social construction of whiteness benefit from legalized rules,

systems, and institutions, which conversely disadvantage minoritized people" (Sampson and Bertrand, "This Is Civil Disobedience"). Sampson and Bertrand apply this concept to their analysis of school board meetings to demonstrate how ostensibly neutral rules and procedures disempower Black participants seeking to advance equity-oriented policies.

84. Wisconsin Joint Finance Committee, "2015–17 Biennial Budget Executive Session (Part 3)." During a 2015 listening session in Milwaukee, Darienne Driver, superintendent of Milwaukee Public Schools, maintained that "education is the civil rights issue of our generation" (Wisconsin Joint Finance Committee, "Public Hearing in Milwaukee [Part 1]"). Driver opposed vouchers, yet, as Janelle Scott explains, contemporary voucher advocates have made a habit of aligning their cause with the struggle for civil rights; see "Rosa Parks Moment?"

85. Wisconsin Joint Finance Committee, "2015–17 Biennial Budget Executive Session (Part 3)."

86. Wisconsin Joint Finance Committee, "2015–17 Budget Briefing."

87. On the one-year anniversary of Eric Garner's death, Kirsten West Savali wrote, "Though the #BlackLivesMatter movement recently celebrated its two-year anniversary, it moved to the forefront of the nation's consciousness during the summer of death that began with Garner's killing on July 17, 2014" ("1 Year After").

88. Flores, "Choosing to Consume," 249.

89. Wisconsin Joint Finance Committee, "2015–17 Budget Briefing."

90. Flores, "Choosing to Consume," 245.

91. Policymakers and participants in the listening sessions opposing vouchers cited reports indicating that the large majority of WPCP students had previously attended private schools. For example, in a 2015 listening session in Reedsburg, Baraboo School Board member Doug Mering referenced the 75 percent statistic of private school students that I cite in the introduction. He urged the committee, "I implore you not to go ahead with this expansion proposal with its middle-class entitlement" (Wisconsin Joint Finance Committee, "Public Hearing in Reedsburg [Part 1]"). Representative Chris Taylor and Senator Lena Taylor also referenced this number during the committee's 2015 executive session; see Wisconsin Joint Finance Committee, "2015–17 Biennial Budget Executive Session (Part 3)."

92. See Asen, *Visions of Poverty*, 25–66.

93. On the school-to-prison pipeline in Wisconsin, see Garton, "Milwaukee Schools," and Spitzer-Resnick, "Student Discipline."

94. For an overview of the OSPP, see Wisconsin Legislative Audit Bureau, *Opportunity Schools and Partnership Program*.

95. Wisconsin Joint Finance Committee, "2015–17 Biennial Budget Executive Session (Part 3)."

96. Ibid.

97. Franklin, "New MU Law Poll."

98. Wisconsin Joint Finance Committee, "2013–15 Biennial Budget Executive Session (Part 4)."

99. Wisconsin Joint Finance Committee, "Public Hearing in Wisconsin Dells (Part 2)."

100. Ibid.

101. Wisconsin Joint Finance Committee, "Public Hearing in Brillion (Part 2)."

102. In addition to the 2013 poll I cite above, a 2015 Marquette Law School poll conducted as the Joint Finance Committee 2015–17 budget listening sessions concluded also found strong support for public education as well as a majority of respondents opposed to voucher expansion. See Franklin, "Marquette Law School Poll."

CHAPTER 5

1. Dewey, *Democracy and Education*, 19.
2. Dewey, "Creative Democracy," 229.
3. To coordinate our approaches, we conducted the first three interviews together, each with an individual advocate. Of the thirty-two additional interviews, Kelly Jensen conducted thirteen of them, while I conducted nineteen. All of these additional interviews were one-on-one, except for one interview with three advocates from the same group, which Kelly Jensen conducted. The analysis of these thirty-five interviews presented in this chapter is entirely my own. In terms of recruiting interviewees, we started by contacting groups with whom I had become familiar by reading about their activities in Wisconsin newspapers and following them through social media. At the conclusion of each interview, we asked everyone to identify other people we should meet. We followed up on some, but not all, of these names to create a manageable interview pool that exhibited diversity and represented the different regions of the state. We also sought to balance the number of interviews with advocates from the state's two largest cities, Milwaukee and Madison, with advocates from smaller cities and rural areas.
4. Of the thirty-seven people we interviewed, seven identified as African American (19 percent of the interview pool), two identified as Latinx (5.4 percent of the interview pool), and two identified as American Indian (5.4 percent of the interview pool). According to the US Census Bureau, the 2018 demographics of the state of Wisconsin, in comparison to the demographics of the interview pool, were 81.1 percent white (non-Hispanic/Latinx), 6.7 percent Black, 6.9 percent Hispanic/Latinx, and 1.2 percent American Indian; see "Quick Facts." We received the names of some Asian American advocates (3 percent of the state population), but we were unsuccessful in our attempts to contact them.
5. Williams, *Keywords*, 75–76.
6. For an intellectual history of the concept of community and its implications for theories of communication, see Depew and Peters, "Community and Communication."
7. Secomb, "Fractured Community," 134, 142.
8. Stuckey and O'Rourke, "Civility, Democracy," 714.
9. Bettez, "Critical Community Building," 7.
10. In her study of fan-based citizenship, Ashley Hinck illuminates a mode of community-building and public engagement that could operate in school settings. For instance, Hinck considers the public engagement of some Harry Potter fans. One could imagine a school book club adopting this model. See Hinck, *Politics for the Love*.
11. Clark, "Rescuing the Discourse," 63. See also Abowitz, "Reclaiming Community."
12. McClish and Bacon, "Taking Agency, Constituting Community," 5, 6.
13. Young, "Ideal of Community," 20, 21.
14. Campbell, "Agency," 4.
15. Wanzer-Serrano, *New York Young Lords*, 171.
16. Dewey, *Public and Its Problems*, 213.
17. Depew and Peters, "Community and Communication," 4–5.
18. Ronald Arnett writes that *"community is both inclusive and exclusive"* ("Communication and Community," 27). Emphasis in original. Michael Hogan holds that "the problem of community is rooted in enduring moral conflicts," and that communities must negotiate tensions between sustaining themselves and "relating constructively to those outside the group" ("Conclusion," 295–96).
19. Bettez, "Critical Community Building," 10.
20. Loehwing, *Homeless Advocacy*, 82, 88–89. In another case, Colette Cann and Eric DeMeulenaere narrate their experiences, with both successes and failures, of

bringing together their mostly white, middle- and upper-middle-class college students with the mostly Black and Brown, poor and working-class high school students living in the towns where their institutions are located. Cann and DeMeulenaere describe their work as creating "a discordant community," which they define as "a community based on difference that serves to challenge assumptions and raise critical (racial) conscious-ness so that individuals can work together across differences for greater social justice" ("Forged in the Crucibles," 49). Here, too, we may discern an effort to reconfigure com-munity boundaries across difference.

21. See "Milwaukee Community Schools Partnership." The program operates through three principles of shared leadership (engaging diverse stakeholders in articu-lating local strategies for educational success), equity (working to generate appropriate resources for local schools), and cultural relevance (attending to the distinctive qualities of schools, neighborhoods, and the people who inhabit them).

22. Tesfamichael, "Hundreds March to Wisconsin."

23. Dewey, *Public and Its Problems*, 216.

24. These tensions in Dewey's writings on race and community have led scholars to varying conclusions about the capacity for his theories to address contemporary rac-ism and anti-racist education. For example, John Rogers and Jeannie Oakes discern in Dewey the materials for an equity-oriented education that may empower low-income parents and parents of color; see "John Dewey Speaks." In contrast, Frank Margonis finds in Dewey's views of education a Eurocentric bias; see "John Dewey's Racialized Visions."

25. See, for example, Center on Wisconsin Strategy, "Wisconsin's Extreme Racial Disparity"; Larsen, "Wisconsin Considered"; "New 'Race in the Heartland'"; Robinson, "Racial Reckoning"; Wisconsin Council on Children and Families, *Race to Equity*.

26. In this formulation, I am invoking "constraint" in the tradition of Lloyd Bitz-er's understanding of the rhetorical situation. In Bitzer's conception, constraints do not necessarily refer to limits on human agency or unjust arrangements—although some constraints, like structural racism, certainly fit this description—but to "persons, events, objects, and relationships" that shape conditions for action ("Rhetorical Situation," 8). Insofar as they do not work from a blank canvas, agency and community-building always engage constraints.

27. For the history and operation of revenue limits, see Blair, "Wis. Districts Chafe"; Kava and Olin, "Local Government Expenditure"; and Reschovsky and Imazeki, "Achiev-ing Educational Adequacy."

28. In an early essay titled "The Ethics of Democracy," Dewey wrote of majority rule, "The heart of the matter is found not in the voting nor in the counting the votes to see where the majority lies. It is in the process by which the majority is formed" (234). See also Rogers, "Dewey and His Vision."

29. One African American advocate from Madison did reject democracy because of her concern that it would inevitably perpetuate societal inequalities. She explained that democracy does not consider "the wholeness and the needs of all involved in that situa-tion starting with the person that is most vulnerable. To me that's justice."

30. Scholars of deliberative democracy also have noted the benefits of collabora-tive processes. See, for example, Benhabib, "Toward a Deliberative Model," and Hicks, "Promise(s)."

31. For a theoretical explication of voice and rhetoric, see Watts, "'Voice' and 'Voicelessness.'"

32. Asen, *Democracy, Deliberation, and Education*, 175–77.

33. See Rai, "Power, Publics," and Tracy, *Challenges of Ordinary Democracy*.

34. Wisconsin Council on Children and Families, *Race to Equity*.

CONCLUSION

1. Burgum, Raza, and Vasquez, "Interview with Wendy Brown," 231. Brown maintains that "white entitlement and white supremacy" have been "savaged by the effects of neoliberalism which has moved jobs to other parts of the world, moved inexpensive labour forces into countries and neighbourhoods and cities that were a bit more homogenous in the past" (231). See also W. Brown, "Apocalyptic Populism," and Hamburger, "Wendy Brown." On the convergence of neoliberalism and "conservative family values," see Dingo, "Securing the Nation."

2. As I explain in chapter 3, given Trump's relative silence on the subject of education, especially in light of his public disagreements with his administration officials on numerous issues, we should regard Betsy DeVos's advocacy for school choice and related policies as the K–12 education preferences that guided the Trump administration.

3. Friedman and Friedman, *Capitalism and Freedom*, 33.

4. Cooper, *Family Values*, 72.

5. DeVos, "Prepared Remarks by Secretary DeVos to the Alfred E. Smith Foundation"; Walker, "2015 State of the State."

6. W. Brown, *In the Ruins of Neoliberalism*, 40.

7. Scott, "Market-Driven Education Reform," 586.

8. Harvey, *Brief History of Neoliberalism*, 37–41. Wendy Brown writes that "freedom without society is a pure instrument of power, shorn of concern for others, the world, or the future" (*In the Ruins of Neoliberalism*, 44–45).

9. Walker, "2011 Inaugural Address"; Walker, "2015 State of the State."

10. US Senate Subcommittee on Labor, Health and Human Services, Education, and Related Agencies, *Appropriations for Fiscal Year 2018*, 43.

11. Kemble, "Wisconsin's Voucher Vultures."

12. US Senate Subcommittee on Labor, Health and Human Services, Education, and Related Agencies, *Appropriations for Fiscal Year 2018*, 35. In his complaint about restricted choices, Senator Kennedy did not acknowledge Louisiana's statewide voucher program. See Cierniak, Stewart, and Ruddy, *Mapping the Growth*.

13. Wisconsin Joint Finance Committee, "2013–15 Budget Briefing."

14. Friedman and Friedman, *Capitalism and Freedom*, 86.

15. DeVos, "Prepared Remarks by US Secretary of Education Betsy DeVos to the US Conference."

16. Wisconsin Joint Finance Committee, "2013–15 Budget Briefing."

17. Means, "Democratic Education," 222–23. See also Boyles, "Privatized Public," and Stengel, "Educating *Homo Oeconomicus?*"

18. Nationally, for the 2019–20 academic year, 90 percent of K–12 students attended public schools; see National Center for Education Statistics, "Back to School Statistics." In Wisconsin, for the 2018–19 academic year, 85.7 percent of K–12 schoolchildren attended public schools; see Wisconsin Department of Public Instruction, "Public Schools."

19. On this score, Wendy Brown notes the endorsement of authoritarian regimes in such countries as Chile by neoliberal stalwarts like Milton Friedman and Friedrich Hayek; see W. Brown, *In the Ruins of Neoliberalism*, 63–73.

20. Judith Suissa values educational counterpublics for challenging "dominant political values and ideas" and developing "new forms of social interaction" that may "enable people to imagine new political structures and to think differently about what these values mean" ("Reflections on the 'Counter,'" 779).

21. Allen, *Education and Equality*, 31.

22. See Darling-Hammond, *Flat World and Education*, 27–65.

23. See Rogers and Oakes, "John Dewey Speaks."

24. For a discussion of efforts to foreground public engagement in the rhetoric classroom, see Rood, "Gap Between Rhetorical Education."

25. For a detailed analysis of the failures of a market education and the comparative successes of public education, see Lubienski and Lubienski, *Public School Advantage.*

26. Allen, *Education and Equality,* 48.

27. Dewey, *Public and Its Problems,* 184.

BIBLIOGRAPHY

Abbott, Blake. "'A Widespread Loss of Confidence': TARP, Presidential Rhetoric, and the Crisis of Neoliberalism." *Communication Quarterly* 66, no. 5 (2018): 463–80.

Abowitz, Kathleen Knight. "Reclaiming Community." *Educational Theory* 49, no. 2 (1999): 143–59.

Allen, Danielle. *Education and Equality*. Chicago: University of Chicago Press, 2016.

American Federation for Children. *2012 Election Impact Report*. 2013. http://www.tpcref .org/wp-content/uploads/AFC_Election_Impact_Report_2012.pdf.

American National Election Studies. "The ANES Guide to Public Opinion and Political Behavior." 2010. https://www.electionstudies.org/nesguide/.

Anderson, Zac. "Rick Scott Wants to Shift University Funding Away from Some Degrees." *Herald-Tribune*, October 10, 2011. http://politics.heraldtribune.com/2011/10/10 /rick-scott-wants-to-shift-university-funding-away-from-some-majors.

Apple, Michael W. "Ideological Success, Educational Failure? On the Politics of No Child Left Behind." *Journal of Teacher Education* 58, no. 2 (2007): 108–16.

Arendt, Hannah. *The Human Condition*. Chicago: University of Chicago Press, 1958.

Arnett, Ronald C. "Communication and Community in an Age of Diversity." In *Communication Ethics in an Age of Diversity*, edited by Josina M. Makau and Ronald C. Arnett, 27–47. Urbana: University of Illinois Press, 1997.

Asen, Robert. *Democracy, Deliberation, and Education*. University Park: Pennsylvania State University Press, 2015.

———. "Imagining in the Public Sphere." *Philosophy and Rhetoric* 35, no. 4 (2002): 345–67.

———. "The Multiple Mr. Dewey: Multiple Publics and Permeable Borders in John Dewey's Theory of the Public Sphere." *Argumentation and Advocacy* 39, no. 3 (2003): 174–88.

———. "Seeking the 'Counter' in Counterpublics." *Communication Theory* 10, no. 4 (2000): 424–46.

———. *Visions of Poverty: Welfare Policy and Political Imagination*. East Lansing: Michigan State University Press, 2002.

Asen, Robert, and Kelly Jensen. "Interviews with Community Advocates for Public Education." January 2020. https://research.commarts.wisc.edu/docs/rbasen/Asen -Jensen-Memo.pdf.

Associated Press. "Former Speakers Lobbying for Vouchers." *La Crosse Tribune*, January 22, 2013. https://lacrossetribune.com/news/local/state-and-regional/former -speakers-lobbying-for-vouchers/article_9afadf36-64a7-11e2-a894-001a4bcf887a .html.

Associated Press–NORC Center for Public Affairs Research. "Education in the United States: Choice, Control, and Quality." April 2017. https://apnorc.org/projects /education-in-the-united-states-choice-control-and-quality/.

Aune, James Arnt. "How to Read Milton Friedman: Corporate Social Responsibility and Today's Capitalisms." In *The Debate over Corporate Social Responsibility*, edited by Steve May, George Cheney, and Juliet Roper, 207–18. New York: Oxford University Press, 2007.

———. *Selling the Free Market: The Rhetoric of Economic Correctness.* New York: Guilford, 2001.

Barkan, Joanne. "The Miseducation of Betsy DeVos." *Dissent* 64, no. 2 (Spring 2017): 141–46.

Bauer, Scott. "Audit: School Voucher Expansion Could Cost $800 Million." *Green Bay Press Gazette*, May 28, 2015. https://www.greenbaypressgazette.com/story /news/education/2015/05/28/audit-wisconsin-school-voucher-expansion -could-cost-800-million/28084239.

Beck, Molly. "Conservative Study: Teachers Make $2k Less in Base Pay Than Before Act 10." *Wisconsin State Journal*, June 22, 2016. https://madison.com/wsj/news /local/govt-and-politics/conservative-study-teachers-make-k-less-in-base-pay-than /article_4ed2349f-344d-5a61-b3f7-92270e1f5051.html.

———. "Memo: State Voucher Expansion Could Cost up to $800M over 10 Years." *Wisconsin State Journal*, May 29, 2015. https://madison.com/wsj/news/local/govt -and-politics/memo-10-year-voucher-expansion-could-shift-up-to-m/article _e7fffc49-7229-5281-89ec-3dc1a10d1f09.html.

Bell, Terrel H. "Education Policy Development in the Reagan Administration." *Phi Delta Kappan* 67, no. 7 (March 1986): 487–93.

———. "Memo to the Secretary of Education: How to Make Education a Top Priority." *Change* 20, no. 6 (1988): 20–23.

Belman, Lary S. "John Dewey's Concept of Communication." *Journal of Communication* 27, no. 1 (1977): 29–37.

Benhabib, Seyla. "Toward a Deliberative Model of Democratic Legitimacy." In *Democracy and Difference: Contesting the Boundaries of the Political*, edited by Seyla Benhabib, 67–94. Princeton: Princeton University Press, 1996.

Berkshire, Jennifer. "A New Public Education Movement Is Emerging in Wisconsin, a Rebuke to Gov. Walker's War on Labor and School Privatization." *Washington Post*, July 3, 2018. https://www.washingtonpost.com/news/answer-sheet/wp/2018/07 /03/a-new-public-education-movement-is-emerging-in-wisconsin-a-rebuke-to -gov-walkers-war-on-labor-and-school-privatization.

Bettez, Silvia Cristina. "Critical Community Building: Beyond Belonging." *Educational Foundations* 25, nos. 3–4 (2011): 3–19.

Bice, Daniel. "Thompson the Governor Touted Collegial Work with Unions." *Milwaukee Journal Sentinel*, January 29, 2012. http://archive.jsonline.com/watchdog /noquarter/thompson-the-governor-touted-collegial-work-with-unions-be401cu -138304009.html.

Biesta, Gert. "'Of All Affairs, Communication Is the Most Wonderful': The Communicative Turn in Dewey's *Democracy and Education*." In *John Dewey and Our Educational Prospect: A Critical Engagement with Dewey's "Democracy and Education,"* edited by David T. Hansen, 23–37. Albany: State University of New York Press, 2006.

Bitzer, Lloyd F. "Rhetoric and Public Knowledge." In *Rhetoric, Philosophy and Literature*, edited by Don M. Burks, 67–93. West Lafayette, IN: Purdue University Press, 1978.

———. "The Rhetorical Situation." *Philosophy and Rhetoric* 1, no. 1 (1968): 1–14.

Blair, Julie. "Wis. Districts Chafe Under State's Revenue Limits." *Education Week*, January 27, 1999. https://www.edweek.org/ew/articles/1999/01/27/20wisc.h18.html.

Bohman, James. "Democracy as Inquiry, Inquiry as Democratic: Pragmatism, Social Science, and the Cognitive Division of Labor." *American Journal of Political Science* 43, no. 2 (1999): 590–607.

Bolick, Clint. "Voting Down Vouchers." *Education Next* 8, no. 2 (Spring 2008): 46–51.

Borchers, Gladys L. "John Dewey and Speech Education." *Western Speech* 32, no. 2 (1968): 127–37.

Boyles, Deron. "The Privatized Public: Antagonism for a Radical Democratic Politics in Schools?" *Educational Theory* 61, no. 4 (2011): 433–50.

Brockriede, Wayne. "Where Is Argument?" *Journal of the American Forensic Association* 11, no. 4 (1975): 179–82.

Brouwer, Daniel C. "Communication as Counterpublic." In *Communication as . . . Perspectives on Theory*, edited by Gregory J. Shepherd, Jeffrey St. John, and Ted Striphas, 195–208. Thousand Oaks, CA: Sage, 2006.

Brouwer, Daniel C., and Robert Asen. "Introduction: Public Modalities, or the Metaphors We Theorize By." In *Public Modalities: Rhetoric, Culture, Media, and the Shape of Public Life*, edited by Daniel C. Brouwer and Robert Asen, 1–32. Tuscaloosa: University of Alabama Press, 2010.

Brown, Emma. "Trump Picks Billionaire Betsy DeVos, School Voucher Advocate, as Education Secretary." *Washington Post*, November 23, 2016. https://www .washingtonpost.com/local/education/trump-picks-billionaire-betsy-devos -school-voucher-advocate-as-education-secretary/2016/11/23/c3d66b94-af96 -11e6-840f-e3ebab6bcdd3_story.html.

Brown, Frank. "Privatization and Urban Education: More Political and Less Educational." *Education and Urban Society* 29, no. 2 (1997): 204–16.

Brown, Wendy. "Apocalyptic Populism." *Eurozine*, August 30, 2017. https://www .eurozine.com/apocalyptic-populism.

———. *In the Ruins of Neoliberalism: The Rise of Antidemocratic Politics in the West*. New York: Columbia University Press, 2019.

———. *Undoing the Demos: Neoliberalism's Stealth Revolution*. New York: Zone Books, 2015.

Bruecker, Ellie. *Assessing the Fiscal Impact of Wisconsin's Statewide Voucher Program*. Boulder, CO: National Education Policy Center, October 2017. https://nepc.colorado .edu/publication/funding.

Bruell, Cornelia, Monika Mokre, and Birte Siim. "Inclusion and Exclusion in the European Public Sphere: Intersections of Gender and Race." *Javnost—The Public* 19, no. 1 (2012): 35–50.

Burch, Patricia. *Hidden Markets: The New Education Privatization*. New York: Routledge, 2009.

Burgin, Angus. "Age of Certainty: Galbraith, Friedman, and the Public Life of Economic Ideas." Supplement, *History of Political Economy* 45 (2013): 191–219.

Burgum, Samuel, Sebastian Raza, and Jorge Vasquez. "An Interview with Wendy Brown: Redoing the Demos?" *Theory, Culture & Society* 34, nos. 7–8 (2017): 229–36.

Burks, Don M. "John Dewey and Rhetorical Theory." *Western Speech* 32, no. 2 (1968): 118–26.

Bush, George H. W. *Public Papers of the Presidents of the United States: George Bush, 1989*. 2 vols. Washington, DC: Government Printing Office, 1990.

Bush, George W. *Public Papers of the Presidents of the United States: George W. Bush, 2001*. 2 vols. Washington, DC: Government Printing Office, 2003.

Campbell, Karlyn Kohrs. "Agency: Promiscuous and Protean." *Communication and Critical/Cultural Studies* 2, no. 1 (2005): 1–19.

Cann, Colette, and Eric DeMeulenaere. "Forged in the Crucibles of Difference: Building Discordant Communities." *Perspectives on Urban Education* 7, no. 1 (2010): 41–53.

Carcasson, Martín, and Leah Sprain. "Beyond Problem Solving: Reconceptualizing the Work of Public Deliberation as Deliberative Inquiry." *Communication Theory* 26, no. 1 (2016): 41–63.

Carey, Kevin. "Dismal Results from Vouchers Surprise Researchers as DeVos Era Begins." *New York Times*, February 23, 2017. https://www.nytimes.com/2017 /02/23/upshot/dismal-results-from-vouchers-surprise-researchers-as-devos-era -begins.html.

Carl, Jim. *Freedom of Choice: Vouchers in American Education*. Santa Barbara, CA: Praeger, 2011.

Carnoy, Martin. "School Vouchers Are Not a Proven Strategy for Improving Student Achievement." Economic Policy Institute, February 28, 2017. http://epi.org /121635.

Carroll, Peter N. *It Seemed Like Nothing Happened: America in the 1970s*. New Brunswick, NJ: Rutgers University Press, 1990.

Carter, Jimmy. *Public Papers of the Presidents of the United States: Jimmy Carter, 1979*. 2 vols. Washington, DC: Government Printing Office, 1980.

Casey, Leo. "When Privatization Means Segregation: Setting the Record Straight on School Vouchers." *Dissent* 64, no. 3 (Summer 2017): 155–59.

Caspary, William R. *Dewey on Democracy*. Ithaca, NY: Cornell University Press, 2000.

———. "'One and the Same Method': John Dewey's Thesis of Unity of Method in Ethics and Science." *Transactions of the Charles S. Pierce Society* 39, no. 3 (2003): 445–68.

Center on Wisconsin Strategy. "Wisconsin's Extreme Racial Disparity." January 2017. https://www.cows.org/_data/documents/1816.pdf.

Chapman, Thandeka, and René Antrop-González. "A Critical Look at Choice Options as Solutions to Milwaukee's Schooling Inequities." *Teachers College Record* 113, no. 4 (2011): 787–810.

Chaput, Catherine. *Market Affect and the Rhetoric of Political Economic Debates*. Columbia: University of South Carolina Press, 2019.

———. "The Rhetorical Situation and the Battle for Public Sentiment: How Friedman Overtook Galbraith at the Dawn of Neoliberalism." In *Communication and the Economy: History, Value and Agency*, edited by Joshua S. Hanan and Mark Hayward, 187–208. New York: Peter Lang, 2014.

Chávez, Karma R. "Counter-Public Enclaves and Understanding the Function of Rhetoric in Social Movement Coalition-Building." *Communication Quarterly* 59, no. 1 (2011): 1–18.

Chingos, Matthew. "Why the Proficiency-Versus-Growth Debate Matters for Assessing School Performance." *Urban Institute*, January 17, 2017. https://www.urban .org/urban-wire/why-proficiency-versus-growth-debate-matters-assessing-school -performance.

Cierniak, Katherine, Molly Stewart, and Anne-Maree Ruddy. *Mapping the Growth of Statewide Voucher Programs in the United States*. Bloomington, IN: Center for Evaluation and Education Policy, 2015.

Cillizza, Chris. "Betsy DeVos' Trainwreck Interview on '60 Minutes.'" *CNN*, March 12, 2018. https://www.cnn.com/2018/03/12/politics/besty-devos-interview-analysis /index.html.

Cintron, Ralph. "Democracy and Its Limitations." In *The Public Work of Rhetoric: Citizen-Scholars and Civic Engagement*, edited by John M. Ackerman and David J. Coogan, 98–116. Columbia: University of South Carolina Press, 2010.

———. *Democracy as Fetish*. University Park: Pennsylvania State University Press, 2020.

Clabaugh, Gary K. "The Educational Legacy of Ronald Reagan." *Educational Horizons* 82, no. 4 (2004): 256–59.

Clark, Gregory. "Rescuing the Discourse of Community." *College Composition and Communication* 45, no. 1 (1994): 61–74.

Clinton, Bill. "Foreword." In *Education Reform: Making Sense of It All*, edited by Samuel B. Bacharach, xi–xii. Needham Heights, MA: Allyn and Bacon, 1990.

Colombini, Crystal Broch. "Energeia, Kinesis, and the Neoliberal Rhetoric of Strategic Default." *Advances in the History of Rhetoric* 21, no. 2 (2018): 178–93.

———. "Speaking Confidence: Bubble Denial as Market Authoritative Rhetorical Decorum." *Rhetoric Society Quarterly* 45, no. 2 (2015): 117–37.

Condit, Celeste. "Crafting Virtue: The Rhetorical Construction of Public Morality." *Quarterly Journal of Speech* 73, no. 1 (1987): 79–97.

Coons, John E. "Give Us Liberty and Give Us Depth." In *Liberty and Learning: Milton Friedman's Voucher Idea at Fifty*, edited by Robert C. Enlow and Lenore T. Ealy, 57–65. Washington, DC: Cato Institute, 2006.

Cooper, Melinda. *Family Values: Between Neoliberalism and the New Social Conservatism*. New York: Zone Books, 2017.

Crick, Nathan. *Democracy and Rhetoric: John Dewey on the Arts of Becoming*. Columbia: University of South Carolina Press, 2010.

Cross, Christopher T. *Political Education: National Policy Comes of Age*. Updated ed. New York: Teachers College Press, 2010.

Curtis, Mary C. "Protests at Bethune-Cookman Graduation Prove Today's Students Know Their History." *The Undefeated*, May 18, 2017. https://theundefeated.com /features/protests-at-bethune-cookman-graduation-prove-todays-students-know -their-history/.

Dahlberg, Lincoln. "Visibility and the Public Sphere: A Normative Conceptualisation." *Javnost—The Public* 25, nos. 1–2 (2018): 35–42.

Danisch, Robert. *Pragmatism, Democracy, and the Necessity of Rhetoric*. Columbia: University of South Carolina Press, 2007.

Darling-Hammond, Linda. *The Flat World and Education: How America's Commitment to Equity Will Determine Our Future*. New York: Teachers College Press, 2010.

Davey, Monica, and Steven Greenhouse. "Angry Demonstrations in Wisconsin as Cuts Loom." *New York Times*, February 16, 2011. https://www.nytimes.com/2011/02/17 /us/17wisconsin.html.

Davidoff, Leonore. "Regarding Some 'Old Husbands' Tales': Public and Private in Feminist History." In *Feminism, the Public and the Private*, edited by Joan B. Landes, 164–94. New York: Oxford University Press, 1998.

Davies, Gareth. *See Government Grow: Education Politics from Johnson to Reagan*. Lawrence: University Press of Kansas, 2007.

Davies, William. "What Is 'Neo' About Neoliberalism?" In *Liberalism in Neoliberal Times: Dimensions, Contradictions, Limits*, edited by Alejandro Abraham-Hamanoiel, Des Freeman, Gholam Khiabany, Kate Nash, and Julian Petley, 13–22. London: Goldsmiths Press, 2017.

Davis, James A., and Tom W. Smith. *General Social Surveys, 1972–2008*. Chicago: National Opinion Research Center, 2009.

Dean, Jodi. "Nothing Personal." In *Rethinking Neoliberalism: Resisting the Disciplinary Regime*, edited by Sanford F. Schram and Marianna Pavlovskaya, 3–22. New York: Routledge, 2018.

DeBray, Elizabeth H. *Politics, Ideology and Education: Federal Policy During the Clinton and Bush Administrations*. New York: Teachers College Press, 2006.

DeBray-Pelot, Elizabeth, and Patrick McGuinn. "The New Politics of Education: Analyzing the Federal Education Policy Landscape in the Post-NCLB Era." *Educational Policy* 23, no. 1 (2009): 15–42.

DeFour, Matthew. "Budget Cuts Hundreds of Millions of Dollars from Schools." *Wisconsin State Journal*, March 2, 2011. https://madison.com/wsj/news/local/education

/local_schools/budget-cuts-hundreds-of-millions-of-dollars-from-schools/article
_de7c67c0-444c-11e0-bfd0-001cc4c03286.html.

Delmont, Matthew F. *Why Busing Failed: Race, Media, and the National Resistance to School Desegregation.* Berkeley: University of California Press, 2016.

Depew, David, and John Durham Peters. "Community and Communication: The Conceptual Background." In *Communication and Community,* edited by Gregory J. Shepherd and Eric W. Rothenbuhler, 3–21. Mahwah, NJ: Lawrence Erlbaum, 2001.

DeVos, Betsy. "Bethune-Cookman 2017 Commencement Address." *C-Span,* May 10, 2017. https://www.c-span.org/video/?428006-2/betsy-devos-delivers-bethune -cookman-university-commencement-address.

———. "Betsy DeVos' Entire CPAC Speech." *CNN,* February 23, 2017. https://www.cnn .com/videos/politics/2017/02/23/cpac-betsy-devos-entire-remarks-sot.cnn.

———. "Bush-Obama School Reform: Lessons Learned." American Enterprise Institute, January 16, 2018. https://www.youtube.com/watch?v=6Ves9rPhnEQ.

———. "Competition, Creativity and Choice in the Classroom." American Federation for Children, March 11, 2015. http://www.federationforchildren.org/wp-content /uploads/2015/03/Betsy-SXSWedu-speech-final-remarks.pdf.

———. "Education Secretary Betsy DeVos Addresses ALEC 44th Annual Meeting." American Legislative Exchange Council, July 20, 2017. https://www.alec.org /article/education-secretary-betsty-devos-address-alec-44th-annual-meeting/.

———. "Keynote Address to the 2017 National Policy Summit." American Federation for Children, May 22, 2017. https://www.federationforchildren.org/event/2017 -national-policy-summit/.

———. "Keynote Address to the Council of Chief State School Officers." *C-Span,* March 5, 2018. https://www.c-span.org/video/?442005-14/council-chief-state-school -officers-education-secretary-betsy-devos.

———. "Keynote at National Summit on Education Reform." Excel*in*Ed, November 30, 2017. https://www.excelined.org/national-summit/2017-agenda/.

———. "Keynote Remarks at the 2016 Education Choice and Competition Index." Brookings Institution, March 29, 2017. https://www.brookings.edu/wp-content /uploads/2017/03/20170329_ecci_devos_transcript.pdf.

———. "Prepared Remarks by Secretary DeVos to Students and Faculty at Woods Learning Center." US Department of Education, September 12, 2017. https://www .ed.gov/news/speeches/prepared-remarks-secretary-devos-students-and-faculty -woods-learning-center.

———. "Prepared Remarks by Secretary DeVos to the Alfred E. Smith Foundation." US Department of Education, May 16, 2018. https://www.ed.gov/news/speeches /prepared-remarks-secretary-devos-alfred-e-smith-foundation.

———. "Prepared Remarks by Secretary of Education Betsy DeVos to the National Lieutenant Governors Association." US Department of Education, March 15, 2017. https://www.ed.gov/news/speeches/prepared-remarks-secretary-education-betsy -devos-national-lieutenant-governors-association.

———. "Prepared Remarks by US Secretary of Education Betsy DeVos to SXSW EDU." US Department of Education, March 6, 2018. https://www.ed.gov/news/speeches /prepared-remarks-us-secretary-education-betsy-devos-sxsw-edu.

———. "Prepared Remarks by US Secretary of Education Betsy DeVos to the 2017 ASU GSV Summit." US Department of Education, May 9, 2017. https://www.ed.gov /news/speeches/prepared-remarks-us-secretary-education-betsy-devos-2017-asu -gsv-summit.

————. "Prepared Remarks by US Secretary of Education Betsy DeVos to the US Conference of Mayors." US Department of Education, January 25, 2018. https://www .ed.gov/news/speeches/prepared-remarks-us-secretary-education-betsy-devos-us -conference-mayors.

————. "Prepared Remarks to the American Enterprise Institute World Forum." US Department of Education, March 12, 2018. https://www.ed.gov/news/speeches /prepared-remarks-american-enterprise-institute-world-forum.

————. "Prepared Remarks to the National Parent Teacher Association Legislative Conference." US Department of Education, March 13, 2018. https://www.ed .gov/news/speeches/prepared-remarks-national-parent-teacher-association -legislative-conference.

————. "President Trump Delivers on Education Promises." *USA Today*, March 3, 2017. https://www.usatoday.com/story/opinion/2017/03/02/betsy-devos-trump -delivers-education-promises-column/98594982/.

————. "Remarks by Secretary DeVos to the Michigan Community College Association Summer Conference." US Department of Education, July 27, 2017. https://www .ed.gov/news/speeches/remarks-secretary-devos-michigan-community-college -association-summer-conference.

————. "Remarks by US Education Secretary DeVos to the Washington Policy Center Annual Dinner." Washington Policy Center, October 26, 2017. https://www .washingtonpolicy.org/publications/detail/remarks-by-us-education-secretary -devos-to-the-washington-policy-center-annual-dinner.

————. "Rethink School Tour: Remarks at US Space and Rocket Center." US Department of Education, October 3, 2018. https://www.youtube.com/watch?v=mak2fLYyjgk.

————. "Secretary Betsy DeVos Prepared Remarks National Alliance for Public Charter Schools." US Department of Education, June 13, 2017. https://www.ed.gov/news /speeches/secretary-betsy-devos-prepared-remarks-national-association-public -charter-schools.

————. "Secretary DeVos Remarks at Kennedy School of Government." *C-Span*, September 29, 2017. https://www.c-span.org/video/?434821-1/education-secretary -betsy-devos-speaks-harvard.

————. "Transcript of Education Secretary DeVos' Interview with AP." *US News and World Report*, August 12, 2017. https://www.usnews.com/news/best-states /michigan/articles/2017-08-12/transcript-of-education-secretary-devos-interview -with-ap.

————. "US Secretary of Education Betsy DeVos Addressed the National Association of State Boards of Education in Washington, D.C." US Department of Education, March 20, 2017. https://www.ed.gov/news/speeches/us-secretary-education-betsy -devos-addressed-national-association-state-boards-education-washington-dc.

————. "US Secretary of Education Betsy DeVos' Prepared Remarks at HBCU Congressional Luncheon in Washington, D.C." US Department of Education, February 28, 2017. https://www.ed.gov/news/speeches/us-secretary-education-betsy -devos-prepared-remarks-hbcu-congressional-luncheon-washington-dc.

————. "US Secretary of Education Betsy DeVos' Prepared Remarks to the Council of the Great City Schools." US Department of Education, March 13, 2017. https://www .ed.gov/news/speeches/us-secretary-education-betsy-devos-prepared-remarks -council-great-city-schools.

Dewey, John. "The Basic Values and Loyalties of Democracy." In *John Dewey: The Later Works, 1925–1953*, vol. 14, *1939–1941*, edited by Jo Ann Boydston, 275–77. Carbondale: Southern Illinois University Press, 1991.

———. "Creative Democracy: The Task Before Us." In *John Dewey: The Later Works, 1925–1953*, vol. 14, *1939–1941*, edited by Jo Ann Boydston, 224–30. Carbondale: Southern Illinois University Press, 1991.

———. *Democracy and Education: An Introduction to the Philosophy of Education.* 1916. Reprint, New York: Free Press, 1944.

———. "Democracy Is Radical." In *John Dewey: The Later Works, 1925–1953*, vol. 11, *1935–1937*, edited by Jo Ann Boydston, 296–99. Carbondale: Southern Illinois University Press, 1987.

———. "The Ethics of Democracy." In *John Dewey: The Early Works, 1882–1898*, vol. 1, *1882–1888*, edited by Jo Ann Boydston, 227–49. Carbondale: Southern Illinois University Press, 1969.

———. *Experience and Education.* In *John Dewey: The Later Works, 1925–1953*, vol. 13, *1938–1939*, edited by Jo Ann Boydston. 1939. Reprint, Carbondale: Southern Illinois University Press, 1991.

———. *Experience and Nature.* In *John Dewey: The Later Works, 1925–1953*, vol. 1, *1925*, edited by Jo Ann Boydston. 1925. Reprint, Carbondale: Southern Illinois University Press, 1988.

———. "Experience, Knowledge and Value: A Rejoinder." In *John Dewey: The Later Works, 1925–1953*, vol. 14, *1939–1941*, edited by Jo Ann Boydston, 3–90. Carbondale: Southern Illinois University Press, 1991.

———. *Freedom and Culture.* In *John Dewey: The Later Works, 1925–1953*, vol. 13, *1938–1939*, edited by Jo Ann Boydston. 1939. Reprint, Carbondale: Southern Illinois University Press, 1991.

———. *Individualism, Old and New.* In *John Dewey: The Later Works, 1925–1953*, vol. 5, *1929–1930*, edited by Jo Ann Boydston. 1930. Reprint, Carbondale: Southern Illinois University Press, 1984.

———. *Liberalism and Social Action.* In *John Dewey: The Later Works, 1925–1953*, vol. 11, *1935–1937*, edited by Jo Ann Boydston. 1935. Reprint, Carbondale: Southern Illinois University Press, 1987.

———. *The Public and Its Problems.* 1927. Reprint, Athens, OH: Swallow Press, 1954.

———. "What I Believe." In *John Dewey: The Later Works, 1925–1953*, vol. 5, *1929–1930*, edited by Jo Ann Boydston, 267–78. Carbondale: Southern Illinois University Press, 1984.

Dingo, Rebecca. *Networking Arguments: Rhetoric, Transnational Feminism, and Public Policy Writing.* Pittsburgh: University of Pittsburgh Press, 2012.

———. "Securing the Nation: Neoliberalism's US Family Values in a Transnational Gendered Economy." *Journal of Women's History* 16, no. 3 (2004): 173–86.

Dingo, Rebecca, Rachel Riedner, and Jennifer Wingard. "Toward a Cogent Analysis of Power: Transnational Rhetorical Studies." *JAC: A Journal of Rhetoric, Culture, and Politics* 33, nos. 3–4 (2013): 517–28.

Dougherty, Jack. *More Than One Struggle: The Evolution of Black School Reform in Milwaukee.* Chapel Hill: University of North Carolina Press, 2004.

Douglas-Gabriel, Danielle, and Tracy Jan. "DeVos Called HBCUs 'Pioneers' of 'School Choice': It Didn't Go Over Well." *Washington Post*, February 28, 2017. https://www.washingtonpost.com/news/grade-point/wp/2017/02/28/devos-called-hbcus-pioneers-of-school-choice-it-didnt-go-over-well.

Duerringer, Christopher Michael. "Rhetorical Arbitrage: The Rhetoric of the Sharing Economy." *Communication Theory* 29, no. 4 (2019): 383–400.

Easter, Makeda, and Paresh Dave. "Remember When Amazon Only Sold Books?" *Los Angeles Times*, June 18, 2017. https://www.latimes.com/business/la-fi-amazon-history-20170618-htmlstory.html.

Education Commission of the States. "ESSA: Quick Guides on Top Issues." August 8, 2016. https://www.ecs.org/essa-quick-guides-on-top-issues/.

"Education Dept. Won't Be Abolished: Reagan Backs Down, Citing Little Support for Killing Agency." *Los Angeles Times*, January 29, 1985. https://www.latimes.com /archives/la-xpm-1985-01-29-mn-13948-story.html.

Eldridge, Michael. "Dewey's Faith in Democracy as Shared Experience." *Transactions of the Charles S. Pierce Society* 32, no. 1 (1996): 11–30.

Endres, Susan. "Baraboo Christian School Administrator Tells Families How to Get State Vouchers Through Loophole." *Madison.com*, December 21, 2019. https:// madison.com/news/local/education/local_schools/baraboo-christian-school -administrator-tells-families-how-to-get-state/article_93667ab3-7cd7-5b75-9cec -88b427c3ec7b.html.

Engels, Jeremy. "Dewey on Jefferson: Reiterating Democratic Faith in Times of War." In *Trained Capacities: John Dewey, Rhetoric, and Democratic Practice*, edited by Brian Jackson and Gregory Clark, 87–105. Columbia: University of South Carolina Press, 2014.

Englund, Tomas. "The Potential of Education for Creating Mutual Trust: Schools as Sites for Deliberation." *Educational Philosophy and Theory* 43, no. 3 (2011): 236–48.

Epps-Robertson, Candace. "The Race to Erase Brown v. Board of Education: The Virginia Way and the Rhetoric of Massive Resistance." *Rhetoric Review* 35, no. 2 (2016): 108–20.

Fernandes, Deirdre, and Jake Johnson. "Hundreds Protest DeVos During Harvard Visit." *Boston Globe*, September 29, 2017. https://www.bostonglobe.com/metro/2017 /09/28/hundreds-protest-education-secretary/20vwZ3gXVzSqtw8LEyl5BL/story .html.

Festenstein, Matthew. "Inquiry as Critique: On the Legacy of Deweyan Pragmatism for Political Theory." *Political Studies* 49, no. 4 (2001): 730–48.

———. "The Ties of Communication: Dewey on Ideal and Political Democracy." *History of Political Thought* 18, no. 1 (1997): 104–24.

Finn, Chester E., Jr. "Education Policy and the Reagan Administration: A Large but Incomplete Success." *Educational Policy* 2, no. 4 (1988): 343–60.

Flanders, Will. "The Facts of School Choice." Wisconsin Institute for Law and Liberty, July 3, 2018. https://www.will-law.org/will-blog-flanders-response-valerie-strauss -washington-post.

Flores, Lisa A. "Choosing to Consume: Race, Education, and the School Voucher Debate." In *The Motherhood Business: Consumption, Communication, and Privilege*, edited by Anne Teresa Demo, Jennifer L. Borda, and Charlotte Kroløkke, 243–65. Tuscaloosa: University of Alabama Press, 2015.

Foley, Megan. "From Infantile Citizens to Infantile Institutions: The Metaphoric Transformation of Political Economy in the 2008 Housing Market Crisis." *Quarterly Journal of Speech* 98, no. 4 (2012): 386–410.

Ford, Chris, Stephenie Johnson, and Lisette Partelow. "The Racist Origins of Private School Vouchers." Center for American Progress, July 12, 2017. https://www .americanprogress.org/issues/education-k-12/reports/2017/07/12/435629/racist -origins-private-school-vouchers.

Ford, Michael R. *The Consequences of Governance Fragmentation: Milwaukee's School Voucher Legacy*. Lanham, MD: Lexington Books, 2017.

———. "Funding Impermanence: Quantifying the Public Funds Sent to Closed Schools in the Nation's First Urban School Voucher Program." *Public Administration Quarterly* 40, no. 4 (2017): 882–912.

Ford, Michael R., and Fredrik O. Andersson. "Determinants of Organizational Failure in the Milwaukee School Voucher Program." *Policy Studies Journal* 47, no. 4 (2016): 1048–68.

Foucault, Michel. *The Birth of Biopolitics: Lectures at the Collège de France, 1978–1979.* Translated by Graham Burchell. New York: Picador, 2008.

Franklin, Charles. "Marquette Law School Poll Finds Walker Job Approval Down." *Marquette University Law School Poll,* April 16, 2015. https://law.marquette.edu/poll/2015/04/16/marquette-law-school-poll-finds-walker-job-approval-down.

———. "New MU Law Poll Looks at Wisc Views on Guns, Education, Economy." *Marquette University Law School Poll,* March 19, 2013. https://law.marquette.edu/poll/2013/03/19/new-mu-law-poll-looks-at-wisc-views-on-guns-education-economy.

Fraser, Nancy. "Feminism, Capitalism, and the Cunning of History." In *Fortunes of Feminism: From State-Managed Capitalism to Neoliberal Crisis,* 209–26. London: Verso, 2013.

———. "Rethinking the Public Sphere: A Contribution to the Critique of Actually Existing Democracy." In *Habermas and the Public Sphere,* edited by Craig Calhoun, 109–42. Cambridge, MA: MIT Press, 1992.

Fraser, Nancy, and Linda Gordon. "A Genealogy of Dependency: Tracing a Keyword of the US Welfare State." *Signs* 19, no. 2 (1994): 309–36.

Friedman, Milton. *Bright Promises, Dismal Performance: An Economist's Protest.* Edited by William R. Allen. New York: Harcourt Brace Jovanovich, 1983.

———. "The Foundations of a Free Society." In *Milton Friedman on Freedom,* edited by Robert Leeson and Charles G. Palm, 197–205. Stanford, CA: Hoover Institution Press, 2017.

———. "Free Markets and Free Speech." In *Milton Friedman on Freedom,* edited by Robert Leeson and Charles G. Palm, 177–88. Stanford, CA: Hoover Institution Press, 2017.

———. "An Interview with Milton Friedman: A *Reason* Interview." In *Milton Friedman on Freedom,* edited by Robert Leeson and Charles G. Palm, 69–92. Stanford, CA: Hoover Institution Press, 2017.

———. "The Line We Dare Not Cross." In *Milton Friedman on Freedom,* edited by Robert Leeson and Charles G. Palm, 101–17. Stanford, CA: Hoover Institution Press, 2017.

———. "Neo-liberalism and Its Prospects." *Farmand,* February 17, 1951, 89–93. https://miltonfriedman.hoover.org/friedman_images/Collections/2016c21/Farmand_02_17_1951.pdf.

———. "Prologue: A Personal Retrospective." In *Liberty and Learning: Milton Friedman's Voucher Idea at Fifty,* edited by Robert C. Enlow and Lenore T. Ealy, vii–x. Washington, DC: Cato Institute, 2006.

———. "The Role of Government in Education." In *Economics and the Public Interest,* edited by Robert A. Solo, 123–44. New Brunswick: Rutgers University Press, 1955.

Friedman, Milton, and Rose Friedman. *Capitalism and Freedom.* Chicago: University of Chicago Press, 1962.

———. *Free to Choose: A Personal Statement.* New York: Harcourt, 1980.

———. *Tyranny of the Status Quo.* New York: Harcourt Brace Jovanovich, 1983.

Fusarelli, Bonnie C., and Lance D. Fusarelli. "Federal Education Policy from Reagan to Obama: Convergence, Divergence, and 'Control.'" In *Handbook of Education Politics and Policy,* edited by Bruce S. Cooper, James G. Cibulka, and Lance D. Fusarelli, 189–210. New York: Routledge, 2015.

Galey, Sarah. "Education Politics and Policy: Emerging Institutions, Interests, and Ideas." *Policy Studies Journal* 43, no. S1 (2015): S12–S39.

Gallup, George H. "The 12th Annual Gallup Poll of the Public's Attitudes Toward the Public Schools." *Phi Delta Kappan* 62, no. 1 (September 1980): 33–46.

Garahan, Katie L. "The Public Work of Identity Performance: Advocacy and Dissent in Teachers' Open Letters." *Rhetoric & Public Affairs* 22, no. 1 (2019): 59–94.

Garton, Nicholas. "Milwaukee Schools: Preparing Kids for Life, or for Life in Prison?" *Madison365*, April 13, 2018. https://madison365.com/milwaukee-schools-preparing -kids-for-life-or-for-life-in-prison.

Gent, Whitney. "When Homelessness Becomes a 'Luxury': Neutrality as an Obstacle to Counterpublic Rights Claims." *Quarterly Journal of Speech* 103, no. 3 (2017): 230–50.

Gilbert, Craig. "Dividing Lines: Already Polarized, Wisconsin's Fault Lines Now Wider." *Milwaukee Journal Sentinel*, December 27, 2014. http://archive.jsonline.com /blogs/news/286923111.html.

Glaude, Eddie S., Jr. *In a Shade of Blue: Pragmatism and the Politics of Black America*. Chicago: University of Chicago Press, 2007.

Glickstein, Howard. "Inequalities in Educational Financing." *Teachers College Record* 96, no. 4 (1995): 722–28.

Goldberg, Milton, and Anita Madan Renton. "*A Nation at Risk*: Ugly Duckling No Longer." In *Commissions, Reports, Reforms, and Educational Policy*, edited by Rick Ginsberg and David N. Plank, 19–39. Westport, CT: Praeger, 1995.

Gooden, Mark A., Huriya Jabbar, and Mario S. Torres, Jr. "Race and School Vouchers: Legal, Historical, and Political Contexts." *Peabody Journal of Education* 91, no. 4 (2016): 522–36.

Goodnight, G. Thomas. "The Personal, Technical, and Public Spheres: A Note on 21st Century Critical Communication Inquiry." *Argumentation and Advocacy* 48, no. 4 (2012): 258–67.

Gordon, Linda. *Pitied but Not Entitled: Single Mothers and the History of Welfare*. Cambridge, MA: Harvard University Press, 1994.

Gordon, Scott. "Western Wisconsin Schools Grapple with Falling Status of Teachers." *WisContext*, March 23, 2017. https://www.wiscontext.org/western-wisconsin -schools-grapple-falling-status-teachers.

Graham, Hugh Davis. *The Uncertain Triumph: Federal Education Policy in the Kennedy and Johnson Years*. Chapel Hill: University of North Carolina Press, 1984.

Graham, Patricia Albjerg. *Schooling America: How the Public Schools Meet the Nation's Changing Needs*. New York: Oxford University Press, 2005.

Green, Erica L. "Bethune-Cookman Graduates Greet Betsy DeVos with Turned Backs." *New York Times*, May 10, 2017. https://www.nytimes.com/2017/05/10/us/politics /betsy-devos-bethune-cookman-commencement.html.

Greene, Ronald Walter. "Rhetorical Capital: Communicative Labor, Money/Speech, and Neo-liberal Governance." *Communication and Critical/Cultural Studies* 4, no. 3 (2007): 327–31.

Habermas, Jürgen. "Discourse Ethics: Notes on a Program of Philosophical Justification." In *Moral Consciousness and Communicative Action*, 57–115. Translated by Christian Lenhardt and Shierry Weber Nelson. Cambridge, MA: MIT Press, 1990.

Hall, Dee J., and Samara Kalk Derby. "Gov. Scott Walker Unveils Agenda for Wisconsin During Speech in California." *Wisconsin State Journal*, November 19, 2012. https://host.madison.com/wsj/news/local/govt-and-politics/gov-scott-walker -unveils-agenda-for-wisconsin-during-speech-in/article_a35a1378-31ed-11e2-bb6c -0019bb2963f4.html.

Hall, Stuart, and Alan O'Shea. "Common-Sense Neoliberalism." *Soundings*, no. 55 (2013): 8–24.

Hamburger, Jacob. "Wendy Brown: 'Who Is Not a Neoliberal Today?'" *Tocqueville21*, January 18, 2018. https://tocqueville21.com/interviews/wendy-brown-not-neoliberal -today.

Hanan, Joshua S., Indradeep Ghosh, and Kaleb W. Brooks. "Banking on the Present: The Ontological Rhetoric of Neo-Classical Economics and Its Relation to the 2008 Financial Crisis." *Quarterly Journal of Speech* 100, no. 2 (2014): 139–62.

Hariman, Robert. *Political Style: The Artistry of Power.* Chicago: University of Chicago Press, 1995.

Harvey, David. *A Brief History of Neoliberalism.* New York: Oxford University Press, 2005.

Hauser, Gerard A. "Rhetorical Democracy and Civic Engagement." In *Rhetorical Democracy: Discursive Practices of Civic Engagement*, edited by Gerard A. Hauser and Amy Grim, 1–14. Mahwah, NJ: Lawrence Erlbaum, 2004.

———. *Vernacular Voices: The Rhetoric of Publics and Public Spheres.* Columbia: University of South Carolina Press, 1999.

Hayek, F. A. *The Road to Serfdom.* 1944. Reprint, Chicago: University of Chicago Press, 1994.

Hayes, William. *No Child Left Behind: Past, Present, and Future.* Lanham, MD: Rowman and Littlefield, 2008.

Healy, Patrick. "How Is Scott Walker Like Ronald Reagan? He'll Tell You." *New York Times*, April 6, 2015. https://www.nytimes.com/2015/04/07/us/politics/2016 -elections-scott-walker-ronald-reagan.html.

Henig, Jeffrey. "Education Policy from 1980 to the Present: The Politics of Privatization." In *Conservatism and American Political Development*, edited by Brian J. Glenn and Steven M. Teles, 291–323. New York: Oxford University Press, 2009.

Hentschke, Gilbert C. "A Brief and Future History of School Choice." In *The Wiley Handbook of School Choice*, edited by Robert A. Fox and Nina K. Buchanan, 28–45. Hoboken, NJ: Wiley, 2017.

Hess, Frederick M. "Does School Choice Work?" *National Affairs*, no. 5 (Fall 2010): 35–53.

Hewitt, Randy. "Democracy and Power: A Reply to John Dewey's Leftist Critics." *Education and Culture* 19, no. 2 (2002): 1–13.

Hicks, Darrin. "The Promise(s) of Deliberative Democracy." *Rhetoric & Public Affairs* 5, no. 2 (2002): 223–60.

Hildreth, R. W. "Reconstructing Dewey on Power." *Political Theory* 37, no. 6 (2009): 780–807.

———. "What Good Is Growth? Reconsidering Dewey on the Ends of Democratic Education." *Education and Culture* 27, no. 2 (2011): 28–47.

Hill, Paul, and Ashley Jochim. *The Power of Persuasion: A Model for Effective Political Leadership by State Chiefs.* Seattle: Center on Reinventing Public Education, 2017. https://www.crpe.org/publications/power-persuasion-state-chiefs.

Hinck, Ashley. *Politics for the Love of Fandom: Fan-Based Citizenship in a Digital World.* Baton Rouge: Louisiana State University Press, 2019.

Hlavacik, Mark. *Assigning Blame: The Rhetoric of Education Reform.* Cambridge, MA: Harvard Education Press, 2016.

Hogan, J. Michael. "Conclusion: Rhetoric and the Restoration of Community." In *Rhetoric and Community: Studies in Unity and Fragmentation*, edited by J. Michael Hogan, 292–302. Columbia: University of South Carolina Press, 1998.

Honneth, Axel. "Democracy as Reflexive Cooperation: John Dewey and the Theory of Democracy Today." *Political Theory* 26, no. 6 (1998): 763–83.

Huetteman, Emmarie, and Yamiche Alcindor. "Betsy DeVos Confirmed as Education Secretary; Pence Breaks Tie." *New York Times*, February 7, 2017. https://www.nytimes .com/2017/02/07/us/politics/betsy-devos-education-secretary-confirmed.html.

Ivie, Robert L. "Enabling Democratic Dissent." *Quarterly Journal of Speech* 101, no. 1 (2015): 46–59.

———. "Rhetorical Deliberation and Democratic Politics in the Here and Now." *Rhetoric & Public Affairs* 5, no. 2 (2002): 277–85.

Jack, Caroline. "Producing Milton Friedman's *Free to Choose*: How Libertarian Ideology Became Broadcasting Balance." *Journal of Broadcasting and Electronic Media* 62, no. 3 (2018): 514–30.

Jackson, Ben. "At the Origins of Neo-liberalism: The Free Economy and the Strong State, 1930–1947." *Historical Journal* 53, no. 1 (2010): 129–51.

———. "Freedom, the Common Good, and the Rule of Law: Lippmann and Hayek on Economic Planning." *Journal of the History of Ideas* 73, no. 1 (2012): 47–68.

Jackson, Sarah J., and Brooke Foucault Welles. "#Ferguson Is Everywhere: Initiators in Emerging Counterpublic Networks." *Information, Communication & Society* 19, no. 3 (2016): 397–418.

———. "Hijacking #myNYPD: Social Media Dissent and Networked Counterpublics." *Journal of Communication* 65, no. 6 (2015): 932–52.

Jaffe, Sarah. "The Fight Against Austerity Started Here." *The Nation*, September 23, 2016. https://www.thenation.com/article/the-fight-against-austerity-started-here.

Jeffrey, Julie Roy. *Education for Children of the Poor: A Study of the Origins and Implementation of the Elementary and Secondary Education Act of 1965*. Columbus: Ohio State University Press, 1978.

Jennings, John F. *Why National Standards and Tests? Politics and the Quest for Better Schools*. Thousand Oaks, CA: Sage, 1998.

Jensen, Kelly. "An Alternative Ideology of Choice: The 'Mother of School Choice' and the Inception of Milwaukee's School Voucher Program." Master's thesis, University of Wisconsin–Madison, 2019.

Johnson, Lyndon Baines. *Public Papers of the Presidents of the United States: Lyndon B. Johnson, 1965*. 2 vols. Washington, DC: Government Printing Office, 1966.

Johnstone, Christopher Lyle. "Dewey, Ethics, and Rhetoric: Toward a Contemporary Conception of Practical Wisdom." *Philosophy and Rhetoric* 16, no. 3 (1983): 185–207.

Jones, Bradley, and Roopali Mukherjee. "From California to Michigan: Race, Rationality, and Neoliberal Governmentality." *Communication and Critical/Cultural Studies* 7, no. 4 (2010): 401–22.

Jones, Daniel Stedman. *Masters of the Universe: Hayek, Friedman, and the Birth of Neoliberal Politics*. Princeton: Princeton University Press, 2012.

Kamenetz, Anya. "Anti-Test 'Opt-Out' Movement Makes a Wave in New York State." *NPR*, April 20, 2015. https://www.npr.org/sections/ed/2015/04/20/400396254/anti-test-opt-out-movement-makes-a-wave-in-new-york-state.

———. "A Rocky Appearance for DeVos on '60 Minutes.'" *NPR*, March 12, 2018. https://www.npr.org/sections/ed/2018/03/12/592860699/a-rocky-appearance-for-devos-on-60-minutes.

Katz, Michael B. *The Undeserving Poor: From the War on Poverty to the War on Welfare*. New York: Pantheon Books, 1989.

Kava, Russ, and Rick Olin. "Local Government Expenditure and Revenue Limits." Informational Paper 12, Wisconsin Legislative Fiscal Bureau, Madison, January 2015. https://docs.legis.wisconsin.gov/misc/lfb/informational_papers/january_2015/0012_local_government_expenditure_and_revenue_limits_informational_paper_12.pdf.

Keith, William M. *Democracy as Discussion: Civic Education and the American Forum Movement*. Lanham, MD: Lexington Books, 2007.

Keith, William M., and Robert Danisch. "Dewey on Science, Deliberation, and the Sociology of Rhetoric." In *Trained Capacities: John Dewey, Rhetoric, and Democratic Practice*, edited by Brian Jackson and Gregory Clark, 27–46. Columbia: University of South Carolina Press, 2014.

Kemble, Rebecca. "Wisconsin's Voucher Vultures." *The Progressive*, July 30, 2013. https://progressive.org/op-eds/wisconsin-s-voucher-vultures.

Klein, Alyson. "Betsy DeVos Finds 'Bully Pulpit' No Easy Perch." *Education Week*, October 9, 2017. https://www.edweek.org/ew/articles/2017/10/11/betsy-devos-finds-bully-pulpit-no-easy.html.

———. "DeVos Would Be First Ed. Sec. Who Hasn't Been a Public School Parent or Student." *Education Week*, December 6, 2016. http://blogs.edweek.org/edweek/campaign-k-12/2016/12/betsy_devos_would_be_first_ed_.html.

———. "Scenes from DeVos' 'Rethink School' Tour." *Education Week*, October 4, 2017. https://www.edweek.org/ew/articles/2017/10/04/scenes-from-devos-rethink-school-tour.html.

Kock, Christian, and Lisa Villadsen, eds. *Rhetorical Citizenship and Public Deliberation*. University Park: Pennsylvania State University Press, 2012.

Krugman, Paul. *The Age of Diminished Expectations*. Cambridge, MA: MIT Press, 1992.

Kuo, Rachel. "Racial Justice Activist Hashtags: Counterpublics and Discourse Circulation." *New Media & Society* 20, no. 2 (2018): 495–514.

Larsen, J. Carlisle. "Wisconsin Considered One of the Worst States for Racial Disparities." *Wisconsin Public Radio*, January 16, 2017. https://www.wpr.org/wisconsin-considered-one-worst-states-racial-disparities.

Larson, Stephanie R. "'Everything Inside Me Was Silenced': (Re)defining Rape Through Visceral Counterpublicity." *Quarterly Journal of Speech* 104, no. 2 (2018): 123–44.

Leadership Conference on Civil and Human Rights. "Civil and Human Rights Groups: Education Secretary Must Enforce Civil Rights Law and Advance Public Education." December 12, 2016. https://civilrights.org/2016/12/12/civil-and-human-rights-groups-education-secretary-must-enforce-civil-rights-law-and-advance-public-education/#.

Leamy, Elisabeth. "You Can Now Use a 529 to Pay for K–12 Tuition—So Should You?" *Washington Post*, February 28, 2018. https://www.washingtonpost.com/lifestyle/on-parenting/you-can-now-use-a-529-to-pay-for-k-12-tuition--so-should-you/2018/02/27/885fb5a4-1aff-11e8-9de1-147dd2df3829_story.html.

Lippmann, Walter. *The Good Society*. 1937. Reprint, New Brunswick, NJ: Transaction, 2005.

———. *The Phantom Public*. 1927. Reprint, New Brunswick, NJ: Transaction, 1993.

Loehwing, Melanie. *Homeless Advocacy and the Rhetorical Construction of the Civic Home*. University Park: Pennsylvania State University Press, 2018.

Lubienski, Christopher, and T. Jameson Brewer. "An Analysis of Voucher Advocacy: Taking a Closer Look at the Uses and Limitations of 'Gold Standard' Research." *Peabody Journal of Education* 91, no. 4 (2016): 455–72.

Lubienski, Christopher, and Gregg Garn. "Evidence and Ideology on Consumer Choices in Education Markets: An Alternative Framework." *Current Issues in Education* 13, no. 3 (2010): 1–19.

Lubienski, Christopher, and Sarah Theule Lubienski. "Is There a 'Consensus' on School Choice and Achievement? Advocacy Research and the Emerging Political Economy of Knowledge Production." *Educational Policy* 23, no. 1 (2009): 161–93.

———. *The Public School Advantage: Why Public Schools Outperform Private Schools*. Chicago: University of Chicago Press, 2014.

Macedo, Stephen. "Property-Owning Plutocracy: Inequality and American Localism." In *Justice and the American Metropolis*, edited by Clarissa Rile Hayward and Todd Swanstrom, 33–58. Minneapolis: University of Minnesota Press, 2011.

Malaby, Thomas. *Making Virtual Worlds: Linden Lab and Second Life*. Ithaca, NY: Cornell University Press, 2009.

Manna, Paul. *Collision Course: Federal Education Policy Meets State and Local Realities*. Washington, DC: CQ Press, 2011.

Margonis, Frank. "John Dewey's Racialized Visions of the Student and Classroom Community." *Educational Theory* 59, no. 1 (2009): 17–39.

Martin, Victoria, and Luis Miguel Lázaro. "The Race to Educational Reform in the USA: The Race to the Top." *Language and Education* 25, no. 6 (2011): 479–90.

Massey, Doreen. "Vocabularies of the Economy." *Soundings*, no. 54 (2013): 9–22.

Mayer, Jane. "Betsy DeVos, Trump's Big-Donor Education Secretary." *New Yorker*, November 23, 2016. https://www.newyorker.com/news/news-desk/betsy-devos-trumps-big-donor-education-secretary.

McCann, Bryan J. "Queering Expertise: Counterpublics, Social Change, and the Corporeal Dilemmas of LGBTQ Equality." *Social Epistemology* 25, no. 3 (2011): 249–62.

McClish, Glen, and Jacqueline Bacon. "Taking Agency, Constituting Community: The Activist Rhetoric of Richard Allen." *Advances in the History of Rhetoric* 11/12, no. 1 (2008/2009): 1–34.

McDermott, Kathryn A. *High-Stakes Reform: The Politics of Educational Accountability*. Washington, DC: Georgetown University Press, 2011.

McDonnell, Lorraine M. "Educational Accountability and Policy Feedback." *Educational Policy* 27, no. 2 (2013): 170–89.

———. "No Child Left Behind and the Federal Role in Education: Evolution or Revolution?" *Peabody Journal of Education* 80, no. 2 (2005): 19–38.

McGuinn, Patrick J. "Education Policy from the Great Society to 1980: The Expansion and Institutionalization of the Federal Role in Schools." In *Conservatism and American Political Development*, edited by Brian J. Glenn and Steven M. Teles, 188–219. New York: Oxford University Press, 2009.

———. *No Child Left Behind and the Transformation of Federal Education Policy, 1965–2005*. Lawrence: University Press of Kansas, 2006.

———. "Stimulating Reform: Race to the Top, Competitive Grants and the Obama Education Agenda." *Educational Policy* 26, no. 1 (2012): 136–59.

McIntush, Holly G. "Defining Education: The Rhetorical Enactment of Ideology in *A Nation at Risk*." *Rhetoric & Public Affairs* 3, no. 3 (2000): 419–43.

———. "Political Truancy: George Bush's Claim to the Mantle of 'Education President.'" In *The Rhetorical Presidency of George H. W. Bush*, edited by Martin J. Medhurst, 102–18. College Station: Texas A&M University Press, 2006.

McKerrow, Raymie E. "Principles of Rhetorical Democracy." *Rétor* 2, no. 1 (2012): 94–113.

Meckler, Laura. "The Education of Betsy DeVos: Why Her School Choice Agenda Has Not Advanced." *Washington Post*, September 4, 2018. https://www.washingtonpost.com/local/education/the-education-of-betsy-devos-why-her-school-choice-agenda-has-crashed/2018/09/04/c21119b8-9666-11e8-810c-5fa705927d54_story.html.

Meens, David E. "Democratic Education Versus Smithian Efficiency: Prospects for a Deweyan Ideal in the 'Neoliberal Age.'" *Educational Theory* 66, nos. 1–2 (2016): 211–26.

Mehta, Jal. *The Allure of Order: High Hopes, Dashed Expectations, and the Troubled Quest to Remake American Schooling*. New York: Oxford University Press, 2013.

————. "How Paradigms Create Politics: The Transformation of American Educational Policy, 1980–2001." *American Educational Research Journal* 50, no. 2 (2013): 285–324.

Meibaum, Debra L. "An Overview of the Every Student Succeeds Act." American Institutes of Research, November 2016. https://eric.ed.gov/?q=source%3A %22Southeast+Comprehensive+Center%22&id=ED573536.

Metz, Joseph G. "Democracy and the Scientific Method in the Philosophy of John Dewey." *Review of Politics* 31, no. 2 (1969): 242–62.

Milewski, Todd D. "Blame Attacks on Public Education for Teacher Shortages, Percy Brown and Tim Slekar Say." *Capital Times*, August 16, 2015. https://madison.com /ct/news/local/writers/todd-milewski/blame-attacks-on-public-education-for -teacher-shortages-percy-brown/article_07e59142-f8f1-51e0-a797-0532a7b42ebf .html.

"Milwaukee Community Schools Partnership." United Way of Greater Milwaukee and Waukesha County, n.d. https://www.unitedwaygmwc.org/Education/Milwaukee -Community-Schools-Partnership.

Miner, Barbara. *Lessons from the Heartland: A Turbulent Half-Century of Public Education in an Iconic American City.* New York: New Press, 2013.

Mirowski, Philip. *Never Let a Serious Crisis Go to Waste: How Neoliberalism Survived the Financial Meltdown.* London: Verso, 2013.

————. "The Political Movement That Dared Not Speak Its Own Name: The Neoliberal Thought Collective Under Erasure." Working Paper 23, Institute for New Economic Thinking, New York, August 2014. https://www.ineteconomics.org /research/research-papers/the-political-movement-that-dared-not-speak-its-own -name-the-neoliberal-thought-collective-under-erasure.

Morris, Debra. "'How Shall We Read What We Call Reality?': John Dewey's New Science of Democracy." *American Journal of Political Science* 43, no. 2 (1999): 608–28.

Mouffe, Chantal. *Agonistics: Thinking the World Politically.* London: Verso, 2013.

————. *The Democratic Paradox.* London: Verso, 2000.

Natanson, Hannah. "Hundreds Protest Education Secretary DeVos at IOP." *Harvard Crimson*, September 29, 2017. https://www.thecrimson.com/article/2017/9/29 /IOP-devos-draws-protest/.

National Center for Education Statistics. "Back to School Statistics." Institute of Education Sciences, n.d. https://nces.ed.gov/fastfacts/display.asp?id=372.

National Commission on Excellence in Education. *A Nation at Risk: The Imperative for Educational Reform.* Washington, DC: Government Printing Office, 1983.

National Conference of State Legislatures. *State Legislative Policymaking in an Age of Political Polarization.* June 15, 2017. http://www.ncsl.org/research/about-state -legislatures/state-legislative-policymaking-in-an-age-of-political-polarization .aspx.

"New 'Race in the Heartland' Report Highlights Wisconsin's Extreme Racial Disparities." *Madison365*, October 10, 2019. https://madison365.com/new-race-in-the -heartland-report-highlights-wisconsins-extreme-racial-disparity.

Norris, Pippa. *Democratic Deficits: Critical Citizens Revisited.* New York: Cambridge University Press, 2011.

Obama, Barack. *Public Papers of the Presidents of the United States: Barack Obama, 2009.* 2 vols. Washington, DC: Government Printing Office, 2013.

————. "Remarks by the President at Every Student Succeeds Act Signing Ceremony." The White House, December 10, 2015. https://obamawhitehouse.archives.gov /the-press-office/2015/12/10/remarks-president-every-student-succeeds-act -signing-ceremony.

Olson, Lester C. "Concerning Judgment in Criticism of Rhetoric." *Review of Communication* 12, no. 3 (2012): 251–56.

Onosko, Joe. "Race to the Top Leaves Children and Future Citizens Behind: The Devastating Effects of Centralization, Standardization, and High Stakes Accountability." *Education and Democracy* 19, no. 2 (2011): 1–11.

Palczewski, Catherine Helen. "Argument in an Off Key: Playing with the Productive Limits of Argument." In *Arguing Communication and Culture*, edited by G. Thomas Goodnight, 1–23. Washington, DC: National Communication Association, 2002.

Peck, Jamie. *Constructions of Neoliberal Reason*. Oxford, UK: Oxford University Press, 2010.

Pennington, Mark. "Against Democratic Education." *Social Philosophy and Policy* 31, no. 1 (2014): 1–35.

Peterson, Paul E. "The End of the Bush-Obama Regulatory Approach to School Reform." *Education Next* 16, no. 3 (Summer 2016): 23–32.

Pezzullo, Phaedra C. "Resisting 'National Breast Cancer Awareness Month': The Rhetoric of Counterpublics and Their Cultural Performances." *Quarterly Journal of Speech* 89, no. 4 (2003): 345–65.

Pfister, Damien Smith. "The Terms of Technoliberalism." In *Theorizing Digital Rhetoric*, edited by Aaron Hess and Amber Davisson, 32–42. New York: Routledge, 2018.

Pfister, Damien Smith, and Misti Yang. "Five Theses on Technoliberalism and the Networked Public Sphere." *Communication and the Public* 3, no. 3 (2018): 247–62.

Plagianos, Irene. "WeWork Is Launching a Grade School for Budding Entrepreneurs." *Bloomberg*, November 6, 2017. https://www.bloomberg.com/news/articles/2017 -11-06/wework-hits-education-with-an-entrepreneurial-school-for-kids.

Posey, Kirby G. "Household Income: 2015." US Census Bureau Survey Brief ACSBR/15-02. September 2016. https://www.census.gov/content/dam/Census/library/pub lications/2016/acs/acsbr15-02.pdf.

Prokop, Andrew. "Scott Walker Loves Ronald Reagan More Than Seems Humanly Possible." *Vox*, July 13, 2015. https://www.vox.com/2015/3/3/8135031/scott-walker -reagan-birthday.

Pugh, Christa. "Estimated Per Pupil Payments for Incoming Pupils in the Statewide Private School Choice Program, 2015–16 to 2024–25." Wisconsin Legislative Fiscal Bureau memo. May 26, 2015.

———. "Private School Choice Programs." Wisconsin Legislative Fiscal Bureau. Informational Paper 25. January 2017.

Rai, Candace. "Power, Publics and the Rhetorical Uses of Democracy." In *The Public Work of Rhetoric: Citizen-Scholars and Civic Engagement*, edited by John M. Ackerman and David J. Coogan, 39–55. Columbia: University of South Carolina Press, 2010.

Ravitch, Diane. *Reign of Error: The Hoax of the Privatization Movement and the Danger to America's Public Schools*. New York: Vintage, 2014.

———. "Why Public Schools Need Democratic Governance." *Phi Delta Kappan* 91, no. 6 (March 2010): 24–27.

Reagan, Ronald. *Public Papers of the Presidents of the United States: Ronald Reagan, 1981*. 2 vols. Washington, DC: Government Printing Office, 1982.

Reckhow, Sarah. *Follow the Money: How Foundation Dollars Change Public School Politics*. New York: Oxford University Press, 2013.

Reilly, Katie. "'I Work 3 Jobs and Donate Blood Plasma to Pay the Bills': This Is What It's Like to Be a Teacher in America." *Time*, September 13, 2018. https://time.com /longform/teaching-in-america.

Reinhoudt, Jurgen, and Serge Audier. *The Walter Lippmann Colloquium: The Birth of Neoliberalism*. Cham, Switzerland: Palgrave Macmillan, 2018.

Reschovsky, Andrew, and Jennifer Imazeki. "Achieving Educational Adequacy Through School Finance Reform." *Journal of Education Finance* 26, no. 4 (2001): 373–96.

Rhim, Lauren Morando, and Sam Redding. "Leveraging the Bully Pulpit: Optimizing the Role of the Chief State School Officer to Drive, Support, and Sustain School Turnaround." In *The State Role in School Turnaround: Emerging Best Practices*, edited by Lauren Morando Rhim and Sam Redding, 31–48. San Francisco: WestEd, 2014.

Richards, Erin, and Andrew Hahn. "Vouchers Could Shift at Least $600 Million from Districts Through 2025." *Milwaukee Journal Sentinel*, May 28, 2015. http://archive.jsonline.com/news/statepolitics/voucher-expansion-could-cost-at-least-600-million-through-2025-b99509041z1-305357651.html.

Richards, Erin, and Matt Kulling. "School Districts Scramble to Find Teachers for Open Positions." *Milwaukee Journal Sentinel*, August 17, 2015. http://archive.jsonline.com/news/education/school-districts-scramble-to-find-teachers-for-open-positions-b99556824z1-322096631.html.

Riley, Richard W. "Reflections on Goals 2000." *Teachers College Record* 96, no. 3 (1995): 380–88.

Robinson, Sue. "A Racial Reckoning of a Progressive Ideology in Public Discourse." *International Journal of Communication* 12 (2018): 4689–707.

Rochester, Chris. "Wisconsin Teachers' Union Leads Nation Again in Membership Losses." MacIver Institute, August 24, 2018. http://www.maciverinstitute.com/2018/08/wisconsin-teachers-union-leads-nation-again-in-membership-losses.

Rogers, John, and Jeannie Oakes. "John Dewey Speaks to Brown: Research, Democratic Social Movement Strategies, and the Struggle for Education on Equal Terms." *Teachers College Record* 107, no. 9 (2005): 2178–203.

Rogers, Melvin L. "Dewey and His Vision of Democracy." *Contemporary Pragmatism* 7, no. 1 (2010): 69–91.

Rood, Craig. "The Gap Between Rhetorical Education and Civic Discourse." *Review of Communication* 16, nos. 2–3 (2016): 135–50.

Rooks, Noliwe. *Cutting School: Privatization, Segregation, and the End of Public Education*. New York: New Press, 2017.

Ryan, James E. *Five Miles Away, a World Apart: One City, Two Schools, and the Story of Educational Opportunity in Modern America*. New York: Oxford University Press, 2010.

Sampson, Carrie, and Melanie Bertrand. "'This Is Civil Disobedience. I'll Continue': The Racialization of School Board Meeting Rules." *Journal of Education Policy*, June 14, 2020. https://doi.org/10.1080/02680939.2020.1778795.

Sandlin, Jennifer A., Jake Burdick, and Trevor Norris. "Erosion and Experience: Education for Democracy in a Consumer Society." *Review of Research in Education* 36 (2012): 139–68.

Saunders, Laura. "The New Tax Law: 529 Education-Savings Accounts." *Wall Street Journal*, February 13, 2018. https://www.wsj.com/articles/the-new-tax-law-529-education-savings-accounts-1518540633.

Savali, Kirsten West. "1 Year After Eric Garner's Death and Black America Still Can't Breathe." *The Root*, July 17, 2015. https://www.theroot.com/1-year-after-eric-garner-s-death-and-black-america-stil-1790860525.

Schneider, Pat. "'Opt-Out' Movement Gaining Ground for Testing in Madison Schools." *Madison.com*, April 15, 2015. https://madison.com/ct/news/local/writers/pat_schneider/opt-out-movement-gaining-ground-for-testing-in-madison-schools/article_83c01e97-b2d8-5fbc-b595-ce437251d1b5.html.

Schulman, Bruce J. *The Seventies: The Great Shift in American Culture, Society, and Politics.* New York: Free Press, 2001.

Scott, Janelle T. "Market-Driven Education Reform and the Racial Politics of Advocacy." *Peabody Journal of Education* 86, no. 5 (2011): 580–99.

———. "Rosa Parks Moment? School Choice and the Marketization of Civil Rights." *Critical Studies in Education* 54, no. 1 (2013): 5–18.

Secomb, Linnell. "Fractured Community." *Hypatia: A Journal of Feminist Philosophy* 15, no. 2 (2000): 133–50.

Seigfried, Charlene Haddock. "John Dewey's Pragmatist Feminism." In *Feminist Interpretations of John Dewey*, edited by Charlene Haddock Seigfried, 47–77. University Park: Pennsylvania State University Press, 2002.

Seltzer, Rick. "Disparaging Interpretive Dance (and More)?" *Inside Higher Education*, September 14, 2017. https://www.insidehighered.com/news/2017/09/14/kentuckys -governor-says-universities-should-think-about-cutting-programs-poor-job.

Sewell, Abby. "Protestors Out in Force Nationwide to Oppose Wisconsin's Antiunion Bill." *Los Angeles Times*, February 26, 2011. http://articles.latimes.com/2011/feb /26/nation/la-na-wisconsin-protests-20110227.

Shuls, James V. "Financing School Choice: How Program Design Impacts Issues Regarding Legality and Equity." *Kansas Journal of Law and Public Policy* 28, no. 3 (2018): 500–514.

Slater, Joseph E. *Public Workers: Government Employee Unions, the Law, and the State, 1900–1962.* Ithaca, NY: Cornell University Press, 2004.

Slater, Robert Bruce. "The First Black Faculty Members at the Nation's Highest-Ranked Universities." *Journal of Blacks in Higher Education*, no. 22 (1998–99): 97–106.

Slosarski, Yvonne. "Jamming Market Rhetoric in Wisconsin's 2011 Labor Protests." *Communication and Critical/Cultural Studies* 13, no. 3 (2016): 250–68.

Smith, Marshall S., Jessica Levin, and Joanne E. Cianci. "Beyond a Legislative Agenda: Education Policy Approaches of the Clinton Administration." *Educational Policy* 11, no. 2 (1997) 209–26.

Sommerhauser, Mark. "New State Data: Post–Act 10, Teachers' Health Care Costs Soared." *Wisconsin State Journal*, July 3, 2018. https://madison.com/wsj/news /local/govt-and-politics/new-state-data-post-act-teachers-health-care-costs-soared /article_b67e5f94-109f-54ea-aa74-ac5b41d2b32f.html.

Sowards, Stacey K., and Valerie R. Renegar. "Reconceptualizing Rhetorical Activism in Contemporary Feminist Contexts." *Howard Journal of Communications* 17, no. 1 (2006): 57–74.

Spitzer-Resnick, Jeffrey D. "Student Discipline and the School-to-Prison Pipeline." *Wisconsin Lawyer*, September 2014. https://www.wisbar.org/NewsPublications /WisconsinLawyer/Pages/Article.aspx?Volume=87&Issue=8&ArticleID=23538.

Springer, Simon. *The Discourse of Neoliberalism: An Anatomy of a Powerful Idea.* London: Rowman and Littlefield, 2016.

Squires, Catherine. "The Black Press and the State: Attracting Unwanted (?) Attention." In *Counterpublics and the State*, edited by Robert Asen and Daniel C. Brouwer, 111–36. Albany: State University of New York Press, 2001.

———. "Rethinking the Black Public Sphere: An Alternative Vocabulary for Multiple Public Spheres." *Communication Theory* 12, no. 4 (2002): 446–68.

Stahl, Lesley. "Interview with Betsy DeVos." *60 Minutes*, CBS, March 11, 2018. https:// www.cbsnews.com/news/secretary-of-education-betsy-devos-on-guns-school -choice-and-why-people-dont-like-her/.

Stallings, D. T. "A Brief History of the US Department of Education, 1979–2002." *Phi Delta Kappan* 83, no. 9 (May 2002): 677–83.

Staton, Ann Q., and Jennifer A. Peeples. "Educational Reform Discourse: President George Bush on 'America 2000.'" *Communication Education* 49, no. 4 (2000): 303–19.

Stein, Jason, and Patrick Marley. *More Than They Bargained For: Scott Walker, Unions, and the Fight for Wisconsin.* Madison: University of Wisconsin Press, 2013.

Stengel, Barbara S. "Educating *Homo Oeconomicus?* 'The Disadvantages of a Commercial Spirit' for the Realization of *Democracy and Education.*" *Educational Theory* 66, nos. 1–2 (2016): 245–61.

Stob, Paul. "Kenneth Burke, John Dewey, and the Pursuit of the Public." *Philosophy and Rhetoric* 38, no. 3 (2005): 226–47.

Stolee, Michael. "The Milwaukee Desegregation Case." In *Seeds of Crisis: Public Schooling in Milwaukee Since 1920,* edited by John L. Rury and Frank A. Cassell, 229–68. Madison: University of Wisconsin Press, 1993.

Stossel, John. "What's So Wrong with Giving Parents School Choices?" *Chicago Sun-Times,* January 1, 2017. http://chicago.suntimes.com/opinion/john-stossel-whats-so-wrong-with-giving-parents-school-choices.

Strauss, Valerie. "Education Secretary Betsy DeVos Stumbles During Pointed '60 Minutes' Interview." *Washington Post,* March 12, 2018. https://www.washingtonpost.com/news/answer-sheet/wp/2018/03/12/education-secretary-betsy-devos-stumbles-during-pointed-60-minutes-interview.

———. "In Front of Kids, Betsy DeVos Says School Is Too Often a 'Mundane Malaise.'" *Washington Post,* September 12, 2017. https://www.washingtonpost.com/news/answer-sheet/wp/2017/09/12/in-front-of-kids-betsy-devos-says-school-is-too-often-a-mundane-malaise.

———. "Omarosa Claims Betsy DeVos Wants to 'Replace Public Education with For-Profit Schools'—and That Trump Calls Her 'Ditzy DeVos.'" *Washington Post,* August 15, 2018. https://www.washingtonpost.com/news/answer-sheet/wp/2018/08/14/omarosa-claims-betsy-devos-wants-to-replace-public-education-with-for-profit-schools-and-that-trump-calls-her-ditzy-devos.

———. "When DeVos Spoke at Harvard, Guests Were Told They Would Be Escorted Out If Disruptive. Some Protested Anyway." *Washington Post,* September 28, 2017. https://www.washingtonpost.com/news/answer-sheet/wp/2017/09/28/devos-speaks-at-harvard-and-guests-were-told-they-would-be-escorted-out-if-disruptive/.

Stroud, Scott R. "John Dewey and the Question of Artful Criticism." *Philosophy and Rhetoric* 44, no. 1 (2011): 27–51.

Stuckey, Mary E., and Sean Patrick O'Rourke. "Civility, Democracy, and National Politics." *Rhetoric & Public Affairs* 17, no. 4 (2014): 711–36.

Suissa, Judith. "Reflections on the 'Counter' in Educational Counterpublics." *Educational Theory* 66, no. 6 (2016): 769–86.

Sunderman, Gail L., and James S. Kim. "The Expansion of Federal Power Implementing the No Child Left Behind Act." *Teachers College Record* 109, no. 5 (2007): 1057–85.

Swalwell, Katy, Simone Schweber, Kristin Sinclair, Jennifer Gallagher, and Eleni Schirmer. "In the Aftermath of Act 10: The Changed State of Teaching in a Changed State." *Peabody Journal of Education* 92, no. 4 (2017): 486–504.

Taylor, Chris. "ALEC's Attack on Public Education: A Report from the Front Lines." *The Progressive,* August 1, 2017. https://progressive.org/dispatches/alec%E2%80%99s-attack-on-public-education-a-report-from-the-frontlin.

Teaching Assistants' Association. "History." TAA-Madison, n.d. http://taa-madison.org/history.

Tesfamichael, Negassi. "Hundreds March to Wisconsin Capitol Demanding Larger Increases to Education Funding." *Capital Times*, June 26, 2019. https://madison .com/ct/news/local/education/hundreds-march-to-wisconsin-capitol-demanding -larger-increases-to-education/article_322f5173-0886-5eee-8193-a6218eead769 .html.

Thernstrom, Abigail. "A Culture of Choice." In *Liberty and Learning: Milton Friedman's Voucher Idea at Fifty*, edited by Robert C. Enlow and Lenore T. Ealy, 35–48. Washington, DC: Cato Institute, 2006.

Toch, Thomas. *In the Name of Excellence: The Struggle to Reform the Nation's Schools, Why It's Failing, and What Should Be Done*. New York: Oxford University Press, 1991.

Tracy, Karen. *Challenges of Ordinary Democracy: A Case Study in Deliberation and Dissent*. University Park: Pennsylvania State University Press, 2010.

Turner, Rachel S. "The 'Rebirth of Liberalism': The Origins of Neo-liberal Ideology." *Journal of Political Ideologies* 12, no. 1 (2007): 67–83.

Turpin, Paul. *The Moral Rhetoric of Political Economy: Justice and Modern Economic Thought*. New York: Routledge, 2011.

Tyack, David, and Larry Cuban. *Tinkering Toward Utopia: A Century of Public School Reform*. Cambridge, MA: Harvard University Press, 1995.

Ujifusa, Andrew. "Civil Rights Groups Blast DeVos' 'Lack of Respect' for Student Diversity." *Education Week*, December 12, 2016. http://blogs.edweek.org/edweek /campaign-k-12/2016/12/civil_rights_groups_blast_devos_diversity.html.

Underwood, Julie. "School Boards Beware." *Wisconsin School News*, May 2013. https:// wasb.org/wp-content/uploads/2017/04/Underwood-Commentary.pdf.

US Census Bureau. "Quick Facts: Wisconsin." 2018. https://www.census.gov/quickfacts /WI.

US House Subcommittee on Labor, Health and Human Services, Education, and Related Agencies. *Departments of Labor, Health and Human Services, Education, and Related Agencies Appropriations for 2018*. 115th Cong., 1st sess., 2017.

———. *Departments of Labor, Health and Human Services, Education, and Related Agencies Appropriations for 2019*. 115th Cong., 2nd sess., 2018.

US Senate Subcommittee on Education. *Elementary and Secondary Education Act of 1965*. 98th Cong., 1st sess., 1965.

US Senate Subcommittee on Health, Education, Labor, and Pensions. *Nomination of Betsy DeVos to Serve as Secretary of Education*. 115th Cong., 1st sess., 2017.

US Senate Subcommittee on Labor, Health and Human Services, Education, and Related Agencies. *Departments of Labor, Health and Human Services, Education, and Related Agencies Appropriations for Fiscal Year 2018*. 115th Cong., 1st sess., 2017.

Van Horn, Rob, and Philip Mirowski. "The Rise of the Chicago School of Economics and the Birth of Neoliberalism." In *The Road from Mont Pèlerin: The Making of the Neoliberal Thought Collective*, edited by Philip Mirowski and Dieter Plehwe, 139–78. Cambridge, MA: Harvard University Press, 2015.

Villadsen, Lisa S. "Progress, but Slow Going: Public Argument in the Forging of Collective Norms." *Argumentation* 34 (2020): 325–37.

Vinovskis, Maris A. "Gubernatorial Leadership and American K–12 Education Reform." In *A Legacy of Innovation: Governors and Public Policy*, edited by Ethan G. Sribnick, 185–203. Philadelphia: University of Pennsylvania Press, 2008.

———. *The Road to Charlottesville: The 1989 Education Summit*. Washington, DC: National Education Goals Panel, 1999.

Walker, Scott. "2011 Budget Address." March 1, 2011. Accessed December 24, 2018. https://walker.wi.gov/speeches/2011-budget-address.

———. "2011 Inaugural Address." January 3, 2011. Accessed December 30, 2018. https://walker.wi.gov/speeches/2011-inaugural-address.

———. "2013 Budget Address: More Prosperity, Better Performance, and True Independence." February 20, 2013. Accessed December 30, 2018. https://walker.wi.gov /speeches/2013-budget-address-more-prosperity-better-performance-and-true -independence.

———. "2013 State of the State Address: Bold Vision and Bright Hope for the Future." January 15, 2013. Accessed December 30, 2018. https://walker.wi.gov/speeches /2013-state-state-bold-vision-and-bright-hope-future.

———. "2015 Budget Address: Freedom and Prosperity." February 3, 2015. Accessed December 30, 2018. https://walker.wi.gov/speeches/freedom-and-prosperity -governor-scott-walkers-2015-budget-address.

———. "2015 State of the State Address: Moving Wisconsin Forward." January 13, 2015. Accessed December 30, 2018. https://walker.wi.gov/speeches/2015-state-state -address-moving-wisconsin-forward.

———. "Excerpt from Governor Scott Walker's Budget Signing Remarks." June 30, 2013. Accessed December 30, 2018. https://walker.wi.gov/speeches/excerpt-governor -scott-walkers-budget-signing-remarks.

———. "Walker: We Changed Broken Education System." *Des Moines Register*, June 9, 2015. http:www.desmoinesregister.com/story/opinion/columnists/caucus/2015 /06/10/walker-changed-broken-education-system/28778201.

———. "Why I'm Fighting in Wisconsin." *Wall Street Journal*, March 10, 2011. https:// www.wsj.com/articles/SB10001424052748704132204576190260787805984.

Wallace, Kelly. "Parents All Over US 'Opting Out' of Standardized Student Testing." *CNN*, April 24, 2015. https://www.cnn.com/2015/04/17/living/parents-movement-opt -out-of-testing-feat/index.html.

Walsh, Camille. "Erasing Race, Dismissing Class: *San Antonio Independent School District v. Rodriguez.*" *Berkeley La Raza Law Journal* 21 (2011): 133–71.

Wanzer-Serrano, Darrel [published as Darrel Enck-Wanzer]. "Barack Obama, the Tea Party, and the Threat of Race: On Racial Neoliberalism and Born Again Racism." *Communication, Culture & Critique* 4, no. 1 (2011): 23–30.

———. *The New York Young Lords and the Struggle for Liberation.* Philadelphia: Temple University Press, 2015.

Wapshott, Nicholas. *Keynes Hayek: The Clash That Defined Modern Economics.* New York: W. W. Norton, 2011.

Watts, Eric King. "Pragmatist Publicity: W. E. B. Du Bois and the New Negro Movement." In *Public Modalities: Rhetoric, Culture, Media, and the Shape of Public Life*, edited by Daniel C. Brouwer and Robert Asen, 33–59. Tuscaloosa: University of Alabama Press, 2010.

———. "'Voice' and 'Voicelessness' in Rhetorical Studies." *Quarterly Journal of Speech* 87, no. 2 (2001): 179–96.

Weiss, Joanne, and Patrick McGuinn. "States as Change Agents Under ESSA." *Phi Delta Kappan* 97, no. 8 (May 2016): 28–33.

Wermund, Benjamin. "Vouchers Have Been a Tough Sell When Put to a Vote." *Politico*, December 2, 2016. https://www.politico.com/tipsheets/morning-education /2016/12/vouchers-have-been-a-tough-sell-when-put-to-a-vote-217673.

Westbrook, Robert B. *John Dewey and American Democracy.* Ithaca, NY: Cornell University Press, 1991.

Will, Madeline. "From 'Rotten Apples' to Martyrs: America Has Changed Its Tune on Teachers." *Education Week*, September 28, 2018. https://www.edweek.org/ew /articles/2018/10/03/from-rotten-apples-to-martyrs-america-has.html.

Williams, Raymond. *Keywords: A Vocabulary of Culture and Society*. Rev. ed. New York: Oxford University Press, 1983.

Wisconsin Council on Children and Families. *Race to Equity: A Baseline Report on the State of Racial Disparities in Dane County*. October 3, 2013. https://racetoequity.net /baseline-report-state-racial-disparities-dane-county.

Wisconsin Department of Public Instruction. "Official Report Shows Cuts to School Staff for 2011–12 School Year." DPI-NR 2012-58. April 28, 2012.

———. "Private School Choice Programs: Frequently Asked Questions for Parents—2020–21 School Year." February 2020. Accessed October 19, 2020. https:// dpi.wi.gov/sites/default/files/imce/sms/Choice/Student_Application_Webpage /PSCP_FAQ_2020-21_Final.pdf.

———. "Public Schools at a Glance." February 2019. https://dpi.wi.gov/sites/default /files/imce/eis/pdf/schools_at_a_glance.pdf.

———. "Statewide Voucher Program Enrollment Counts." DPI-NR 2015-103. October 27, 2015.

———. "Summary of 2011 Wisconsin Act 32 Final 2011–13 Budget with Vetoes." July 2011. https://dpi.wi.gov/sites/default/files/imce/policy-budget/pdf/budsum1113lite.pdf.

Wisconsin Joint Finance Committee. "2013–15 Biennial Budget Executive Session (Part 4)." June 5, 2013. https://wiseye.org/2013/06/04/joint-committee-on-finance -part-4-of-4-3.

———. "2013–15 Budget Briefing." March 21, 2013. https://wiseye.org/2013/03/21/joint -committee-on-finance-59.

———. "2015–17 Biennial Budget Executive Session (Part 3)." May 19, 2015. https:// wiseye.org/2015/05/19/joint-committee-on-finance-part-3-2.

———. "2015–17 Budget Briefing." March 3, 2015. https://wiseye.org/2015/03/03/joint -committee-on-finance-budget-briefing.

———. "Public Hearing in Brillion (Part 1)." March 18, 2015. https://wiseye.org/2015 /03/18/joint-committee-on-finance-public-hearing-part-1.

———. "Public Hearing in Brillion (Part 2)." March 18, 2015. https://wiseye.org/2015 /03/18/joint-committee-on-finance-public-hearing-part-2.

———. "Public Hearing in Green Bay (Part 1)." April 8, 2013. https://wiseye.org/2013 /04/08/joint-committee-on-finance-green-bay-part-1-of-3.

———. "Public Hearing in Greendale (Part 1)." April 4, 2013. https://wiseye.org/2013 /04/04/joint-committee-on-finance-public-hearing-greendale-part-1-of-3.

———. "Public Hearing in Milwaukee (Part 1)." March 20, 2015. https://wiseye.org /2015/03/20/joint-committee-on-finance-public-hearing-part-1-2.

———. "Public Hearing in Milwaukee (Part 2)." March 20, 2015. https://wiseye.org /2015/03/20/joint-committee-on-finance-public-hearing-part-2-2.

———. "Public Hearing in Milwaukee (Part 3)." March 20, 2015. https://wiseye.org /2015/03/20/joint-committee-on-finance-public-hearing-part-3.

———. "Public Hearing in Reedsburg (Part 1)." March 26, 2015. https://wiseye.org /2015/03/26/joint-committee-on-finance-public-hearing-part-1-4.

———. "Public Hearing in Rice Lake (Part 1)." March 23, 2015. https://wiseye.org/2015 /03/23/joint-committee-on-finance-public-hearing-part-1-3.

———. "Public Hearing in Rice Lake (Part 2)." March 23, 2015. https://wiseye.org/2015 /03/23/joint-committee-on-finance-public-hearing-part-2-3.

———. "Public Hearing in Wisconsin Dells (Part 2)." April 10, 2013. https://wiseye.org /2013/04/10/joint-committee-on-finance-public-hearing-wisconsin-dells-part-2 -of-3.

Wisconsin Legislative Audit Bureau. *Opportunity Schools and Partnership Program*. Report 17-13. August 2017. https://legis.wisconsin.gov/lab/media/2644/17-13full.pdf.

Witte, John F. *The Market Approach to Education: An Analysis of America's First Voucher Program*. Princeton: Princeton University Press, 2000.

Wolfe, Joel. "Does Pragmatism Have a Theory of Power?" *European Journal of Pragmatism and American Philosophy* 4, no. 1 (2012): 1–19.

Young, Iris Marion. "The Ideal of Community and the Politics of Difference." *Social Theory and Practice* 12, no. 1 (1986): 1–26.

———. *Inclusion and Democracy*. New York: Oxford University Press, 2000.

Zernike, Kate. "Betsy DeVos, Trump's Education Pick, Has Steered Money from Public Schools." *New York Times*, November 23, 2016. https://www.nytimes.com/2016/11/23/us/politics/betsy-devos-trumps-education-pick-has-steered-money-from-public-schools.html.

INDEX

achievement measures, 81, 83
Acomb, John, 129
Aid to Families with Dependent Children
     program (AFDC), 54
Allen, Danielle, 173, 175
Allen, Richard, 137–38
American Federation for Children, 11,
     121–22
American Legislative Exchange Council
     (ALEC), 91, 123
A Nation at Risk report, 71, 78–80,
     188nn17–18
anti-government views
     DeVos, Betsy, 77, 98
     Reagan, Ronald, 77, 79, 113
     Walker, Scott, 113–14, 167
Antrop-González, René, 124
Arendt, Hannah, 5, 41–42, 184n23
Arnett, Ronald, 197n18
Aune, James, 47
authoritarianism, 170, 199n19

Bacon, Jacqueline, 137
Baldwin, James, 44
Belman, Larry, 180n30
Bender, Jim, 121–22
Bertrand, Melanie, 195n83
Bethune, Mary McLeod, 99
Bettez, Silvia Cristina, 137, 139–40
Biesta, Gert, 181n56
Bitzer, Lloyd, 180n45, 198n26
Bohman, James, 182n90
Bolick, Clint, 108–9, 194n33
Brewer, T. Jameson, 192n2
Brooks, Kaleb, 179n46
Brouwer, Daniel, 45
Brown, Wendy
     democratic values, 7–8
     freedom, 199n8
     individualism, 166
     market relationships, 11
     neoliberalism, 162, 199n1, 199n19
     Thatcher, Margaret, 184n24
bully pulpits, 85–88, 102, 189n54
Burks, Don, 35

Bush, George H. W., 80
Bush, George W., 76, 80
busing, 78
Byrd, Harry, 104

Campbell, Karlyn Kohrs, 138
Cann, Colette, 197n20
Carl, Jim, 106–7
Carter, Jimmy, 78–79
Caspary, William, 180n44, 182n85
Chapman, Thandeka, 124
Chaput, Catherine, 14, 65
Chitester, Robert, 64
choice
     American identity, 70–71
     collective consequences, 168
     consumer identity, 167–68
     context-free, 168
     democratic, 171
     DeVos's rhetoric of, 95–97, 167
     the Friedmans on, 57–58, 166
     in market ideologies, 168
     in market publics, 103
     problem of persuasion, 170
     relationality, 58
     voucher advocacy rhetoric, 70–71,
          125–26
     See also individual-freedom-choice;
          parental choice; school choice
Cintron, Ralph, 9
civil rights language appropriations,
     99–100, 124
Clark, Gregory, 137
Clark, Katherine, 84
Clinton, Bill, 80
coercion, 55, 60, 167
collective bargaining, 2, 109–11, 194n37
collectives
     decision-making, 41, 67
     Dewey on, 8, 22–24, 26–27
     empowering individuals, 165–66
     the Friedmans on, 50–52
     identities, 165–66
     wisdom, 68
     See also community

RHETORICAND**DEMOCRATIC**DELIBERATION